AF890481

Cybersecurity

Cybersecurity

Data Privacy in the Age of Digital Communication

First Edition

Dr. Lamia Zia, Dr. Shane McNeil, and Dr. Tiffany Ceasor

cognella
SAN DIEGO

Bassim Hamadeh, CEO and Publisher
Mieka Portier, Supervising Senior Acquisitions Editor
Skyler Bryant, Project Editor
Jeanine Rees, Production Editor
Summer Fitzgerald, Editorial Associate
Jessica Delia, Graphic Design Associate
Tiffany Mok, Senior Content Marketing Specialist
Natalie Piccotti, Director of Marketing
Kassie Graves, Senior Vice President, Editorial
Alia Bales, Director of Project Editorial & Production

Printed in the United States of America.

Contents

Contents

Preface

How to Stay Safe in a World That Runs on Wi-Fi

Shane McNeil, PhD

This book began with a spark of curiosity. Three of us—an academic, a techie, and a government expert—came together with a shared mission: to make cybersecurity and data privacy not only understandable but engaging. We wanted to go beyond the typical academic textbook and create something that's informative, approachable, and maybe even a little bit fun. We didn't want to write just another textbook something that gets read in a classroom, crammed for a final exam, and then forgotten the moment a student graduates. No, we wanted something different. We wanted a book that talks to you, not at you. One that helps you understand why your IP address is like your home address, why oversharing on social media might just open the gates to trouble, and why multi-factor authentication is the modern-day equivalent of a deadbolt.

This book offers real-life examples, practical strategies, and answers to questions you didn't know you had—like what's really happening when you click "I agree" without reading anything, or how your smart fridge could be smarter than it should be. This book is our invitation to you: to become cyber literate, digitally confident, and ready to surf the internet jungle without getting eaten alive by cyber lions (read: hackers, trackers, and shady data miners).

Whether you're a student, a working professional, or just someone who loves their Wi-Fi but doesn't want it spying on them, we wrote this for you. This book is written for everyone navigating today's digital world. It's for students looking to gain real-world skills and a competitive digital edge, both in the classroom and in their future careers. It's for professionals who need to protect their data, maintain client trust, and stay ahead of compliance demands. And it's for everyday digital citizens who simply want to understand what's happening behind their screens—and how to stay safe while staying connected.

And we hope that by the time you reach the last page, you'll feel a little more in control—and a lot more empowered—in your digital life. So, grab a cup of coffee, get comfy, and let's dive into the world where privacy matters, and cyber knowledge is your strongest firewall.

Overview

This book is designed to be your practical guide through the digital landscape, offering simple explanations, real-life examples, and cyber tips to help you stay informed and protected.

We've structured the content to bridge technical cybersecurity knowledge with everyday digital relevance. Each chapter breaks down key concepts in cybersecurity and data privacy, from understanding how hackers operate to learning how to protect personal data, navigate digital threats, and make smarter choices online. Along the way, we include scenarios, checklists, and case studies to ground the information in real-world application.

Whether you're studying, working, or simply using a smartphone, this book aims to empower you with the knowledge and confidence to stay safe in a world that runs on Wi-Fi. And along the way, we hope to shift your mindset. Because data privacy isn't just about defense—it's about empowerment. It's about taking ownership of your digital life and becoming a confident, informed communicator in a world that doesn't always make that easy.

At its core, the book teaches you the importance of data privacy, also known as information privacy, the practice of protecting personal and sensitive information from unauthorized access, misuse, or exposure. It also emphasizes your right to control who can access your data and how it is used.

Data privacy matters for several key reasons:

- Personal Rights: Data privacy is a fundamental human right recognized by international laws and treaties. It intersects with freedoms of expression, association, and autonomy. Respecting data privacy means protecting individual dignity.
- Security: When your personal data is exposed, it can lead to identity theft, fraud, blackmail, or cyberattacks. Protecting your privacy is essential to safeguarding yourself and others from harm.
- Trust: Sharing data is an act of trust. Whether you're interacting with apps, services, or institutions, you expect your information to be handled responsibly. Data privacy is the foundation of that trust—and of accountability in the digital world.

Through real-world examples, case studies and expert guidance, this book helps you understand not just what data privacy is, but why it's worth protecting and how to do it.

Each chapter in this book engages with a distinct theme, offering readers both theoretical knowledge and practical tools. Collectively, the chapters stimulate reflection and discussion around the core challenges of cybersecurity and data privacy, unpacking not only technical mechanisms but also ethical, legal, and social considerations. The book argues that while data privacy is a fundamental right and a critical security concern, it remains difficult to achieve in today's data-driven world.

In our daily lives, we generate vast amounts of data through our digital communications, financial transactions, online behaviors, wearable devices, and more. These data streams, while often enabling convenience and personalization, also pose serious risks. Personal information can reveal intimate details about our preferences, locations, identities, and even our health and political beliefs. As such, the stakes of data privacy extend beyond individual users to institutions and entire societies.

This book identifies and explores three central challenges to achieving effective data privacy:

- Lack of Awareness: Many individuals are unaware of how their data is collected, stored, or used. They often accept privacy policies without fully understanding them, remain unfamiliar with privacy settings, or underestimate the long-term consequences of their digital footprints.
- Lack of Control: Once data is shared, users frequently have limited ability to access, edit, delete, or restrict further use of their information. This disempowerment is compounded by opaque data practices, complex terms of service, and limited regulatory recourse.
- Lack of Protection: The digital ecosystem is vulnerable to a range of threats, including unauthorized access, cyberattacks, data breaches, and malware. Additionally, the exploitation of data by governments or corporations for surveillance, manipulation, or discriminatory practices presents significant societal risks.

Despite these challenges, Data Privacy in a Digital World maintains a solutions-oriented focus. It introduces strategies for developing a layered privacy plan, using encryption, securing communication technologies, and navigating ethical dilemmas. Readers are also guided through real-world case studies to contextualize theoretical knowledge and assess the effectiveness of different privacy practices.

By combining foundational concepts with cyber knowledge, this book equips students, professionals, educators, and everyday users with the skills and confidence necessary to understand and protect their digital identities. Far from being just another classroom text, it is a timely and enduring resource designed to spark informed dialogue and create responsible digital citizenship in an era where data privacy is both a right and a responsibility.

So, why should you read this book?

Academically, it's your backstage pass to mastering cyber literacy and digital privacy without falling asleep in the process. You'll walk away with practical know-how, critical thinking skills, and the ability to spot sketchy sources like a pro. Whether it's for an assignment, a class debate, or just outsmarting that one friend who thinks incognito mode is foolproof, you'll be ready.

Personally, this book will teach you how to keep your digital life on lockdown. From choosing passwords that aren't your pet's name to sidestepping phishing scams like a cybersecurity ninja, you'll learn how to keep your identity (and sanity) intact.

Professionally, we've got your future self-covered. Whether you're building a portfolio, launching a startup, or just trying to survive a group project without leaking everyone's data, you'll learn how to protect your digital reputation and play by the privacy rules. Bonus: it looks really good on a resume when you understand encryption and ethics.

By the end of this book, you won't just know how to dodge data disasters—you'll understand why it all matters. Because privacy is for everyone. It's personal, it's professional, it's political. And it's yours to protect.

So, buckle up, power on, and get ready to own your digital life like a true cybersecurity pro!

Chapter 1

Introduction to Data Privacy in Digital Communications

Shane McNeil, PhD

Learning Outcomes

1. **Understand the Concept of Data Privacy**: Gain a comprehensive understanding of what data privacy means, its significance in the digital age, and its relevance in both personal and professional contexts.
2. **Identify Common Security Threats**: Learn about various digital security threats such as malware, phishing, and social engineering, and understand their impact on data privacy.
3. **Grasp the Fundamentals of Data Privacy**: Comprehend key principles like data classification, consent, transparency, anonymization, and pseudonymization in the context of protecting personal data.
4. **Recognize the Role of Encryption**: Understand the basics of encryption technologies, including the importance of end-to-end encryption in securing digital communications.
5. **Explore Digital Communication Technologies**: Develop an awareness of different types of digital communication technologies and their specific data privacy challenges and solutions.
6. **Examine Privacy and Ethical Considerations**: Evaluate the ethical dilemmas and privacy considerations in digital communications, focusing on the balance between privacy, utility, security, and freedom.
7. **Analyze Real-World Case Studies**: Analyze case studies to understand the real-world implications of data privacy practices, successes, and failures.
8. **Construct a Layered Data Privacy Plan**: Learn how to build a comprehensive, multilayered approach to data privacy, incorporating various strategies for robust protection.
9. **Understand Data Privacy in Social Media**: Recognize the unique challenges and considerations of managing data privacy in the context of social media.

10. **Appreciate the Global Nature of Data Privacy**: Acknowledge the complexities and intricacies of managing data privacy in a global context, understanding diverse data laws, cultural perspectives, and cross-border data transfer issues.

Key Terms

- **Data Privacy**: The right and ability to control access and use of personal information.
- **Encryption**: The process of converting information or data into a code to prevent unauthorized access.
- **Pseudonymization**: The processing of personal data in such a manner that the data can no longer be attributed to a specific data subject without the use of additional information.
- **VPN (Virtual Private Network)**: A service that encrypts your internet traffic and protects your online identity.
- **GDPR (General Data Protection Regulation)**: A regulation in European Union (EU) law on data protection and privacy in the EU and the European Economic Area.
- **Digital Sovereignty**: The concept that states or individuals have the right to manage and control their digital information.

1.1 Understanding Data Privacy

In the digital age, the concept of data privacy has become increasingly significant. At its most fundamental level, data privacy refers to the right and ability of individuals and organizations to maintain control over their personal information. This concept encompasses more than just the protection of data from unauthorized access; it's about ensuring that personal information is handled in a manner that respects the individual's preferences and expectations.

Data privacy is a multifaceted concept, touching on various aspects of digital life. It includes considerations about what data is collected, how it is stored, who has access to it, and how it is used. The proliferation of digital technologies has led to an explosion of data generation, making the concept of privacy in the digital realm complex and dynamic.

Personal Versus Professional Context

In a personal context, data privacy pertains to the protection of sensitive information such as Social Security numbers, financial records, health information, and personal communications. This protection extends to digital footprints left on social media, search engines, and online shopping. The rise of the digital age has blurred the boundaries between public and private life, making it increasingly challenging to keep personal information out of the public domain.

In a professional context, data privacy takes on a different dimension. Organizations are tasked with safeguarding not only employee data but also sensitive business information, trade secrets, and customer data. This protection is crucial for maintaining competitive advantage, complying with legal requirements, and fostering customer trust. The stakes in the professional realm are high, as data breaches can lead to significant financial losses, legal ramifications, and reputational damage.

Legal and Ethical Aspects

Legal frameworks play a critical role in shaping the landscape of data privacy. Laws such as the General Data Protection Regulation (GDPR) in the EU and the California Consumer Privacy Act (CCPA) in the United States have set benchmarks for data protection. These laws regulate the ways in which personal data can be collected, processed, stored, and shared. They also provide individuals with rights over their data, including the right to access, correct, and, in some cases, request the deletion of their data.[1]

However, the legal aspect is just one side of the coin. Ethical considerations are equally important. Respecting data privacy is about recognizing and valuing individual autonomy and the right to control one's personal information. It's about understanding the power dynamics at play in the collection and use of data and striving for a balance where data is used responsibly and transparently.

The ethical aspect becomes particularly significant when considering the impact of technology on privacy. Technologies like artificial intelligence and machine learning can analyze vast amounts of data, making it difficult to ensure privacy and consent. The ethical use of such technologies involves a commitment to transparency, accountability, and the protection of individual rights.

The Evolution of Data Privacy

Data privacy has evolved significantly over the past few decades. Initially, concerns about data privacy were primarily focused on preventing unauthorized access to data. However, as digital technologies have become more integrated into daily life, the focus has shifted to the broader implications of data collection and use.

This evolution has been driven by several factors, including technological advancements, changing societal norms, and growing awareness of privacy issues. The rise of social media, e-commerce, and smart devices has led to new privacy challenges, such as the tracking of online behavior and the collection of personal data for targeted advertising.

As digital communication continues to evolve, so too will the concept of data privacy. Future challenges may include privacy in the context of augmented reality, the Internet of

1. Orla Lynskey, "Complete and Effective Data Protection," *Current Legal Problems* 76, no. 1 (November 27, 2023): 297–344, https://doi.org/10.1093/clp/cuad009.

Things (IoT), and other emerging technologies. These challenges will require continuous adaptation and refinement of privacy principles and practices.

Understanding data privacy in the digital age requires a comprehensive approach that encompasses legal, ethical, and practical considerations. As digital technologies continue to advance, the importance of protecting personal information will only grow. For individuals and organizations alike, navigating the complexities of data privacy is an ongoing challenge that requires vigilance, awareness, and a commitment to ethical principles.

Digital Shadows: The Unseen Impact of Data Privacy Violations

In our increasingly digital world, understanding the nuances of data privacy is not just a luxury but a necessity. For college students and young professionals stepping into this interconnected realm, the stakes are higher than ever. This narrative delves into the often-overlooked consequences of data privacy violations, offering a glimpse into the digital challenges faced by today's youth.

Imagine a typical day in the life of a college student, Alex: posting on social media, ordering books online, and participating in virtual classrooms. Unbeknownst to Alex, each digital interaction leaves a trail of personal data—a digital shadow that is constantly growing. From preferences in music to personal chats, bits of Alex's digital identity are perpetually harvested, often without clear consent or understanding.

Alex's routine takes a jarring turn when a popular social media platform announces a massive data breach. Personal information, including Alex's, has been compromised. Suddenly, Alex is faced with unauthorized transactions on their credit card, a barrage of targeted phishing emails, and a palpable sense of vulnerability. The breach not only disrupts Alex's financial stability but also instills a deep-seated unease about online activities.

The repercussions of this incident extend far beyond immediate distress. As Alex graduates and enters the job market, they find that the breach has left a lasting imprint. Potential employers question Alex's credibility due to a tarnished online reputation, stemming from identity theft linked to the breach. The psychological toll is equally daunting, with Alex becoming increasingly wary of digital platforms, a significant hindrance in our technology-driven age.

Transitioning into a young professional, Alex's perspective on data privacy shifts from personal inconvenience to a critical professional obligation. In their role, Alex becomes acutely aware of the importance of safeguarding client data. A single lapse in data security could erode client trust and tarnish the company's reputation, echoing Alex's personal experience but on a much larger scale.

In the backdrop of these experiences are evolving legal frameworks like the GDPR and CCPA, aiming to protect personal data. Yet, as Alex learns, legal compliance is just the baseline. Ethical responsibility in handling data—respecting privacy and prioritizing consent—becomes a core professional and personal value.

Alex's journey underscores the multifaceted impact of data privacy violations, serving as a cautionary tale for college students and young professionals alike. In a world where our digital and physical identities are increasingly intertwined, understanding and advocating for data privacy is not just about navigating the present; it's about safeguarding our future. For the digital natives at the dawn of their careers, embracing this challenge is not just a choice but an imperative.

1.2 Common Security Threats

In the dynamic and ever-evolving landscape of digital communication, the presence of various security threats has become a constant challenge. These threats, ranging from sophisticated malware attacks to clever social engineering tactics, pose significant risks to both individuals and organizations. Understanding these threats is the first step toward effective data privacy and cybersecurity.

The Menace of Malware

Malware, a term that encompasses various forms of harmful software like viruses, worms, ransomware, and spyware, poses a significant threat in the digital realm. These malicious programs can infiltrate systems silently, often without the user's knowledge, leading to a range of harmful consequences. From stealing sensitive data and encrypting files for ransom to hijacking computer resources for malicious purposes, the impact of malware can be devastating.

One notable aspect of malware is its constantly evolving nature. Cybercriminals continuously develop new strains and tactics to bypass security measures, making it a game of cat and mouse between attackers and defenders. The infamous WannaCry ransomware attack, for instance, affected thousands of computers worldwide, encrypting data and demanding ransom for its release. This incident highlights the destructive potential of malware and the need for robust cybersecurity measures.[2]

The Deceptive World of Phishing

Phishing attacks, where cybercriminals impersonate legitimate entities to trick individuals into divulging sensitive information, have become increasingly common. These attacks often take the form of deceptive emails, appearing to be from reputable sources, such as banks or popular online services. The goal is to lure the recipient into clicking on a malicious link or attachment, leading to data theft or malware installation.

The sophistication of phishing attacks has grown remarkably. Attackers now use social engineering and personalization techniques to make their emails more convincing.

2. Lawrence J. Trautman and Peter Ormerod, "Wannacry, Ransomware, and the Emerging Threat to Corporations," *Tennessee Law Review* 86, no. 503 (August 24, 2018), https://doi.org/10.2139/ssrn.3238293.

They often leverage current events or personal information gleaned from social media to create a sense of urgency or legitimacy. The success of phishing attacks lies in exploiting human psychology rather than technical vulnerabilities, making them particularly challenging to combat.

Social Engineering: The Human Element of Cybersecurity

Social engineering attacks are a testament to the adage that the weakest link in cybersecurity is often the human element. These attacks manipulate individuals into breaking standard security procedures, revealing sensitive information, or granting access to restricted areas. Techniques like pretexting, baiting, and tailgating showcase the diverse ways attackers exploit human trust and curiosity.

A classic example of social engineering is the "CEO fraud," where attackers pose as company executives and urge employees to transfer funds or share confidential data. This form of attack relies on the authority and urgency implied by the supposed sender's position, leading to hasty decisions without proper verification.

The Vulnerabilities of Networks

Networks, the backbone of digital communication, are not immune to security threats. Vulnerabilities can arise from various sources, including outdated software, poorly configured hardware, and inadequate security policies. These weak points can be exploited by cybercriminals to gain unauthorized access, intercept communications, or launch attacks against other systems.

The consequences of network vulnerabilities can range from minor disruptions to catastrophic data breaches. For instance, the exploitation of a single vulnerability in a widely used software can lead to widespread compromise of systems worldwide. The importance of regular network assessments, timely software updates, and robust security protocols cannot be overstated.

The Continuous Battle Against Cyber Threats

In the face of these diverse and evolving threats, both individuals and organizations must adopt a multifaceted approach to cybersecurity. This includes not only technical solutions like firewalls, antivirus programs, and encryption but also organizational measures such as regular security audits, incident response plans, and employee training programs.

Awareness and education play a crucial role in mitigating the risk of cyber threats. Regular training sessions can help individuals recognize potential threats and respond appropriately. Simulated phishing exercises, for example, can be an effective tool for teaching employees how to spot and avoid phishing emails.

The Future of Cybersecurity Threats

As technology advances, so do the methods and tactics of cyber attackers. The emergence of new technologies like artificial intelligence and the IoT opens up new frontiers for cyber threats. Future-oriented security measures, therefore, need to be adaptive, proactive, and comprehensive, encompassing not only technological solutions but also human-centric approaches.

The landscape of common security threats in digital communication is complex and requires a vigilant and informed approach to ensure effective data privacy and security. Understanding these threats is the foundation upon which robust cybersecurity strategies are built. By staying informed and proactive, individuals and organizations can navigate the digital world with greater confidence and resilience against these evolving threats.

1.3 Fundamentals of Data Privacy

Data privacy is essential in our digital age, focusing on principles and practices to protect personal information from unauthorized access and misuse. Let's dive into the foundational elements of effective data privacy strategies for individuals and organizations.

The Concept of Data Classification

Data classification involves categorizing data based on its sensitivity and required protection level. This process helps determine how different types of data should be managed. Typically, data is classified into categories like public, internal-only, confidential, and highly confidential.

For example, highly confidential data such as financial records or personal health information demands stricter protection compared to public information. Effective data classification enhances security and helps meet regulatory compliance, as many privacy laws require specific protection measures for certain data types.

Why is data classification so critical? It acts as the backbone of an organization's data governance strategy. By systematically categorizing data, organizations can allocate resources more effectively, ensuring that the most sensitive information receives the highest level of security. This prioritization helps in crafting targeted security policies, deploying specific encryption standards, and conducting regular audits tailored to the data's sensitivity level.

Understanding Consent and Transparency in Data Privacy

Consent and transparency are vital components of data privacy. They involve informing individuals about how their data is collected, used, and shared, and obtaining their explicit permission for these activities.

Informed consent means that individuals fully understand what they are agreeing to. It must be given freely, without coercion. Transparency requires organizations to be open about their data handling practices, providing clear privacy policies, promptly disclosing data breaches, and being transparent about third-party data processors.

Recent regulations like the GDPR highlight the importance of consent and transparency, setting new standards for how organizations should approach the collection and use of personal data.

The role of transparency goes beyond just compliance. It's about building trust with users, ensuring they feel confident in how their personal information is managed. Clear communication about data policies, straightforward consent mechanisms, and honest breach notifications form the core of an ethical data privacy approach. This trust is crucial not only for regulatory reasons but also for maintaining a positive relationship with users, who are increasingly aware of and concerned about their privacy rights.

Anonymization and Pseudonymization Techniques

Anonymization and pseudonymization are techniques to protect individuals' identities and personal information. Anonymization alters data so that individuals cannot be identified, while pseudonymization replaces private identifiers with pseudonyms.

These techniques are invaluable in data privacy. Anonymization is useful for research or statistical purposes, allowing data to be used while protecting individual privacy. Pseudonymization is often used in data processing and storage, reducing risks associated with data breaches.

When to use which technique? Anonymization is preferred when data needs to be shared for public research, ensuring no personal identifiers remain. Pseudonymization, however, is used in scenarios where some level of identification is necessary, but full exposure of personal data is too risky. For instance, in medical studies where patient records are used, pseudonyms can help maintain a link to the patient if needed for follow-up, while still protecting the patient's identity.

The Principles of Data Minimization and Purpose Limitation

Data minimization and purpose limitation advocate for minimal data collection and use. Data minimization involves collecting only the necessary data, while purpose limitation ensures data is used only for its intended purpose.

These principles build trust and maintain data privacy integrity. Adhering to them reduces data handling risks and ensures personal information is not misused.

How do these principles translate into practice? Organizations need to conduct regular data audits to ensure that only necessary data is collected and retained. This might involve revisiting data collection forms, evaluating the necessity of each data point, and implementing automated systems that flag unnecessary data. Purpose limitation requires clear documentation of data use purposes and rigorous checks to prevent data from being repurposed without consent.

Data Subject Rights and Access Control

Data subject rights allow individuals to control their personal information. These rights include accessing, rectifying inaccuracies, erasing data under certain conditions, and restricting or objecting to data processing.

Access control manages who can access data and what they can do with it. Effective access control prevents unauthorized access and ensures appropriate data use, including user authentication, authorization, and auditing mechanisms.

Empowering data subjects means providing user-friendly mechanisms for individuals to exercise their rights. For example, organizations should offer simple online portals where users can view and manage their data, request corrections, or delete their information. On the access control front, multifactor authentication and role-based access controls are critical measures to ensure that only authorized personnel can access sensitive data.

The Role of Privacy by Design and Default

Privacy by design and privacy by default emphasize incorporating data privacy considerations into products, services, and business practices from the outset.

Privacy by design proactively includes privacy measures during the design phase of systems and processes. Privacy by default mandates the highest level of privacy settings automatically, safeguarding users' privacy without intervention.

These principles are best practices in data privacy, ensuring privacy is a core aspect of operations rather than an afterthought. They enhance regulatory compliance and build user trust, demonstrating that personal information is handled with care.

Why are these principles transformative? They shift the focus from reactive to proactive privacy management. Instead of patching privacy loopholes after a breach occurs, organizations anticipate and mitigate privacy risks from the start. This forward-thinking approach not only prevents potential breaches but also ingrains a culture of privacy within the organization.

The Intersection of Data Privacy and Technology

The relationship between data privacy and technology is complex and evolving. Advances in technology like big data analytics, artificial intelligence, and the IoT present new challenges and opportunities for data privacy. These technologies can enhance privacy protection through improved security measures and data anonymization techniques but also create new risks, such as increased surveillance and potential privacy infringements.

Understanding the interplay between data privacy and technology is crucial for managing privacy risks. This involves staying informed about technological advancements, assessing their implications, and adapting privacy strategies accordingly.

Balancing innovation and privacy is a key challenge. As technologies like artificial intelligence (AI) and IoT continue to evolve, organizations must develop robust frameworks to manage these tools responsibly. This might include implementing privacy impact assessments for new technologies, ensuring transparency in AI decision-making processes, and developing secure IoT devices that prioritize user data protection.

Global Data Privacy Regulations and Compliance

Data privacy is a legal issue, with various countries enacting laws that set standards for handling personal information. These laws often include requirements for data protection, breach notification, and data subject rights.

Compliance with these regulations is essential for organizations in the global digital marketplace. This involves understanding different privacy laws, like the GDPR in Europe and the CCPA in California, and implementing policies to meet legal requirements.

Navigating the regulatory landscape requires continuous learning and adaptation. Organizations must invest in legal expertise, maintain up-to-date compliance programs, and actively monitor changes in privacy regulations. Leveraging technology, such as automated compliance tools, can also help streamline regulatory adherence and reduce the risk of noncompliance.[3]

The Future of Data Privacy: Trends and Challenges

The future of data privacy will face new trends and challenges. The growing importance of data, the sophistication of cyber threats, and evolving privacy laws will shape the field. Emerging technologies like quantum computing and blockchain may transform data protection and management.

Navigating these trends requires a proactive approach to data privacy. Staying informed about developments, continuously evaluating privacy practices, and adapting to change are key.

The fundamentals of data privacy provide a framework for managing personal information in the digital world. Embracing principles like data classification, consent, transparency, and privacy by design, and staying informed about technological and regulatory developments, helps navigate the complexities of data privacy and protect valuable information in our digital society.

3. Danielle Kucera, "CCPA vs. GDPR: Similarities and Differences Explained," Okta, accessed October 24, 2024, https://www.okta.com/blog/2021/04/ccpa-vs-gdpr/; IEEE Digital Privacy, "Emerging Data Privacy Laws and Regulations Around the World," accessed October 24, 2024, https://digitalprivacy.ieee.org/publications/topics/emerging-data-privacy-laws-and-regulations-around-the-world; Deloitte US, "A Quick Reference Guide for CCPA Compliance," accessed October 24, 2024, https://www2.deloitte.com/us/en/pages/advisory/articles/ccpa-compliance-readiness.html.

1.4 Encryption and E2EE

In the vast and intricate world of digital communication, encryption stands as a guardian of privacy and security. It is a process that transforms readable data into a coded form, ensuring that only those with the right "key" can access its true meaning. This section delves into the intricate workings of encryption, its various forms, and the pivotal role it plays in protecting data within the digital realm.

Decrypting the Basics of Encryption

The concept of encryption is not new; it dates back to ancient times when secret messages were written in codes and ciphers. In the digital age, this practice has evolved into complex algorithms designed to secure everything from emails to financial transactions. Encryption serves a dual purpose: It maintains the confidentiality of data and ensures its integrity, verifying that it hasn't been tampered with during transmission.

The two primary types of encryption in use today are symmetric and asymmetric encryption. Symmetric encryption, the older of the two, uses the same key for encrypting and decrypting data. This method is fast and efficient, making it suitable for encrypting large volumes of data. However, the key exchange process poses a security risk. Asymmetric encryption, also known as public-key cryptography, employs a pair of keys—a public key for encryption and a private key for decryption. This method enhances security by eliminating the need to share the private key, but it requires more computational resources.

The Mechanics of Encryption Algorithms and Keys

Encryption algorithms are the heart of the encryption process. They are the complex mathematical formulas that convert plaintext into ciphertext and vice versa. Popular algorithms like the Advanced Encryption Standard (AES) and the Rivest–Shamir–Adleman (RSA) algorithm have been rigorously tested and are widely trusted for their security.

The role of keys in encryption is analogous to a password or a secret code. The strength and complexity of the key are critical to the security of the encryption. Longer keys provide a higher level of security but require more processing power to encrypt and decrypt. The management of these keys is a vital aspect of encryption; if a key is lost or falls into the wrong hands, the encrypted data can be compromised.

End-to-End Encryption (E2EE) in Depth

E2EE represents the gold standard in secure communication. It ensures that data is encrypted at its source and remains so until it reaches the intended recipient, who possesses the key to decrypt it. This form of encryption is particularly crucial in safeguarding sensitive communications such as personal messages, business communications, and financial transactions.

The implementation of E2EE in applications like messaging services and email platforms has been a game-changer in digital privacy. It gives users the assurance that their conversations are private and secure from any potential eavesdropping, including by the service providers themselves.

Implementation and Mechanics of E2EE

At its core, E2EE works by generating encryption keys at the endpoints of communication. When a message is sent, it is encrypted using a key that only the sender and receiver have access to. This process involves complex algorithms that transform the data into an unreadable format. Only the recipient's key can decrypt this data back into its original form, ensuring that no third party, including the service provider, can intercept and read the message.[4]

Applications of E2EE

- **Messaging Services:** Applications like WhatsApp, Signal, and Sudo use E2EE to protect user conversations. This ensures that messages, voice calls, and video calls remain confidential.
- **Email Platforms:** Services like ProtonMail offer E2EE for email communications, ensuring that sensitive information shared via email remains private.
- **Financial Transactions:** E2EE is used in online banking and payment services to protect financial data from being intercepted during transactions.

Benefits of E2EE

- **Enhanced Privacy:** By ensuring that only the communicating parties can access the message content, E2EE provides a high level of privacy, protecting users from unauthorized access.
- **Security Against Cyberattacks:** E2EE makes it extremely difficult for hackers to intercept and decipher communications, thereby reducing the risk of data breaches.
- **Trust in Digital Platforms:** Knowing that their data is secure encourages users to trust and engage with digital platforms, fostering a safer online environment.

Challenges and Limitations of E2EE

Despite its advantages, E2EE is not without challenges:

4. Ksenia Ermoshina, Francesca Musiani, and Harry Halpin, "End-to-End Encrypted Messaging Protocols: An Overview," in *Lecture Notes in Computer Science*, vol. 9934, ed. (Springer, 2016), 244–54, https://doi.org/10.1007/978-3-319-45982-0_22; Valentin Mulder, Alain Mermoud, Vincent Lenders, and Bernhard Tellenbach, eds., *Trends in Data Protection and Encryption Technologies* (Springer, 2023), https://doi.org/10.1007/978-3-031-33386-6.

1. **Metadata Exposure:** While E2EE protects the content of communications, it does not hide metadata, such as the time of communication and the identities of the participants. This metadata can still be exploited for surveillance and analysis.
2. **Key Management:** The security of E2EE depends heavily on the proper management and protection of encryption keys. If keys are compromised, the encrypted data becomes vulnerable.
3. **Law Enforcement Access:** E2EE can hinder legitimate access to data for law enforcement and national security purposes, as even service providers cannot decrypt the messages.
4. **User Error and End-Point Security:** E2EE cannot protect against vulnerabilities at the end points. If a user's device is compromised, their communications can still be intercepted and accessed.

Future of E2EE

As digital communication continues to evolve, the importance of E2EE will only grow. Emerging technologies such as quantum computing present both challenges and opportunities for E2EE. Researchers are exploring quantum-resistant encryption algorithms to future-proof E2EE against potential threats posed by quantum decryption capabilities.

The Critical Role of Encryption in Data Privacy

The importance of encryption extends beyond just securing data; it is a fundamental component of trust in the digital ecosystem. In an age where data breaches and cyber threats are rampant, encryption acts as a robust barrier, protecting personal and sensitive information from unauthorized access and cyberattacks.

Encryption also plays a significant role in regulatory compliance. Many data protection laws and regulations, including the GDPR, mandate the use of encryption to safeguard personal data, highlighting its significance in the contemporary digital landscape.

Navigating the Challenges of Encryption Implementation

Implementing encryption effectively is not without its challenges. One of the key considerations is achieving a balance between strong encryption and user-friendliness. Overly complex encryption systems can be cumbersome for users, reducing their practicality and adoption.

The management of encryption keys is another critical area. Key management involves securely generating, storing, distributing, and revoking keys. Poor key management practices can undermine the security benefits of encryption, leading to vulnerabilities and potential data loss.

The Evolving Landscape of Encryption Technologies

The field of encryption is continually advancing, with new developments aimed at enhancing security and efficiency. Quantum computing presents a significant future challenge to current encryption methods, potentially having the capability to break widely used cryptographic algorithms. This looming threat is driving research into quantum-resistant encryption methods.

Emerging technologies like homomorphic encryption, which enables computation on encrypted data without needing to decrypt it first, are poised to revolutionize data privacy. This technology offers the promise of secure data processing and analysis, opening up new possibilities in fields such as cloud computing and data analytics.

Legal and Ethical Implications of Encryption

The widespread use of encryption has sparked complex legal and ethical debates. On one hand, encryption is essential for protecting privacy and security. On the other hand, it can be used to conceal illegal activities, posing challenges for law enforcement and national security.

The debate over encryption backdoors, which would allow authorities to access encrypted data, encapsulates this dilemma. While such backdoors could aid in criminal investigations, they also introduce vulnerabilities that could be exploited by malicious actors, potentially compromising the security of all users.

Balancing the benefits of encryption with the needs of law enforcement and public safety requires careful consideration of privacy rights, security risks, and the potential societal impact of weakening encryption standards.

Future Directions in Encryption Technology

As digital technologies continue to advance, so too will encryption. The emergence of new computing paradigms, increasing data volumes, and evolving cyber threats will shape the future trajectory of encryption technologies.

One area of future development is in user-centric encryption solutions—systems that provide robust security while being intuitive and easy to use. Another area is the integration of AI and machine learning in encryption, potentially leading to more adaptive and intelligent encryption systems.

Encryption, particularly E2EE, is a vital component of modern digital communications, offering a critical shield against intrusion and ensuring the confidentiality of data. Its role in safeguarding privacy and building trust in the digital sphere cannot be overstated. As we move forward in the digital age, the understanding and effective implementation of encryption will continue to be paramount in protecting the fundamental right to privacy in our increasingly connected world.

1.5 Types of Digital Communication Technologies

In our interconnected world, digital communication technologies have become integral to our daily lives. They facilitate a myriad of interactions, from personal conversations to business communications. However, with the convenience and ubiquity of these technologies come significant data privacy challenges. This section explores various digital communication technologies, focusing on their privacy aspects and the measures taken to secure them.

Email Security: The Backbone of Digital Communication

Email is one of the oldest and most widely used forms of digital communication. Despite its age, email remains a fundamental tool in personal and professional contexts. However, its popularity also makes it a prime target for cyber threats like phishing attacks, malware distribution, and data breaches.

Securing email communications involves multiple layers of protection. This includes the use of encryption technologies like Transport Layer Security (TLS) to secure email in transit and encryption methods like Pretty Good Privacy (PGP) for end-to-end encrypted email. Additionally, robust email security involves spam filters, anti-malware software, and user education to identify and avoid malicious emails.

Instant Messaging Apps: Real-Time Communication and Privacy

Instant messaging apps have revolutionized the way we communicate, offering real-time text, voice, and video communication. However, the personal and often informal nature of instant messaging can lead to privacy concerns, especially when sensitive information is shared.

Many modern messaging apps employ E2EE to ensure that only the communicating parties can read the messages. However, this technology varies among platforms, and users should be aware of the privacy policies and encryption standards of the apps they use. Features like message expiration, where messages are automatically deleted after a certain period, and screenshot detection, are additional privacy-enhancing features found in some messaging apps.

Voice over Internet Protocol (VoIP): Securing Voice Communications

VoIP technology, which allows voice communication over the internet, has become a staple in both personal and business settings. While it offers cost-effectiveness and flexibility, VoIP also presents unique privacy challenges, particularly in terms of eavesdropping and call interception.

Securing VoIP calls involves encryption, both for the call itself and for the data transfer involved in initiating and maintaining the call. Technologies like Secure Real-time Transport Protocol (SRTP) and ZRTP are used for encrypting voice data, while TLS is used for securing the signaling data. Additionally, strong authentication methods and network security measures are crucial for protecting VoIP systems from unauthorized access.

Social Media Platforms: Balancing Openness and Privacy

Social media platforms are at the heart of modern digital communication, fostering connections and content sharing. However, the open nature of these platforms poses significant privacy risks, from data collection practices to potential oversharing by users.

Privacy on social media is a complex issue, requiring both platform-level measures and user vigilance. Platforms use various security measures, including data encryption and robust access controls, to protect user data. However, users also play a crucial role in protecting their privacy by managing their privacy settings, being cautious about the information they share, and understanding the data use policies of the platforms.

Cloud-Based Collaboration Tools: Privacy in the Workplace

Cloud-based collaboration tools have transformed the workplace, enabling remote work and efficient teamwork. These tools include document sharing platforms, project management software, and virtual meeting rooms. While they offer significant productivity benefits, they also raise privacy concerns, particularly regarding data access and storage.

Ensuring privacy in cloud-based collaboration involves a combination of encryption, access controls, and secure data storage practices. Service providers often implement encryption both in transit and at rest to protect data. Organizations should also establish strong access control policies and conduct regular audits to ensure that sensitive information is only accessible to authorized individuals.

Online Forums and Communities: Anonymity and Privacy Concerns

Online forums and communities are platforms where individuals can share knowledge, opinions, and experiences. While these forums can provide valuable spaces for discussion and learning, they also present privacy challenges, particularly regarding anonymity and personal data exposure.

Privacy in online forums involves measures like anonymization, where users can participate without revealing their real identities, and data protection policies that govern the collection and use of personal information. Users should be cautious about the information they share in these forums and understand the privacy implications of their participation.

E-Commerce Platforms: Securing Financial Transactions

E-commerce platforms have become a dominant mode of shopping, requiring the exchange of personal and financial information. Ensuring the privacy and security of this information is critical, given the risks of financial fraud and identity theft.

Securing e-commerce platforms involves encryption of financial transactions, robust authentication methods, and compliance with data protection regulations like the Payment Card Industry Data Security Standard (PCI DSS). Consumers should also be aware of the privacy policies of e-commerce platforms and use secure payment methods to protect their financial information.

The Future of Digital Communication Technologies: Emerging Trends and Privacy Implications

As digital communication technologies continue to evolve, new trends like augmented reality communication, blockchain-based messaging, and AI-driven personal assistants are emerging. These technologies offer exciting possibilities but also bring new privacy challenges.

Navigating the privacy implications of these emerging technologies requires a proactive approach, involving continuous assessment of privacy risks, adoption of advanced security measures, and user education on privacy best practices.

Digital communication technologies are an integral part of our modern world, offering unprecedented connectivity and convenience. However, ensuring the privacy and security of communications across these varied platforms is a complex and ongoing challenge. From securing email and instant messaging to protecting communications on social media and VoIP, a multilayered approach to privacy is essential. As technology continues to advance, staying informed and vigilant about privacy practices and potential risks will remain a key priority for individuals and organizations alike.

1.6 Privacy and Ethical Considerations

The realm of digital communication is not just a technological domain but also an ethical battleground. As we navigate the complexities of data privacy, we are constantly confronted with ethical dilemmas that test the balance between privacy, security, convenience, and freedom. This section explores these ethical considerations, offering insights into the nuanced world of privacy ethics in digital communications.

Balancing Privacy and Utility in the Digital Age

One of the fundamental ethical dilemmas in digital privacy is the trade-off between privacy and utility. On one hand, there is a growing demand for personalized services, convenience, and security, which often require access to personal data. On the other hand, there is the inherent right to privacy, advocating for the protection of personal information from unwarranted intrusion.

Navigating this balance is complex. It involves considering the benefits of data collection and use—such as improved services, targeted content, and enhanced security measures—against the potential risks to individual privacy. It also requires an understanding of the context in which data is collected and used, as well as the expectations of the individuals whose data is involved.

The Ethics of Consent in Data Collection

The concept of consent is central to the ethical handling of personal data. Ethical data practices require that consent is informed, freely given, specific, and unambiguous. However, obtaining true informed consent in the digital age is challenging. Terms of service and privacy policies are often lengthy and complex, making it difficult for users to fully understand what they are consenting to.

The ethical dilemma lies in ensuring that consent is meaningful and not merely a formality. This involves making privacy policies more accessible and understandable, providing clear options for consent, and respecting the user's choice, including the option to opt-out of data collection.

Ethical Implications of Data Mining and Profiling

Data mining and profiling have become commonplace in the digital economy, used for everything from personalized marketing to predictive analytics. While these practices can offer significant benefits, they also raise ethical concerns, particularly regarding privacy and potential discrimination.

The ethical challenge is to ensure that data mining and profiling are conducted responsibly, without infringing on individual privacy rights or leading to discriminatory outcomes. This requires transparency about how data is collected and used, as well as safeguards to prevent misuse and bias in data analysis.

Privacy Versus Security: An Ethical Balancing Act

In the context of national security and law enforcement, the tension between privacy and security becomes particularly pronounced. Governments and security agencies often argue for access to personal data and communication channels to prevent crime and terrorism. However, this can conflict with the right to privacy and freedom of expression.

The ethical dilemma here revolves around finding a balance that respects individual privacy rights while addressing legitimate security concerns. This involves establishing clear legal frameworks, oversight mechanisms, and checks and balances to prevent abuse of surveillance powers.

The Role of Anonymity and Pseudonymity

Anonymity and pseudonymity offer individuals the ability to communicate and interact online without revealing their true identities. These practices protect privacy and freedom of expression, especially in situations where revealing one's identity could lead to harm or persecution.

However, anonymity also presents ethical challenges, as it can be used to shield harmful or illegal activities. Balancing the benefits of anonymity with the need to prevent its misuse is a complex ethical issue, requiring nuanced policies and technological solutions.

Ethical Data Stewardship in Organizations

Organizations that collect and handle personal data have an ethical responsibility to act as stewards of that data. This involves implementing robust privacy and security measures, being transparent about data practices, and respecting the privacy rights of individuals.

Ethical data stewardship also entails accountability. Organizations should be accountable for their data practices, including how they respond to data breaches and how they address privacy concerns raised by users or regulatory bodies.

Emerging Technologies and Ethical Considerations

Emerging technologies like AI, facial recognition, and the IoT introduce new ethical dimensions to privacy. These technologies can enhance privacy protection but also have the potential to intrude on personal privacy in unprecedented ways.

Addressing the ethical challenges posed by these technologies requires a forward-thinking approach. It involves anticipating potential privacy implications, engaging in public discourse about acceptable uses of technology, and developing ethical guidelines and regulations to guide their deployment.

Privacy and ethical considerations are at the heart of the digital communication landscape. Navigating these considerations requires a delicate balance, taking into account the rights and expectations of individuals, the benefits of technological advancements, and the broader societal implications. As digital technologies continue to evolve, so too will the ethical debates surrounding them, making it essential for individuals, organizations, and policymakers to engage in continuous reflection and dialogue about the ethical dimensions of digital privacy.

1.7 Real-World Case Studies

Real-world case studies serve as valuable tools in comprehending the complexities of data privacy in digital communications. They provide practical insights into how theoretical principles are applied, challenges are addressed, and mistakes are rectified in real-life scenarios. This section examines a selection of notable case studies that highlight significant aspects of data privacy and security.

Case Study 1: The Facebook-Cambridge Analytica Data Scandal

One of the most infamous data privacy incidents in recent history is the Facebook-Cambridge Analytica scandal. This case illustrated the consequences of lax data privacy controls and the unethical use of personal data for political profiling and targeting.

Cambridge Analytica, a political consulting firm, accessed the personal data of millions of Facebook users without their consent. This data was used to create targeted political advertisements during the 2016 US presidential election and the Brexit referendum. The scandal raised serious questions about consent, data sharing practices, and the responsibility of social media platforms in protecting user data.

Key Lessons:

- The critical importance of obtaining informed consent for data collection and use.
- The need for robust data sharing agreements and oversight mechanisms.
- The role of regulatory bodies in enforcing data privacy laws and penalizing violations.

Case Study 2: The Equifax Data Breach

The Equifax data breach, which occurred in 2017, exposed the personal information of approximately 147 million consumers, including names, Social Security numbers, birth dates, addresses, and driver's license numbers. This breach was a result of vulnerabilities in Equifax's network security, which were not promptly addressed.

The aftermath of the breach highlighted the far-reaching consequences of failing to implement adequate cybersecurity measures and the importance of rapid response and transparency in the event of a data breach.

Key Lessons:

- The necessity of regular security assessments and timely patching of vulnerabilities.
- The importance of having a comprehensive incident response plan.
- The need for clear and prompt communication with affected parties and regulatory authorities in the event of a breach.

Case Study 3: The GDPR and Its Impact on Global Data Privacy Practices

The GDPR, implemented in the EU in 2018, represents a significant case study in the evolution of global data privacy regulations. The GDPR introduced stringent data protection requirements, including provisions for data subject rights, data breach notifications, and hefty fines for noncompliance.

The regulation has had a global impact, influencing data privacy practices beyond the EU. Many international companies have had to overhaul their data handling practices to comply with the GDPR, leading to a de facto global standard in many aspects of data privacy.

Key Lessons:

- The importance of comprehensive data privacy regulations in protecting personal data.
- The impact of such regulations on global business practices and the need for international compliance.
- The role of regulatory bodies in shaping and enforcing data privacy standards.

Case Study 4: The Sony Pictures Entertainment Hack

The hack of Sony Pictures Entertainment in 2014, attributed to a group called "Guardians of Peace," led to the release of a large amount of confidential data, including personal employee information, emails, and unreleased films. This cyberattack highlighted vulnerabilities in corporate cybersecurity practices and the far-reaching consequences of such breaches.

The incident underscored the need for robust cybersecurity measures, employee training in data privacy practices, and the importance of having an effective crisis management strategy.

Key Lessons:

- The necessity of comprehensive cybersecurity measures, including employee awareness and training.
- The impact of data breaches on reputation and the importance of crisis management and communication.
- The need for continual assessment and upgrading of security practices in response to evolving threats.

These real-world case studies provide invaluable lessons in the field of data privacy and digital communications. They illustrate the diverse challenges faced in protecting personal data, the consequences of security lapses, and the importance of ethical and legal compliance in data handling practices. As digital communication technologies continue to evolve, these case studies serve as important references for understanding the complexities of data privacy and guiding future practices.

1.8 Understanding the Landscape of Data Privacy in Social Media

In the contemporary digital landscape, social media platforms stand as central pillars in our daily digital interactions. These platforms have transformed communication, fostering global connections and community building. However, alongside these benefits, they bring forth significant challenges in data privacy. This introductory section sets the stage for understanding the intricate relationship between social media usage and the safeguarding of personal information.

The intertwining of social media with daily life has elevated the importance of data privacy. Every interaction, post, and share potentially contributes to the digital footprint of users, making it crucial to comprehend how this data is managed and protected. This section underlines the need to balance the advantages of social media with the imperative to protect personal privacy in these highly networked spaces.

Evolution of Social Media Platforms

The history of social media reflects a journey from simple online networking tools to multifaceted platforms that shape public opinion, culture, and individual behavior. Initially, these platforms served as spaces for connecting with friends and sharing experiences. Over time, they have evolved into complex ecosystems that not only facilitate social interaction but also play a pivotal role in news dissemination, marketing, and political campaigns.

This evolution has seen a significant shift in how social media platforms function as data repositories. The user-generated content that forms the backbone of these platforms has turned into a valuable resource for data analysis and monetization strategies. Understanding this transformation is key to grasping the role of user data in the current social media landscape, where personal information drives much of the platforms' functionality and business models.

The Nature of Data on Social Media

Social media platforms are treasure troves of user data, encompassing a wide array of information types. This data ranges from basic personal details to intricate records of user interactions, preferences, and behavioral patterns. The platforms gather this information through various methods, including direct user input, analysis of interactions within the network, and sophisticated tracking technologies.

Despite the extensive data collection, a significant challenge lies in user awareness. Many social media users remain partially or entirely unaware of the extent of data collection and its subsequent use. This gap in understanding raises critical concerns about informed consent and the ethical responsibilities of social media platforms. Enhancing user awareness and understanding of data collection practices is a crucial step toward more transparent and responsible data management in social media.

Privacy Policies and User Agreements

Privacy policies and user agreements are foundational documents that govern the relationship between social media platforms and their users. These documents detail the platforms' data collection, usage, and sharing practices. However, the complexity and length of these policies often lead to a lack of clarity and understanding among users, who may unknowingly consent to extensive data collection and usage.

Demystifying these policies and agreements is essential for users to make informed decisions. This involves breaking down the legal jargon and highlighting key clauses that impact user privacy. Understanding what users are signing up for when they agree to these terms is pivotal in empowering them to take control of their personal data and make choices aligned with their privacy preferences.

Major Data Privacy Concerns in Social Media

Social media platforms, with their vast user bases and extensive data collection, are ripe targets for privacy breaches and misuse of data. Notable incidents in recent years have brought to light the vulnerabilities in these platforms' data privacy practices. These breaches not only expose personal user information but also erode trust in the platforms.

The consequences of such breaches extend beyond the immediate exposure of personal information. They often lead to a broader discussion about the role of social media in society and the ethical responsibilities these platforms have toward their users. Understanding these incidents and their fallout is crucial in shaping future data privacy practices and regulations in the social media domain.

The User's Role in Data Privacy

While social media platforms bear a significant responsibility for protecting user data, users themselves play a critical role in safeguarding their personal information. Awareness of privacy settings, mindful sharing of information, and understanding the tools and options provided by these platforms are essential practices for users.

Empowering users to make informed decisions about their data involves education and transparency. Platforms need to provide clear, accessible information about privacy controls, while users must proactively manage their settings and remain vigilant about their online behavior. The collective effort of both users and platforms is necessary to create a more secure and privacy-conscious social media environment.

In conclusion, the landscape of data privacy in social media is complex and ever-evolving. Balancing the benefits of these platforms with privacy concerns is an ongoing challenge. This section underscores the importance of understanding the changing dynamics of social media, the evolving nature of data collection and usage, and the shared responsibility between users and platforms in protecting personal data.

Looking ahead, the social media landscape is likely to continue evolving, with emerging technologies and changing user behaviors shaping the future of data privacy.

Staying informed and adaptable is crucial for both users and platforms to navigate these changes effectively and responsibly.

1.9 Data Privacy in a Global World

In the interconnected world of the twenty-first century, data flows across borders as seamlessly as it traverses local networks. This global nature of data and the internet introduces a complex web of challenges in managing data privacy. This introduction sets the stage for exploring the multifaceted and intricate landscape of global data privacy, highlighting the need to navigate various legal, cultural, and ethical dimensions.

The rapidly evolving digital landscape has transformed the way data is handled, shared, and protected, necessitating a nuanced understanding of global data privacy dynamics. This section underscores the importance of addressing these complexities in an increasingly connected world where data transcends geographical boundaries.

The Global Data Landscape

Data's ability to transcend borders has revolutionized communication and commerce, making information exchange a truly global phenomenon. This section delves into the international flow of data, examining how it has become a cornerstone of the modern digital economy. We explore the roles of major global data centers that act as hubs of information exchange, influencing economic, social, and political dynamics worldwide.

The concept of digital sovereignty is introduced, shedding light on how countries and regions are grappling with the control and regulation of data within their borders. The implications of digital sovereignty for global data privacy are profound, raising questions about jurisdiction, control, and access in an increasingly digital world.

Diverse Data Privacy Laws and Regulations

Navigating the patchwork of data privacy laws and regulations across different countries and regions is a central challenge in global data privacy. This section offers a comparative analysis of key data privacy regulations, such as the EU's GDPR and the CCPA in the United States. We highlight the differences and similarities in these regulations, focusing on how they shape global data handling practices.

The challenges faced by multinational companies in complying with diverse laws are also examined. This part of the section considers the operational, legal, and ethical challenges in maintaining compliance across different jurisdictions, emphasizing the need for adaptable and comprehensive global data privacy strategies.

Cross-Border Data Transfer and Its Challenges

Cross-border data transfer is a critical aspect of the global data landscape, involving the movement of data across national boundaries. This section explores the mechanisms of cross-border data transfer, such as cloud storage and international servers, and the legal and technical challenges associated with it. The complexities of ensuring data privacy and security in these transfers are discussed, with an emphasis on the need for robust protection measures and compliance with varying legal requirements.

We also present case studies highlighting issues faced by companies in handling international data. These examples illustrate the practical difficulties and considerations in managing data privacy in a global context, offering insights into best practices and strategies for effective cross-border data management.

Cultural Perspectives on Privacy

Data privacy is not only a legal and technical issue but also a cultural one. This section explores how cultural values and norms influence perceptions and expectations of data privacy. We discuss the variation in privacy concerns across different cultural contexts, examining how these differences impact data privacy policies and practices of international organizations.

The section highlights examples of how cultural impacts shape data privacy initiatives and user behaviors. Understanding these cultural nuances is crucial for developing data privacy practices that are sensitive to the diverse expectations and norms of users around the world.

Data Privacy in Developing Nations

Developing nations face unique challenges in the realm of data privacy. This part of the section delves into the specific issues encountered by these countries, including limited resources, infrastructure challenges, and differing priorities in the context of data protection. The implications of the digital divide on data privacy are also discussed, considering how disparities in access to technology can impact data protection efforts.

Case studies of data privacy initiatives in emerging economies are presented, offering insights into the strategies and approaches being adopted to address these unique challenges. These examples highlight the importance of tailored solutions and international cooperation in advancing data privacy in developing regions.

Reflecting on the interconnectedness of global data privacy, this section concludes with thoughts on balancing national interests with global data privacy needs. It emphasizes the importance of a harmonized approach to data privacy that respects the diverse legal, cultural, and ethical considerations present in the global landscape.

Looking to the future, the section presents a vision for a unified global approach to data privacy. This vision encompasses collaborative efforts, shared standards, and mutual understanding, aiming to create a framework that respects individual rights while accommodating the global nature of data and the internet.

1.10 Building a Layered Data Privacy Plan

In the ever-evolving landscape of digital communication, relying on a singular approach to data privacy is insufficient. A layered data privacy plan, incorporating multiple strategies and defenses, is essential for robust protection in the digital realm. This introductory section emphasizes the importance of a comprehensive and multifaceted approach to safeguard personal and organizational data against a variety of threats and vulnerabilities.

The concept of a layered approach recognizes that data privacy challenges are diverse and dynamic, requiring a range of tools and tactics to address effectively. This section sets the stage for exploring the various components that make up a well-rounded data privacy plan.

IP Address Protection

The concealment of IP addresses is a fundamental aspect of maintaining online privacy and preventing unwanted tracking. IP addresses can reveal a user's location and internet usage patterns, making them a valuable target for data collectors and cyberattackers. This section delves into the techniques for masking IP addresses, including the use of Virtual Private Networks (VPNs), proxy servers, and the Tor network.

Each method offers different levels of protection and anonymity. VPNs, for instance, encrypt internet traffic and route it through remote servers, effectively hiding the user's real IP address. Proxy servers serve a similar function but may not offer the same level of security as VPNs. The Tor network provides enhanced anonymity by routing traffic through multiple servers. The pros and cons of each method are discussed, guiding users in choosing the right approach for their needs.

MAC Address Security

MAC (Media Access Control) addresses are unique identifiers assigned to network interfaces for communication on the physical network segment. These addresses play a crucial role in internet connectivity, ensuring that data packets are correctly routed between devices on a network.[5]

While MAC addresses are essential for network functionality, they also pose significant privacy risks. Because each MAC address is unique, they can be used to track devices and, by extension, individuals. For example, Wi-Fi access points and Bluetooth beacons can log the MAC addresses of nearby devices, creating a digital trail of a device's movements and interactions. Over time, this data can be compiled to create detailed profiles of individuals' habits and locations.

5. Mathieu Cunche, "I Know Your MAC Address: Targeted Tracking of Individual Using Wi-Fi," *Journal of Computer Virology and Hacking Techniques* 10 (December 27, 2013): 219–27, https://doi.org/10.1007/s11416-013-0196-1.

Securing MAC addresses is an essential aspect of broader data privacy efforts. By protecting MAC addresses from unauthorized tracking and exploitation, individuals can maintain a higher level of privacy and security in their digital lives. These measures help ensure that personal data remains private and protected from potentially malicious actors, contributing to overall data privacy and security.

By understanding the risks associated with MAC address exposure and implementing these protective strategies, users can better safeguard their privacy in an increasingly connected world.

DNS Privacy

Domain Name System (DNS) queries are an often-overlooked aspect of online privacy. Every time a user visits a website, a DNS query is made, potentially revealing their browsing habits. Protecting DNS queries is, therefore, crucial for maintaining online privacy. This section discusses the use of encrypted DNS services, such as DNS over HTTPS (DoH) or DNS over TLS (DoT), which secure DNS queries and prevent eavesdropping by third parties.[6]

The implementation of encrypted DNS services enhances user privacy by ensuring that internet activity is not easily accessible to ISPs, governments, or malicious actors. The section outlines how users can implement these technologies in their personal and professional digital environments.

Implementing E2EE Communications

End-to-end encryption (E2EE) is a critical component of a layered data privacy plan. E2EE ensures that only the communicating parties can access the content of messages or calls, protecting data from interception by third parties, including service providers. This section explores the factors to consider when choosing E2EE communication apps, guiding users toward making informed decisions.

Key considerations include the app's security reputation, whether the app is open-source, the encryption protocol used, the size of the user base, cross-platform support, and usability. The section reviews various E2EE apps, comparing their features and security measures. The importance of using reputable and thoroughly vetted communication tools is underscored, highlighting their role in a comprehensive data privacy strategy.

In conclusion, building a layered data privacy plan is an essential endeavor in today's digital age. By adopting a multifaceted approach that includes IP address protection, MAC address security, DNS privacy, and the implementation of E2EE communications, individuals and organizations can create a robust framework for safeguarding sensitive information.

6. "Encrypted DNS Factsheet," *Internet Society* (blog), accessed October 24, 2024, https://www.internetsociety.org/resources/doc/2023/fact-sheet-encrypted-dns/.

The section closes with a forward-looking perspective, emphasizing the need for ongoing vigilance and adaptation in response to evolving technologies and threats. The layered approach to data privacy is not static but requires continuous assessment and refinement to remain effective in protecting against a diverse array of digital privacy challenges.

Chapter Conclusion: Navigating the Complexities of Data Privacy in Digital Communications

This chapter has embarked on a comprehensive journey through the multifaceted world of data privacy in the digital age, addressing the challenges, strategies, and evolving dynamics of protecting personal and organizational information. From understanding the foundational concepts of data privacy to exploring the global landscape of data regulations and practices, the chapter has provided a panoramic view of the field.

We began by defining data privacy, distinguishing its significance in both personal and professional contexts, and examining the legal and ethical frameworks that underpin it. Recognizing common security threats, such as malware, phishing, and social engineering, we underscored the importance of awareness and proactive defense mechanisms in safeguarding digital communications.

Delving into the fundamentals of data privacy, we explored the principles of data classification, consent, transparency, and techniques like anonymization and pseudonymization. The critical role of encryption in securing digital communications was highlighted, with a special focus on E2EE as a gold standard for privacy.

The chapter then navigated the various types of digital communication technologies, examining the unique privacy challenges and protective strategies associated with each, from email and instant messaging to VoIP and social media. We also considered the ethical dilemmas inherent in balancing privacy with utility, security, and freedom, emphasizing the user's agency and responsibility in data protection.

Real-world case studies offered valuable lessons, demonstrating the consequences of data privacy failures and the importance of robust privacy practices. Building on this practical understanding, we outlined a layered approach to data privacy, integrating multiple strategies to create a comprehensive defense against diverse threats.

Sections focusing on social media and the global context of data privacy shed light on the specific challenges and considerations in these areas, revealing the nuances of managing data privacy amid evolving technologies and diverse cultural landscapes.

In conclusion, the journey through the complexities of data privacy in digital communications underscores the need for continuous learning, vigilance, and adaptation. As digital technologies advance and the landscape of data privacy evolves, staying informed and proactive is crucial. By embracing a layered approach to data privacy, understanding the global intricacies of data protection, and acknowledging the user's pivotal role, we can navigate this dynamic field more effectively, fostering a safer and more privacy-conscious digital world.

This chapter lays the groundwork for a deeper exploration of specific aspects of data privacy in subsequent chapters, each building on the foundational knowledge and perspectives established here, guiding readers toward a comprehensive understanding of data privacy in the digital age.

Key Takeaways

- Data Privacy Fundamentals: Understanding the definition and significance of data privacy in the digital age, including its application in personal and professional contexts.
- Awareness of Security Threats: Recognizing various digital security threats such as malware, phishing, and social engineering, and their impact on data privacy.
- Importance of Encryption: Grasping the role of encryption and end-to-end encryption (E2EE) in protecting digital communications.
- Digital Communication Technologies and Privacy: Identifying the unique data privacy challenges and solutions associated with different digital communication technologies like email, instant messaging, and social media.
- Ethical Considerations in Data Privacy: Evaluating the balance between privacy, utility, and security, and understanding the ethical implications in digital communications.
- Learning from Real-World Scenarios: Analyzing case studies to comprehend the practical implications and consequences of data privacy practices.
- Layered Approach to Data Privacy: Building a comprehensive, multilayered data privacy plan that incorporates various strategies for robust protection.
- Global Context of Data Privacy: Appreciating the complexities of data privacy in a global landscape, including diverse legal frameworks and cultural perspectives.
- Data Privacy in Social Media: Recognizing the challenges of managing data privacy within social media platforms and the importance of user awareness and behavior.
- Adaptive Strategies for Data Privacy: Emphasizing the need for continuous learning and adaptation in data privacy strategies to address evolving technologies and threats.

Chapter Review Questions

1. What are some common security threats in digital communications, and how do they impact data privacy?

    - Answer: Common security threats in digital communications include malware, phishing attacks, and social engineering.[7]

        - Malware: This refers to malicious software designed to harm or exploit

any programmable device, service, or network. Malware breaches can lead to unauthorized access to personal data, loss of sensitive information, and can compromise the integrity of a system.
    - Phishing Attacks: Phishing involves deceiving individuals into revealing personal information, such as passwords or credit card numbers, often through misleading emails or websites. This can lead to identity theft and unauthorized access to private data.
    - Social Engineering: This is the psychological manipulation of people into performing actions or divulging confidential information. It often exploits human error and can lead to significant data breaches.

2. How does E2EE contribute to data privacy, and what are its limitations?

    - Answer: E2EE is a method of secure communication that prevents third parties from accessing data while it is transferred from one end system to another. It contributes to data privacy by ensuring that only the communicating users can access the message content, thereby protecting it from interception by external parties, including service providers.[8]

        - Limitations:

            - It does not protect against the collection of metadata (such as time of communication, participants, etc.).
            - E2EE is effective only if the encryption keys are properly managed and kept secure.
            - In some cases, it can hinder legitimate access to data for law enforcement and security purposes.
            - User error or weak end-point security can still compromise the data.

3. Compare and contrast the data privacy challenges in social media platforms with those in global data management. What unique considerations apply to each?

    - Answer:

        - Social Media Platforms: Challenges include managing the vast amounts of personal data generated by users, protecting this data from unauthorized access, and handling issues related to consent and user awareness. Unique considerations include the need to balance user

7. Kashif Ishaq and Sidra Fareed, "Mitigation Techniques for Cyber Attacks: A Systematic Mapping Study" (arXiv, August 25, 2023), http://arxiv.org/abs/2308.13587.
8. Ermoshina et al., "End-to-End Encrypted Messaging."

experience with privacy protections, the influence of advertising and marketing strategies on data use, and the societal impact of data handling practices.[9]

- Global Data Management: The challenges involve navigating diverse data privacy laws and regulations across different countries, managing cross-border data transfers, and addressing the varying expectations of privacy in different cultural contexts. Unique considerations include legal compliance in multiple jurisdictions, the logistics of data storage and transfer across borders, and addressing the digital sovereignty concerns of different nations.[10]\

9. Alexandra Olteanu, Carlos Castillo, Fernando Diaz, and Emre Kiciman, "Social Data: Biases, Methodological Pitfalls, and Ethical Boundaries," *Frontiers in Big Data* 2 (July 11, 2019), https://doi.org/10.3389/fdata.2019.00013.
10. Sara Marcucci, Natalia González Alarcón, Stefaan G. Verhulst, and Elena Wüllhorst, "Informing the Global Data Future: Benchmarking Data Governance Frameworks," *Data & Policy* 5 (2023): e30, accessed October 24, 2024, https://www.cambridge.org/core/journals/data-and-policy/article/informing-the-global-data-future-benchmarking-data-governance-frameworks/23C5B7F8C65F21602DD5175DDE49E3BF.

Chapter 2

From Bytes to Bites

Understanding Cybersecurity in Digital Life

Lamia Zia, PhD

Learning Outcomes

- Define cyberspace and explain its physical and virtual components using accessible analogies.
- Distinguish between cyber literacy and cybersecurity, understanding the roles each plays in maintaining digital safety.
- Recognize common cyber threats, including malware, phishing, ransomware, social engineering, insider threats, and man-in-the-middle attacks.
- Identify real-world case studies that illustrate the impact of various cyberattacks, including the Bangladesh Bank heist, the WannaCry ransomware attack, and the Equifax breach.
- Describe the evolution of cyberspace, from early networking concepts to modern digital infrastructures.
- Apply foundational concepts of cyber literacy to protect personal identity, data, and systems in a connected world.
- Explain the importance of cyber literacy in digital communication field and how "cyber literates" can to bridge the gap between technical expertise and public understanding.

Key Terms

- **Cyberspace**: The interconnected digital environment consisting of virtual data, hardware infrastructure, and communication networks.
- **Cyber Literacy**: The knowledge and skills necessary to navigate, understand, and engage safely with digital technologies and platforms.
- **Cybersecurity**: The practice of protecting systems, networks, and programs from digital attacks.
- **Phishing**: A fraudulent attempt to obtain sensitive information by disguising as a

trustworthy entity in digital communication.

- **Ransomware**: Malicious software that encrypts data and demands payment for its release.
- **Social Engineering**: Psychological manipulation used to trick individuals into divulging confidential information.
- **Insider Threat**: Security risks that originate from within an organization, typically involving misuse of access.
- **Malware**: Software designed to disrupt, damage, or gain unauthorized access to computer systems.
- **DNS Spoofing**: A cyberattack where a user is misled into visiting a fraudulent website disguised as a legitimate one.
- **Man-in-the-Middle (MitM) Attack**: An attack where a third party intercepts communication between two entities to steal or manipulate data.
- **Digital Literacy**: Broader than cyber literacy, encompassing the ability to use digital tools effectively and responsibly.

Introduction

What does it mean to be "secure" in a world where your life is increasingly lived through a screen?

Cybersecurity is often introduced as a technical discipline, firewalls, encryption, passwords, and code. But for anyone growing up online today, this definition feels incomplete. You don't just use the internet, you build relationships on it, submit assignments through it, run businesses on it, and trust it with your money. Your identity, reputation, and opportunities are all intertwined with digital spaces. In that sense, cybersecurity is no longer just about protecting systems; it is about protecting people.

Think about your daily routine. You message friends, collaborate with classmates, shop, bank, and perhaps even work online. Each of these actions creates a digital footprint, tiny fragments of your life that, when combined, form a detailed portrait of who you are. Cybersecurity, therefore, is not simply a technical safeguard; it is a social, psychological, economic, and even political necessity. It shapes how safely you interact, how confidently you express yourself, and how much control you retain over your own data.

This shift means that cybersecurity is no longer the exclusive domain of IT professionals. It is a shared responsibility. In fact, one of the most important lessons in cybersecurity is that expertise does not guarantee immunity. Consider the case of Madhu Gottumukkala, the acting head of the United States' cyber defense agency, who in 2025 reportedly uploaded sensitive government contracting documents into a public AI system. Despite deep technical knowledge and experience, a simple lapse in judgment triggered multiple internal security warnings (Politico, 2026).

If a cybersecurity expert can make such a mistake, what does that say about the rest of us?

The reality is clear: vulnerability in the digital world is not just about lacking technical skills, it is about human behavior. Curiosity, convenience, trust, and even haste can override knowledge. This is why cybersecurity must be understood not only as a technical field but as a human-centered discipline. It involves awareness, decision-making, ethics, and critical thinking.

For students, professionals, and everyday citizens, the stakes are high. A weak password can compromise a bank account. A careless click can expose personal data. A misleading message can damage relationships or reputations. Cybersecurity, therefore, is not an abstract concept, it is deeply personal.

This chapter begins with a simple but powerful idea: cybersecurity is about understanding how we live, think, and act in the digital world. It is about recognizing that every online action carries risk and that every individual, regardless of expertise, plays a role in managing that risk.

Scenario: Imagine this: You're Ali, a diligent student, logging into your trusted online study platform, "StudyHub.com," as you do every evening. But tonight feels different. The familiar login page is replaced by one that looks slightly off the logo isn't quite right, and instead of asking for your usual username and password, it requests your email and a verification code. Confused, you double-check the web address and spot the subtle difference: "StuddyHub.com," with an extra "d." Without realizing it, you've become the latest victim of a Domain Name System (DNS) spoofing attack. A cybercriminal has carefully set up a fake website to steal your login information. This complex scenario highlights how easy it is to fall prey to cyber threats in our digital world.

While Ali's situation may seem hypothetical, the consequences of such attacks in the real world can be devastating on a personal, financial, and even global scale. In 2016, employees at Bangladesh Bank noticed something odd: a discrepancy in their financial records. They soon discovered that hackers had infiltrated their systems and attempted to steal nearly $1 billion from their account at the Federal Reserve Bank of New York. Through clever use of malware and exploiting weak cybersecurity protocols, the hackers managed to withdraw $81 million before being stopped. The money disappeared into the ether of cyberspace, laundered through casinos in the Philippines, and most of it was never recovered (Krishna & Jonathan, 2016).

This wasn't a typical heist involving guns, ski masks, or getaway cars. Instead, the criminals armed themselves with laptops and exploited the internet as their weapon of choice. This shift marks a profound transformation in how crimes are carried out, turning the digital world into a new kind of battleground—one where anyone can be a target. Whether you're casually shopping online, sharing photos on social media, or working with sensitive corporate data, you're an active participant in this vast and interconnected cyberspace.

While this digital domain has unlocked unprecedented opportunities offering global communication, innovation, and accessibility, it also comes with significant risks. Cybercriminals are constantly evolving their strategies, targeting individuals, organizations, and even governments. Phishing schemes, ransomware attacks, data breaches, and misinformation campaigns are just some examples of how the online world can be weaponized.

In this digital environment, developing a deep understanding of cyberspace and becoming cyber literate is no longer optional; it is essential. Cyber literacy equips you with the ability to recognize potential threats, adopt safe online practices, and critically evaluate digital information. It empowers individuals to protect themselves, their data, and their organizations against the growing number of cyber threats. In essence, understanding cyberspace and mastering its risks is not just a skill, it's a form of digital survival. Engaging with cyberspace is much like Alice's journey in *Alice in Wonderland*, where she ventures into a world full of challenges, often questioning reality and adapting creatively. Her best survival skill lies in thinking critically to make wise decisions that defy the chaos around her. Similarly, mastering these skills in the digital realm is not just an advantage, it's a necessity for survival and success in our ever-evolving online world.

In this chapter, we explore what cyberspace really is, why cyber literacy is essential, and how you can begin to understand this complex digital world safely and effectively. Like the Bangladesh Bank employees learned the hard way, understanding cyberspace is no longer optional, it's a skill that can protect you, your data, and even your future.

According to the US Security Magazine, "much of the existing cybersecurity literature centers around defending the complex digital systems belonging to large corporations. Much less attention is paid to providing the average user with the basic knowledge and technical skills they should have to defend their personal computers or small business systems. However, individual users and small businesses are just as vulnerable to cyber threats" (LeClair 2016).

This highlights a critical issue: the significant knowledge gap between the field of cybersecurity and the everyday user. While cybersecurity experts dedicate their efforts to defending complex systems for large corporations, the average person, a small business owner, or a young student growing up with digital gadgets and social media platforms often lacks the foundational knowledge and tools to protect themselves. This gap leaves individuals and small organizations alarmingly vulnerable to increasingly sophisticated cyber threats.

For instance, consider a small business owner managing their operations online or a young student actively engaging on social media. Both may unknowingly expose themselves to risks by relying on weak passwords, neglecting software updates, or failing to recognize phishing attempts. These seemingly minor oversights can have devastating consequences, from data breaches to financial loss or identity theft.

The knowledge gap, however, is not just a technological challenge, it is a communication challenge. Cybersecurity professionals must bridge this divide by translating their expertise into clear, actionable advice that resonates with everyone. By making cybersecurity education accessible and relatable, even the least technical among us can be equipped with the tools and awareness needed to stay safe in an increasingly digital world. As the line between bytes and bites continues to blur, developing cyber literacy becomes not just an individual skill but a critical tool for safeguarding the digital spaces we rely on every day.

> What is Cyberspace?
>
> Cyberspace is first and foremost an information environment. It is made up of digitized data that is created, stored, and, most importantly, shared. This means that it is not merely a physical place and thus defies measurement in any kind of physical dimension. But cyberspace isn't purely virtual. It comprises the computers that store data plus the systems and infrastructure that allow it to flow. This includes the Internet of networked computers, closed intranets, cellular, technologies, fiber optic cables, and space-based communications (Singer and Friedman 2014, 13).

As Singer and Friedman (2014) argue, cyberspace defies physical measurement because it is not merely a tangible place. Instead, it represents a dual nature both virtual and physical. According to Singer and Friedman, cyberspace is not confined to a single dimension; instead, it exists as an intricate web of information and technology that drives modern communication, commerce, and innovation. From the vast infrastructure of fiber-optic cables and cellular networks to the boundless flow of digitized data, cyberspace underpins every aspect of our digitally connected world.

Imagine it like the world of Minecraft. In the game, you build intricate structures and share creations with others, but everything relies on the game's code (virtual) and the computers, servers, and networks that make the game run (physical). Without both elements working together, your blocky worlds wouldn't exist.

Now, think about what happens if someone hacks the game and floods your world with creepers or steals your prized builds. That's a simplified version of a cyberattack targeting both the software (virtual) and the server systems (physical). Just like in Minecraft, where understanding how the game works helps you protect your creations, cyber literacy helps people to stay safe and secure the complex environment of cyberspace.

This chapter invites readers to embark on a journey through the fascinating, often perilous landscape of cyberspace and cyber literacy. Along the way, it illuminates the essential tools needed to safeguard one's presence and work in this interconnected world. Through the lens of historical events, real-world case studies, and forward-thinking insights, readers will uncover the layers of cyberspace: its infrastructure, vulnerabilities, and the proactive measures necessary to thrive within it.

Key milestones on this journey include the following:

- Defining and contextualizing cyberspace, unraveling its complexity and the systems that sustain it.
- Highlighting the power of cyber literacy as both a compass and shield in the digital age.
- Examining the most pressing security threats, malware, phishing schemes, and ransomware, each a reminder of the stakes in this invisible battlefield.

- Offering cyber strategies to mitigate risks and cultivate a culture of cybersecurity awareness, empowering readers to protect themselves and their digital endeavors.

Understanding cyberspace is not merely a technical exercise; it is an imperative for safeguarding the interconnected systems that define modern life. The future of communication, innovation, and creativity depends on those who dare to explore this web—not as mere participants but as informed and empowered guardians of the digital age (Castells 2009).

2.1 What Is Cyber Literacy?

The illiterate of the 21st century will not be those who cannot read and write, but those who cannot learn, unlearn, and relearn.

Alvin Toffler

According to Cyburanus (2023), cybersecurity awareness is often best conveyed through powerful, memorable quotes. This timeless quote by Alvin Toffler (1970) provides a profound lens through which to understand cyber literacy. In today's rapidly evolving digital world, traditional literacy, the ability to read and write—is no longer enough. Cyber literacy extends this concept, emphasizing the ability to adapt, understand, and responsibly engage with the complex systems of cyberspace. It requires learning how to navigate digital environments, unlearning outdated practices, and relearning to keep pace with technological advancements.

Imagine this: one day, you find out someone has created a fake Facebook account using your name and photos. This impostor starts reaching out to your friends, family, and colleagues, possibly spreading false information or even attempting scams. Naturally, your first reaction is to take action. You quickly report the fake profile to Facebook, providing all the necessary details. To protect your connections, you also post an announcement on your real account, warning your friends about the impersonator and advising them to be cautious.

But then, you receive Facebook's response to your report:

"We didn't remove the profile. To keep our review process as fair as possible, we use the same set of Community Standards to review all reports. We've taken a look and found that the profile doesn't go against our Community Standards. We understand that this might be upsetting, so we recommend exploring the options available to control what you see. If you want us to review something specific within a profile, be sure to report the content (example: photo), not the entire profile. You can also request a review within 180 days if you disagree with the decision to not take this down."

Frustrating, right? Despite your genuine concern, the system has determined the fake account doesn't violate any guidelines. This scenario highlights a significant challenge in digital spaces—platforms' automated or rigid content moderation processes sometimes fail to address real threats. In such cases, you're left wondering: How can you protect your identity and ensure your digital safety when even official avenues fall short? It's situations like this that underscore the importance of cyber literacy and proactive vigilance in navigating cyberspace.

Definition and Scope of Cyber Literacy

In the 1950s and 1960s, media literacy began to take shape as a critical academic response to the rapidly expanding influence of mass media—particularly through dominant channels such as radio, television, film, and print newspapers. During this period, the media became a central force in shaping public opinion, social norms, and cultural values. Scholars and educators recognized that the public was increasingly exposed to a steady stream of mediated messages that could subtly shape behavior, attitudes, and beliefs.

Pioneering communication theorists like Marshall McLuhan and Harold Innis emerged as foundational voices in this discourse. McLuhan, in particular, revolutionized media studies with his assertion that "the medium is the message." This provocative idea challenged conventional thinking by suggesting that the form of a medium whether it was television, print, or radio played a more significant role in shaping human experience and societal change than the actual content delivered through that medium. His work emphasized that the technology of communication itself alters human perception and social organization. Building on this foundation, media literacy in this era aimed to equip individuals with the critical tools necessary to navigate and interpret media messages consciously.

While cyber literacy, as defined by contemporary scholars such as Magomedov et al. (2020), represents an advanced stage in the evolution of literacy in the communication age. This involves understanding the structure and functioning of cyberspace, recognizing and mitigating cyber threats, and engaging responsibly and ethically in online activities. The authors emphasize the importance of cyber literacy as a discipline in modern educational institutions to prepare individuals for the challenges posed by the digital age. In their study, Magomedov and colleagues highlight that cyber literacy is not merely about technical proficiency but also involves critical thinking, awareness of digital rights, and the ability to discern credible information from misinformation. They argue that as technology becomes increasingly integrated into all aspects of life, from education to commerce, the need for comprehensive cyber literacy education becomes paramount. By equipping individuals with these skills, society can better safeguard against cyber threats and promote a more informed and secure digital community. This definition of cyber literacy highlights the nature of cyber literacy, combining technical skills with ethical considerations and critical analysis, making it a crucial competency in today's interconnected world.

While it builds on the foundational concepts introduced by media literacy, cyber literacy responds to a fundamentally different technological and social landscape, one that is highly interactive, networked, and increasingly governed by data and algorithms.

In contrast to the passive media consumption model of the mid-20th century, cyber literacy is concerned with how individuals now actively engage with digital platforms. Users are no longer just recipients of media messages—they are content creators, curators, and distributors. For instance, through platforms like YouTube, TikTok, Twitter, and Reddit, users are constantly generating and reshaping digital content, often unaware of how their behavior is being influenced or surveilled by platform algorithms. The digital environment has become participatory and two-way, requiring a new set of competencies to navigate its complexities.

Cyber literacy, therefore, emphasizes the following core areas:

A cyber-literate individual has a working knowledge of the infrastructure of the internet and the technological mechanisms that drive online experiences. This includes understanding how algorithms curate information, how data is collected and monetized, and how platforms shape the visibility and spread of content. For example, recognizing why certain videos are recommended on YouTube or how a social media feed is ordered is central to understanding one's digital environment.

In today's digital landscape, where data breaches, phishing attacks, and identity theft are common, cyber literacy must include the ability to protect one's personal information. This involves understanding digital footprints, managing privacy settings, using secure passwords, and recognizing suspicious online behavior.

With the rise of cyberbullying, misinformation, trolling, and digital harassment, there is a growing need for ethical awareness in online interactions. Cyber literacy promotes digital citizenship, where individuals communicate respectfully, fact-check information, and understand the moral consequences of their online actions. Similar to media literacy, cyber literacy encourages users to think critically about the information they consume and share. However, this now involves evaluating the credibility of online sources, understanding filter bubbles, and resisting manipulation by targeted advertising or propaganda, often powered by artificial intelligence and algorithmic profiling. Perhaps one of the most important features of cyber literacy is its emphasis on adaptability. The digital world evolves rapidly with new platforms, tools, and threats emerging regularly. A cyber-literate individual embraces continuous learning, staying updated with new technologies, digital trends, and cybersecurity practices.

In contrast to media literacy's focus on centralized media institutions and linear communication flows, cyber literacy addresses a world where control is decentralized and information flows are nonlinear, real-time, and user-driven. Communication is not only shaped by traditional media producers but by millions of individuals whose digital actions have immediate social and political impact. Furthermore, while media literacy traditionally dealt with the analysis of content presented through radio, television, and newspapers, cyber literacy requires an awareness of the invisible systems—algorithms, surveillance networks, data analytics, and AI—that now mediate human interaction and information exchange.

Thus, cyber literacy goes beyond the basic ability to use computers or browse the internet. It refers to a broad and evolving set of skills and knowledge that enable individuals to understand, navigate, and engage effectively in the digital world. In essence, a cyber-literate person not only knows how to use digital tools but also *why* they work the way they do, *what* risks and responsibilities are involved, and how to adapt to new technologies in a rapidly evolving digital world. Below are the core areas that define cyber literacy, each explained with practical, real-life examples:

Understanding the Cyber World

At its core, cyber literacy involves knowing how digital systems function. When you stream a movie on a platform like Netflix, there's more happening than just pressing play. Behind the scenes, data is being transmitted through servers, internet infrastructure, and your local network. A cyber-literate individual understands these basic concepts—such as how data travels, what networks do, and how devices connect helping them appreciate the technology that powers everyday digital experiences.

Digital Communication and Engagement

Being able to communicate and behave responsibly online is a key component of cyber literacy. Whether you're sharing ideas on social media, participating in a group chat, or commenting on a public forum, it's important to know how to engage respectfully and thoughtfully. For example, recognizing misinformation, avoiding online harassment, and understanding the tone and impact of digital messages are all part of being a cyber-literate communicator.

Protecting Personal Identity and Data

With the rise of cyber threats, protecting your online identity and personal information is more important than ever. Cyber-literate individuals know how to create strong passwords, enable two-factor authentication (2FA), and recognize suspicious emails or websites that may be phishing attempts. For instance, when you shop online, cyber literacy ensures you understand the importance of secure payment systems and safe browsing habits.

Navigating Complex Digital Systems

Today's digital world is built on complex systems like cloud storage, algorithms, and collaborative platforms. Tools such as Google Drive or Microsoft Teams are common in academic and professional settings. Understanding how these tools work—and how to use them efficiently enables students to collaborate, manage files, and organize their digital workspaces effectively. Similarly, knowing how recommendation algorithms work on YouTube or TikTok helps users critically assess the content they consume.

2.2 History of Cyber: A Brief Overview

The concept of cyber" originates from the term cybernetics, introduced by Norbert Wiener in the 1940s. Wiener defined cybernetics as the study of communication and control in machines and living organisms (Wiener 2019). This term laid the foundation for understanding interconnected systems, which would later evolve into what we now call cyberspace. Later, William Gibson introduced the term "cyberspace" in his 1984 novel *Neuromancer* (Gibson 1984), in which he described a virtual reality world accessed through networks. While initially fictional, Gibson's vision became a reality with the development of the internet and modern digital networks.

Key Historical Milestones in Cyber Development:

- 1960s: The Birth of Networking. The groundwork for cyberspace was laid with the development of ARPANET in 1969, a precursor to the internet. Researchers like Lawrence Roberts and Leonard Kleinrock played critical roles in demonstrating the potential of interconnected systems to share data and resources (Abbate 2000).
- 1970s: The Rise of Personal Computing. The 1970s saw the emergence of personal computers, making digital technology accessible to individuals. This democratization of computing paved the way for a future where digital literacy became a necessity (Isaacson 2015).
- 1980s: The Internet Takes Shape. The DNS was introduced in 1983, making the internet more user-friendly. Around this time, researchers began to explore the vulnerabilities of interconnected systems, leading to early discussions on cybersecurity (Levy 1984).
- 1990s: The World Wide Web. Tim Berners-Lee's creation of the World Wide Web in 1989 and its public introduction in the 1990s revolutionized communication and commerce. As cyberspace expanded, so did cyber threats, with the first major malware, the Morris Worm, appearing in 1988 (Hafner and Markoff 1995).
- 2000s: The Digital Age. With the proliferation of social media, smartphones, and e-commerce, cyberspace became integral to daily life. This era also saw the rise of sophisticated cyberattacks, such as the Stuxnet worm in 2010, highlighting the growing need for robust cybersecurity measures (Singer and Friedman 2014).
- 2010s and Beyond: The Age of Cyber Threats and Resilience.

As cyber technologies became more advanced, so did the threats. Nations, organizations, and individuals faced challenges like ransomware attacks, data breaches, and cyber warfare. The literature increasingly emphasized the importance of cyber literacy to navigate these threats (Clarke and Knake 2011). The history of cyberspace is one of rapid innovation, evolving from theoretical concepts in cybernetics to becoming an integral part of modern life. As cyberspace expands, so does the urgency to understand its complexities, vulnerabilities, and the role of cyber literacy in addressing its ever-changing challenges. It is not merely a product of technological advancement but an emerging field of knowledge that continues to evolve, shaping and being shaped by the way we communicate, innovate, and interact in the digital age.

2.3 Cyber Literacy Versus Cybersecurity

There are two sides of the same coin: one is cybersecurity, and the other is cyber literacy. Cybersecurity is like building a fortress. IT professionals construct strong walls, install surveillance, and design defenses to keep attackers out. Their work revolves around creating tools, software, and systems to guard against cyber threats. It's highly technical and focused on the mechanisms of protection.

Now, flip the coin to the other side, cyber literacy. This isn't about building the fortress; it's about teaching the people living inside it how to stay safe. Cyber literacy focuses on the human element, helping individuals understand the risks in the digital world and how to act responsibly. It's not about designing security systems but fostering awareness, teaching safe practices, and ensuring that everyone knows how to avoid common pitfalls, like phishing scams or weak passwords.

For students in media and communication, this distinction is especially important. Think of them as translators—they don't need to be the engineers building the fortress (cybersecurity experts), but they are essential in communicating how to use the fortress effectively. Their role is to take complex cybersecurity concepts and turn them into accessible knowledge for the public. They create a culture of cyber literacy, enabling people to live and work safely in a world where everything is connected. By doing this, they bridge the gap between technical defenses and everyday digital behaviors.

Why Cyber Literacy Matters?

Cyber literacy equips individuals to not just survive but excel in an interconnected world. Whether it's staying safe from ransomware, collaborating with colleagues globally, or simply understanding how a smartphone connects to a Wi-Fi network, being cyber literate ensures one remains adaptable and informed. Through cyber literacy, we can all become active participants in shaping the digital future not just as users, but as empowered and responsible stewards of the cyberspace we inhabit

While developing sophisticated cybersecurity tools is essential, it is equally important to ensure that individuals understand how to use them effectively. Cyber literacy bridges this gap, equipping people with the knowledge to

- identify threats like malware, phishing, and ransomware;
- use encryption and privacy tools to secure communication; and

- develop critical thinking skills to navigate the complexities of cyberspace responsibly.

In essence, cyber literacy empowers individuals to be active, informed participants in the digital age, complementing the technical efforts of cybersecurity professionals. Together, these domains ensure the safety and integrity of the cyber world for all its users.

In the rapidly evolving digital age, where technology integrates deeply into our personal, academic, and professional lives, cyber literacy emerges as an essential skill. Cyber literacy encompasses the knowledge, skills, and awareness required to navigate, use, and secure digital platforms effectively. For students preparing to engage with the dynamic fields of media and communication, understanding cyber literacy is not merely a technical necessity but a critical competency to safeguard data, reputation, and resources.

By exploring the evolution of cyber threats and examining specific challenges such as malware, phishing, and ransomware, the chapter highlight the pressing need for robust cyber literacy in today's interconnected world. It also envisions the future landscape of digital security, encouraging proactive and adaptive approaches to emerging technologies and threats.

The biggest threat to digital communication today is not merely the prevalence of cyberattacks; rather, it is the widespread lack of knowledge and understanding of how to function securely and responsibly in the cyber world. This gap in awareness and skills is what we term cyber literacy, and it represents a foundational weakness in our collective ability to protect our data and navigate the complexities of the digital landscape.

Cyberattacks thrive in environments where individuals and organizations are uninformed or ill-equipped to recognize and respond to threats. For instance, phishing scams, ransomware attacks, and data breaches often succeed because of user errors clicking malicious links, using weak passwords, or failing to update software. These vulnerabilities stem not from a lack of technological solutions but from a lack of understanding about basic cybersecurity principles.

Furthermore, the rapid evolution of technology means that threats are constantly changing, and the only way to keep pace is through ongoing education. Teaching individuals and organizations how to protect their data, identify potential threats, and adopt best practices for secure communication is critical. This involves integrating cybersecurity education into schools, workplaces, and public awareness campaigns to ensure that everyone, regardless of their background, has the tools to navigate the digital world safely.

The Role of "Cyber Literates"

Students in media and communication are uniquely positioned to bridge the knowledge gap in cybersecurity, acting as vital agents of change in cyber literacy. Their deep engagement with digital platforms and networks places them at the forefront of addressing and mitigating risks in both personal and professional digital activities. By developing a nuanced understanding of cyberspace and its vulnerabilities, these "cyber literates" are equipped to advocate for secure digital practices within organizations and communities, ensuring that technology is used responsibly and safely. Moreover, their ability to communicate complex concepts in accessible ways enables them to contribute to a broader understanding of how to explore and live safely in an increasingly cyber-connected world.

2.4 Common Cyber Threats

Cyber threats refer to malicious activities aimed at compromising the integrity, confidentiality, or availability of digital systems and data. Here's a breakdown of some common cyber threats, along with real-world examples and events to illustrate their impact:

Malware: The Sneaky Saboteur

Definition: Malware, short for "malicious software," includes viruses, worms, ransomware, spyware, and trojans designed to disrupt, damage, or gain unauthorized access to systems. Malware often infiltrates systems via malicious email attachments, suspicious links, infected websites

Defensive Measures

- Installed antivirus software.
- Avoided downloading from shady websites.
- Enabled automatic updates to patch vulnerabilities.

Case Study: Malware: The ILOVEYOU Worm

In May 2000, the ILOVEYOU worm emerged as one of the most destructive malware attacks in history. Disguised as a love letter, it spread via email with the subject line "ILOVEYOU" and an attachment named "LOVE-LETTER-FOR-YOU.txt.vbs." When recipients opened the attachment, the worm executed a Visual Basic script that overwrote files, stole passwords, and propagated itself to the victim's email contacts. Within ten days, it infected approximately 45 million computers worldwide, causing an estimated $10 billion in damages.

Phishing: The Master Impersonator

Phishing is a deceptive practice where cybercriminals pose as trustworthy entities, such as banks or companies, to trick individuals into providing sensitive information like usernames, passwords, or credit card details. For instance, Abdul received an email that appeared to be from his bank, urgently requesting him to "verify" his account. Without double-checking, he clicked the link and entered his login credentials, unknowingly handing them over to a cyber thief. Phishing schemes often use fake emails, websites, or messages to exploit trust and steal personal data. To avoid falling victim, it's crucial to watch for red flags such as suspicious sender addresses, generic greetings like "Dear Customer," and urgent demands for immediate action. Staying safe involves adopting best practices, including verifying links before clicking, directly contacting organizations to confirm unusual requests, and enabling multifactor authentication for added security. Awareness and vigilance are your best defenses against phishing attempts.

Case Study: Phishing: Google and Facebook Scam

Between 2013 and 2015, Evaldas Rimasauskas, a Lithuanian national, orchestrated a phishing scheme that defrauded tech giants Google and Facebook of over $100 million. By impersonating a hardware manufacturer through spoofed emails and fake invoices, he deceived the companies into transferring substantial funds to his controlled bank accounts. The scam exploited weaknesses in business processes and highlighted the effectiveness of targeted phishing attacks (CNBC 2019).

Case Study: When the FBI Rings... and It's Not Really the FBI

In May 2025, the FBI's Cyber Division issued an urgent warning that perfectly illustrates why cyber literacy is more important now than ever. Posted on their official LinkedIn page and widely circulated across law enforcement and cybersecurity networks, the alert revealed an ongoing malicious messaging campaign that began in April 2025—and it was unlike anything we've seen before.

Hackers had leveled up.

In this campaign, malicious actors impersonated senior U.S. federal and state government officials—yes, actual top-level officials and used smishing (fraudulent SMS texts) and vishing (voice phishing) techniques to target individuals, including current and former government personnel and their contacts.

But here's the twist: they weren't using simple scam calls. These cybercriminals deployed AI-generated voices—cloned to mimic real people—and convincing text messages to establish credibility. Then, under the guise of switching platforms or continuing a conversation, they'd drop a malicious link designed to capture login credentials or gain access to sensitive accounts.

Once inside, the hackers didn't just stop. They used the compromised accounts to reach further into the professional networks of their victims leveraging trusted relationships to gather even more private data, elicit funds, or impersonate contacts.

This campaign was more than just a scam; it was a masterclass in social engineering.

What Does This Mean for Cyber Literacy?

This case study shows how modern cyberattacks blur the line between reality and manipulation making it harder than ever to tell what's real. It also shows how important it is to recognize and understand tactics like:

- Smishing: Targeted text messages designed to trick you into clicking harmful links or sharing data.
- Vishing: Fake voice messages (increasingly AI-generated) designed to build trust and extract sensitive information.
- Spear Phishing: Highly personalized attacks that exploit familiarity and known relationships to manipulate you.

These aren't abstract threats. They're real, they're current, and they're increasingly sophisticated.

Why This Matters to You

You may not be a government official (yet), but your personal data, social connections, and digital identity are still valuable targets. If hackers can impersonate officials and fool federal agents, imagine how easily they could target a student, a professor, or an employee who doesn't know the warning signs. This case proves why cyber literacy isn't optional—it's essential. Being able to spot red flags, question authenticity, and protect your information are now part of digital survival.

Lesson: If a message claims to be from someone important, pause. Think. Verify. Because in today's world, even the FBI might not be the FBI.

How to Protect Yourself from Smishing and Vishing Scams

Here's how to stay safe from these increasingly sophisticated social engineering attacks:

- Don't trust caller ID or message headers. Phone numbers and names can be spoofed.
- Independently confirm the identity using a contact method you already know—such as an official website, previously saved number, or direct in-person contact.
- If someone claims to be from an organization, call the organization yourself using their official contact number to confirm.
- If a message contains a link and feels even slightly off, don't click it.
- Hover over the link to preview the URL. Look for misspellings, strange domains, or unexpected redirects.
- When in doubt, go directly to the site by typing the URL in your browser—don't follow the link.

- Even if your login credentials are stolen, MFA can stop unauthorized access. Never share MFA codes with anyone—not even someone claiming to be tech support or a company representative.
- AI-generated voices may sound "off" robotic tone, lagging responses, unnatural phrasing.
- Trust your gut. If something sounds strange, hang up or stop the conversation.
- Messages or calls that create a sense of urgency, secrecy, or guilt are classic manipulation tactics.
- Follow cybersecurity news and stay updated on current scams (like this 2025 campaign from the FBI).

Ransomware: The Digital Hostage Taker

Ransomware attacks are a chilling reminder of the vulnerabilities in our digital systems. One high-profile example is the Colonial Pipeline attack, where cybercriminals locked the company's systems and demanded millions in ransom to restore access, causing widespread disruptions (Cybersecurity and Infrastructure Security Agency 2023). This incident illustrates the devastating potential of ransomware. Imagine being locked out of your family photos or critical work files, only to find a ransom note demanding payment to regain access. To combat such threats, preventive measures are essential. Regularly backing up data ensures critical files are not lost, strong network defenses minimize vulnerabilities, and training employees to recognize suspicious emails can help stop an attack before it starts. The Colonial Pipeline attack serves as a stark warning of the importance of these proactive steps.

Case Study: The WannaCry Ransomware Attack

The WannaCry ransomware attack, which began in Europe in May 2017, quickly became one of the most widespread and damaging cyberattacks in history that sent shockwaves through the cybersecurity community (Natasha, 2023). Over the course of a single weekend, the malicious software infected more than 300,000 computers across more than 150 countries. Victims were confronted with a screen demanding a $300 ransom in Bitcoin to unlock their encrypted files. The attack impacted critical infrastructure, including hospitals, businesses, and government systems, causing widespread disruption and financial loss (Bill 2017).

Spread and Impact

The attack leveraged a vulnerability in Microsoft Windows systems known as EternalBlue, which had been previously disclosed in leaked documents from the US National Security Agency (NSA). Despite Microsoft releasing a patch for the vulnerability prior to the attack, many systems remained unpatched, allowing the ransomware to spread rapidly. High-profile victims included the United Kingdom's National Health Service (NHS), where hospital operations and patient care were severely disrupted, and major corporations such as FedEx (BBC News 2017)

Global Scope

While the initial outbreak primarily affected European systems, the malware quickly spread to Asia, with significant impacts reported in Japan and China. The attack's global nature highlighted vulnerabilities in cybersecurity practices worldwide. White House Homeland Security Adviser Tom Bossert noted that the rate of infection slowed over the weekend, but the damage had already been done (Bill 2017). Furthermore, the success of WannaCry inspired copycat attacks, posing ongoing threats to systems that remained vulnerable.

Key Lessons Learned

The WannaCry incident underscored the critical importance of timely software updates and patch management. Organizations that had applied Microsoft's security patch were unaffected, while those that had not suffered severe consequences. Additionally, the attack highlighted the need for robust backup strategies, as many victims lacked alternative access to their encrypted data.

Social Engineering: The Smooth Talker

Social engineering is a cyber threat that involves manipulating individuals into divulging sensitive information, such as passwords or financial details, or performing actions that compromise security. Instead of relying on technical hacking methods, attackers exploit human psychology, such as trust, fear, or urgency, to achieve their goals. For example, an attacker calls an employee, pretending to be from the company's IT department, and claims there's an urgent issue with their account. Exploiting the employee's fear of losing access, the attacker persuades them to share their password, gaining unauthorized access to the company's systems.

Case Study: Social Engineering: 2016 US Election Phishing

According to CNN (2024), the 2016 presidential campaign was targeted by hackers using advanced social engineering techniques. During the 2016 US presidential election, Russian intelligence officers conducted spear-phishing attacks against members of Hillary Clinton's campaign. Disguised as legitimate Google security alerts, these emails tricked recipients into revealing their passwords, leading to the leak of thousands of private emails and documents. This incident highlighted the profound impact of social engineering on political processes.

CNN reported, "Hackers create a fake email account and use it to send spear-phishing emails to more than thirty Clinton staffers, according to investigators. In the emails, the hackers embed a link purporting to direct the recipient to a document titled "hillaryclinton-favorable-rating.xlsx." The link directs the recipients' computers to a website operated by the hackers. That same month, hackers use stolen credentials to access the Democratic Congressional Campaign Committee computer network, stealing data with malware. They ultimately access 33 DNC computers and anonymously register a website called DC Leaks to publicize the release of documents" (2024).

Insider Threats: The Double Agent

Sometimes, the biggest threat to an organization doesn't come from hackers or cybercriminals on the outside but from people on the inside. Imagine this: an unhappy employee at a tech company, upset with their job or employer, decides to sell sensitive company information to a competitor. This can cause serious harm to the business, such as financial losses or a damaged reputation. This is called an insider threat, and it's particularly dangerous because employees already have access to important systems and data. They don't need to "**hack**" into anything—they already have the keys. To protect against these kinds of risks, companies take certain precautions. For example, they limit access to sensitive information so only those who really need it can view it. They also use tools to monitor employee activity, which helps spot unusual behavior before it becomes a bigger problem.

Case Study: Insider Threats: Snowden Revelations

In 2013, Edward Snowden, a former NSA contractor, leaked classified information revealing global surveillance programs. His insider access allowed him to download vast amounts of sensitive data, which he subsequently shared with journalists. The incident underscored the significant risks posed by insider threats and the challenges in safeguarding against unauthorized disclosures by trusted individuals (BBC News 2014).

Network Hacking: The Gatecrasher

Network hacking is when someone gains unauthorized access to a computer network. It's like breaking into a locked house but in the digital world. Hackers look for weaknesses, such as weak passwords, outdated software, or unprotected Wi-Fi, to get into the network. Once inside, they can steal information, spy on activities, or disrupt the systems. For example, a small business might have a Wi-Fi network with a simple password like "12345." A hacker nearby can easily guess that password, get into the network, and access private information like customer details or company files. All because that company's network wasn't properly secured! That's why it's so important to secure your network—use strong passwords, keep software updated, and regularly check for weaknesses.

Case Study: The Holiday Heist: A Tale of Cyber Intrusion

As the holiday season buzzed in November and December of 2013, shoppers across the United States flocked to Target stores, searching for gifts and good deals. What these unsuspecting customers didn't know was that, behind the scenes, a group of cyber thieves was plotting one of the most infamous digital heists in retail history.

Like master burglars in a high-stakes movie, these attackers didn't use crowbars or masks. Instead, they wielded sophisticated malware and exploited weak spots in Target's computer network. Quietly and methodically, they infiltrated the system, gaining access to sensitive information: names, addresses, credit card numbers, and even email accounts. This was the digital equivalent of breaking into a vault.

According to the report published by US Senate Committee on Commerce, Science, and Transportation (2014), the breach was massive affecting as many as 110 million Target customers. But the story didn't end there. Once the data was stolen, the thieves didn't keep it on Target's servers. They whisked it away, like a getaway car speeding from a crime scene, to a remote server in Eastern Europe. From there, the stolen data was ready to be sold on the black market to the highest bidder. This breach caused chaos. Customers felt betrayed, Target's reputation took a massive hit, and the company faced financial and legal repercussions. It was a stark reminder of the risks lurking in the cyber world, even for well-established corporations.

Man-in-the-Middle (MitM) Attacks: The Eavesdropper

To explain this common cyber threat in simple terms, imagine a typical scene at a coffee shop where many people are working or browsing online using public Wi-Fi. Now, suppose you decide to check your bank account while connected to this public network. Without your knowledge, a hacker on the same Wi-Fi network intercepts the communication between your device and the bank's server. As you log in, the hacker captures your username and password. This is known as a MitM attack where the attacker secretly positions themselves between you and the website you're accessing, stealing your sensitive information. To protect yourself from such attacks, take precautions like using only secure websites (look for "HTTPS" in the web address), avoiding public Wi-Fi for sensitive activities such as online banking, and using a VPN (Virtual Private Network). A VPN encrypts your internet connection, making it much more difficult for hackers to intercept your data.

Case Study: The Tale of the Equifax Breach: A Man-in-the-Middle Attack

Imagine you're running a gigantic library filled with the personal information of millions of people names, birthdates, Social Security numbers, and financial records. This library is Equifax, one of the largest credit reporting agencies in the world. People trust you to keep their information safe, like locking it in a secure vault.

But one day in 2017, a group of clever thieves found a tiny crack in the wall. This wasn't a physical vault but a digital one, part of Equifax's web application framework. The crack? A vulnerability that Equifax hadn't patched—a problem the company knew about but hadn't fixed. These attackers, using what's known as an MitM attack, slipped through the crack, intercepted communications, and accessed the sensitive data inside.

What did the thieves find? Everything. Names, addresses, birthdates, Social Security numbers, driver's license numbers, and even credit card information. They didn't take just a few files—they took data from over 143 million people. To put it into perspective, that's nearly half the US population.

The breach left a profound sense of helplessness among those affected. Consumers were not only upset about the breach itself but also felt betrayed by Equifax's indifferent response. Diane Beeney, a resident of York, Nebraska, captured this unease, stating, "I'm not very tech savvy, but I'm very tech wary. There is just too much of this stuff out there that nobody has any control over" (Ron, 2017).

For many, it wasn't just about the data stolen—it was about the realization that they were ensnared in a system they couldn't opt out of. Equifax and its counterparts, Experian and TransUnion, profit from consumers' data without granting them meaningful control or rights over it. People couldn't even freeze their credit files easily, a basic measure to prevent fraud, without paying a fee.

How Did It Happen?

The attackers exploited the web application's vulnerability to position themselves as a "man in the middle." Think of it as if someone intercepted a secret note being passed between you and a friend and then made copies without you realizing. They didn't just steal the note—they copied it quietly, over and over.

The Fallout

When the breach was finally discovered, the damage was done. People's most sensitive information was out there, available for identity thieves to use. The company faced lawsuits, government investigations, and public outrage. For many individuals, the breach was a ticking time bomb years later, someone could still use their stolen data to open fake accounts, take out loans, or commit fraud.

What Can We Learn?

The Equifax breach is a powerful reminder of why timely software updates are crucial. Fixing the "crack in the wall" (patching vulnerabilities) should never be delayed. It's also a lesson in proactive defense: encryption, monitoring, and secure coding practices could have made this attack much harder to pull off.

Conclusion

The chapter concludes by emphasizing that cyber literacy is an essential component of cybersecurity. In many cases, the failure to prevent cyber threats isn't just due to flawed technology but a lack of focus on cybersecurity itself. This highlights an important lesson for everyone whether managing a company, running a library, or simply navigating your personal digital life: always remain vigilant, address vulnerabilities promptly, and never underestimate the creativity and determination of cyber attackers.

Ultimately, the greatest challenge in ensuring secure digital communication isn't the complexity of cyberattacks but the widespread lack of understanding of how to live and operate safely in the digital age. By prioritizing cyber literacy, individuals and organizations can learn to recognize threats, adopt better practices, and significantly reduce risks. As Bruce Schneier, a renowned cybersecurity expert, reminds us: "Security is not a product, but a process." It is through continuous education, awareness, and proactive action that we can create a safer digital world for all.

References

Abbate, J. 2000. *Inventing the Internet.* MIT Press.

BBC News. 2014. "Edward Snowden: Leaks That Exposed US Spy Programme. BBC, January 14. Accessed January 10, 2025. https://www.bbc.com/news/world-us-canada-23123964.

BBC News. 2017. "Cyber-Attack: Ransomware Cases Slow but Fears Remain." BBC, May 15. https://www.bbc.com/news/technology-39920141.

Bill, C. 2017. "WannaCry Ransomware: What We Know Monday." NPR, May 15. https://www.npr.org/sections/thetwo-way/2017/05/15/528451534/wannacry-ransomware-what-we-know-monday.

Castells, M. 2009. *The Rise of the Network Society*. Wiley-Blackwell.

Clarke, R. A., and R. K. Knake. 2011. *Cyber War: The Next Threat to National Security and What to Do About It.* HarperCollins.

CNBC. 2019. "Phishing Email Scam Stole $100 Million from Facebook and Google." Last modified March 27. https://www.cnbc.com/2019/03/27/phishing-email-scam-stole-100-million-from-facebook-and-google.html.

CNN. 2024. "2016 Presidential Campaign Hacking Fast Facts." Last modified October 17. Accessed January 10, 2025. https://www.cnn.com/2016/12/26/us/2016-presidential-campaign-hacking-fast-facts/index.html.

Cybersecurity and Infrastructure Security Agency. 2023. "Attack on Colonial Pipeline: What We've Learned & What We've Done over the Past Two Years." U.S. Department of Homeland Security, May 7. https://www.cisa.gov/news-events/news/attack-colonial-pipeline-what-weve-learned-what-weve-done-over-past-two-years.

Cyburanus. 2023. "51 Powerful Cybersecurity Quotes." Accessed January 10, 2025. https://cyburanus.com/blog/51-powerful-cybersecurity-quotes/.

Federal Bureau of Investigation. Senior US Officials Impersonated in Malicious Messaging Campaign. 15 May 2025, https://www.ic3.gov/PSA/2025/PSA250515.

Gibson, W. (1984). *Neuromancer*. Ace Books.

Hafner, K., and J. Markoff. 1995. *Cyberpunk: Outlaws and Hackers on the Computer Frontier*. Simon & Schuster.

Isaacson, W. 2015. *The Innovators: How a Group of Hackers, Geniuses, and Geeks Created the Digital Revolution.* Simon & Schuster.

Krishna, N. D., and S. Jonathan. 2016. "How the New York Fed fumbled over the Bangladesh Bank Cyber-Heist." Reuters, July 21. https://www.reuters.com/investigates/special-report/cyber-heist-federal/.

LeClair, J. A. 2016. "Cyber Literacy in the Age of Attacks." *U.S. Cybersecurity Magazine.* https://www.uscybersecurity.net/csmag/cyber-literacy-in-the-age-of-attacks/.

Levy, S. 1984. *Hackers: Heroes of the Computer Revolution.* Anchor Press/Doubleday.

Magomedov, I. A., H. A. Murzaev, and A. L. Zolkin. "Cyber Literacy as One of the Main Disciplines Necessary in Modern Time." The European Proceedings of Social and Behavioural Sciences, vol. 90, 2020, pp. 892–899. https://doi.org/10.15405/epsbs.2020.10.03.117.

Natasha, D. 2023. "Case Studies: How Top Companies Tackled Malware Threats." Malware Brains. Accessed January 10, 2025. https://malwarebrains.com/malware-case-studies/?utm_source=chatgpt.com.

Politico. (2026, January 27). Trump's acting cyber chief uploaded sensitive files into a public version of ChatGPT. https://www.politico.com/news/2026/01/27/cisa-madhu-gottumukkala-chatgpt-00749361

Ron, L. 2017. "Why the Equifax Breach Stings So Bad." *New York Times*, September 22. Accessed January 10, 2025. https://www.nytimes.com/2017/09/22/your-money/equifax-breach.html.

Singer, P. W., and A. Friedman. 2014. *Cybersecurity and Cyberwar: What Everyone Needs to Know.* Oxford University Press.

Toffler, A. 1970. *Future Shock.* Random House.

US Senate Committee on Commerce, Science, and Transportation. 2014. A "Kill Chain" Analysis of the 2013 Target Data Breach. Accessed January 10, 2025. https://www.commerce.senate.gov/services/files/24d3c229-4f2f-405d-b8db-a3a67f183883.

Wiener, N. 2019. *Cybernetics: Or Control and Communication in the Animal and the Machine.* MIT Press.

Chapter 3

Fundamental Concepts of Data Privacy

Shane McNeil, PhD

In the interconnected landscape of digital communication, the safeguarding of personal and organizational data has become paramount. As we navigate through the vast digital world, our information continuously interacts with various networks, systems, and devices. This interaction, while facilitating unprecedented levels of connectivity and convenience, also exposes data to various risks and vulnerabilities. This chapter aims to demystify the principles and practices essential for protecting data privacy in today's digital age. Designed with undergraduate communications students in mind, this chapter requires no prior technical knowledge, instead focusing on conveying complex cybersecurity concepts through engaging, relatable content.

As we explore the foundational aspects of data privacy, including confidentiality, security measures, and compliance with data privacy laws, our goal is to equip you with a comprehensive understanding of how data privacy impacts both individuals and organizations. Through real-world examples, case studies, and straightforward explanations, we will delve into the significance of data privacy, the threats that jeopardize it, and the strategies employed to safeguard sensitive information. By the end of this chapter, you will have gained not only a deeper appreciation of the importance of data privacy but also practical knowledge that can be applied in both personal and professional contexts.

Learning Outcomes

- **Understand the Importance of Data Confidentiality:** Recognize the significance of keeping data private and the impact of confidentiality breaches on individuals and organizations.
- **Identify Data Security Measures:** Describe basic security measures like firewalls and encryption, and understand how they protect against threats and vulnerabilities.
- **Recognize Limitations in Data Collection:** Explain the principles of purpose limitation, consent requirements, and transparency in the context of data collection.

- **Navigate Compliance with Data Privacy Laws:** Understand the basics of General Data Protection Regulation (GDPR) and other relevant data privacy laws, and their implications for data collection, storage, and processing.
- **Distinguish Between Anonymization and Pseudonymization:** Describe techniques for anonymizing and pseudonymizing personal data, including the benefits and limitations of each.
- **Assess the Accuracy of Data:** Understand the importance of data quality and the rights of individuals to correct inaccuracies in their personal data.
- **Implement Data Storage Limits:** Determine appropriate data retention policies and the balance between archiving and deletion in the context of privacy concerns.
- **Ensure Data Integrity and Confidentiality:** Outline strategies to prevent unauthorized data modification and safeguard sensitive information from unauthorized disclosure.

Key Terms

- **Data Confidentiality:** Ensuring that personal and sensitive information is kept secure from unauthorized access or disclosure.
- **Encryption:** The process of converting data into a coded form to prevent unauthorized access.
- **Access Controls:** Mechanisms implemented to restrict access to data, ensuring only authorized users can view sensitive information.
- **Data Security:** The measures and practices employed to protect data from unauthorized access, theft, or damage.
- **GDPR (General Data Protection Regulation):** A comprehensive data protection law in the European Union (EU) that sets guidelines for the collection and processing of personal information.
- **Anonymization:** The process of removing personally identifiable information from datasets, so that individuals cannot be easily identified.
- **Pseudonymization:** The replacement of private identifiers with pseudonyms, allowing data to be matched with its source without revealing the actual source.
- **Data Integrity:** The accuracy and consistency of data over its life cycle, ensuring it is not altered or corrupted by unauthorized parties.
- **Incident Response:** The approach taken by organizations to prepare for, detect, and respond to security breaches or data incidents.

3.1 Data Confidentiality

Understanding Confidentiality: The importance of keeping data private and limiting access.

Data confidentiality refers to the principle of ensuring that personal and sensitive information is kept secure from unauthorized access, disclosure, or theft.[1] In the digital age, where vast amounts of information are transmitted and stored online, the importance of data confidentiality cannot be overstated. It's akin to the privacy we expect in our personal conversations and communications; just as we wouldn't want our private discussions to be overheard by strangers, we also don't want our digital data to be accessible to those without the right to view it. This expectation of privacy is fundamental to the trust that users place in companies and organizations with their personal information. When confidentiality is breached, it can lead to a myriad of problems, including identity theft, financial loss, and erosion of trust in digital systems.

Protecting confidentiality involves a combination of technical measures, policies, and practices designed to control access to information and ensure that only authorized individuals can view sensitive data. This is crucial not just for individual privacy but also for maintaining the integrity and reputation of businesses and organizations. A breach of confidentiality can damage a company's reputation, lead to legal consequences, and erode user trust, which can be far more costly to recover than implementing robust security measures in the first place.

Access Controls: Implementing mechanisms to restrict data access to authorized users.

Access controls are one of the primary mechanisms used to ensure data confidentiality. They act as gatekeepers, determining who can access certain pieces of information based on predefined criteria. Imagine access controls as the bouncers of the digital world; just as a bouncer checks IDs before allowing entry into a club, access control systems verify the identity of users and their authorization levels before granting them access to data. These systems can be as simple as a username and password or as complex as biometric authentication methods, like fingerprint or facial recognition.

Implementing effective access controls requires a careful balance. On one hand, data must be accessible enough to ensure that authorized users can perform their duties without unnecessary hindrance. On the other hand, restrictions must be tight enough to prevent unauthorized access. This is often achieved through the principle of least privilege, which means users are granted only the access necessary to perform their job functions and no more. Regular audits and updates to access controls are also essential to adapt to changing roles, responsibilities, and threats, ensuring that data confidentiality is maintained over time.

Encryption: How encryption ensures data confidentiality during transmission and storage.

Encryption is a critical tool for protecting data confidentiality, serving as the digital equivalent of a secret code. It transforms readable data, or plaintext, into a scrambled

1. Sebastian Karcher, Sefa Secen, and Nic Weber, "Protecting Sensitive Data Early in the Research Data Lifecycle," *Journal of Privacy and Confidentiality* 13, no. 2 (2023), https://doi.org/10.29012/jpc.846.

format known as ciphertext. This process, facilitated by algorithms and encryption keys, ensures that even if data is intercepted during transmission or accessed in storage, it remains unintelligible and useless without the corresponding decryption key. Think of it as sending a sealed, coded letter; while the letter can still be stolen or intercepted, the contents remain a secret to anyone without the key to decode it.

The beauty of encryption lies in its ability to protect data's confidentiality across various stages of its life cycle, from the moment it is created until it is securely deleted. Whether data is in transit over the internet or at rest on a server, encryption acts as a robust barrier against unauthorized access. Moreover, advancements in encryption technology have made these tools more accessible and easier to implement, enabling even small organizations and individuals to secure their data effectively. By understanding and utilizing encryption, individuals and organizations can significantly enhance the confidentiality and security of the sensitive information they handle.

3.2 Data Security

Imagine data security as a fortress that guards against myriad threats and vulnerabilities. These threats come in various forms, including malware, phishing attacks, and even insider threats, each capable of compromising the integrity and availability of data. Understanding these risks is the first step toward fortifying our digital defenses. For example, malicious software is designed to damage or disable computers and computer systems, potentially leading to data theft or loss. Phishing attacks, on the other hand, trick individuals into revealing sensitive information, such as passwords and credit card numbers, through deceptive emails or messages that mimic legitimate sources.

Vulnerabilities, or weaknesses in a system that can be exploited, further complicate the landscape of data security. These can range from software bugs to inadequate security policies. The recent surge in remote work has exposed additional vulnerabilities, such as unsecured home networks and the use of personal devices for professional tasks. Addressing these vulnerabilities requires not only technological solutions but also awareness and education to recognize and mitigate risks effectively.

Data security threats are not just theoretical; they manifest in real-world incidents that can have significant consequences. For instance, the WannaCry ransomware attack in 2017 affected hundreds of thousands of computers across 150 countries, encrypting files and demanding ransom payments in Bitcoin.[2] This attack highlighted the global scale of cybersecurity threats and the importance of maintaining updated and secured systems.

Phishing attacks, too, have become increasingly sophisticated. A notable example is the attack on a major social media platform's employees in 2020, leading to the

2. Lawrence J. Trautman and Peter Ormerod, "Wannacry, Ransomware, and the Emerging Threat to Corporations," *Tennessee Law Review* 86, no. 503 (August 24, 2018), https://doi.org/10.2139/ssrn.3238293.

compromise of high-profile accounts.[3] The attackers used social engineering to manipulate employees into providing access to the platform's internal systems. This incident underscores the need for ongoing education and vigilance against seemingly innocuous requests for information.

Vulnerabilities can also stem from seemingly benign sources. The Heartbleed bug, a security flaw in the OpenSSL cryptographic software library, allowed attackers to read the memory of systems protected by vulnerable versions of OpenSSL, exposing sensitive data including passwords and encryption keys.[4] This vulnerability demonstrated the critical importance of regular software updates and patches as part of a comprehensive security strategy.

Security Measures

To shield data from the threats and vulnerabilities mentioned above, a variety of security measures are employed. Firewalls serve as the gatekeepers of computer networks, monitoring and controlling incoming and outgoing network traffic based on predetermined security rules. Think of them as the walls of a castle, designed to keep out invaders while allowing authorized residents to come and go freely.

The implementation of firewalls can be illustrated by the case of a university network that segments its network traffic between administrative operations, student access, and public services. By setting strict rules on what types of traffic are allowed to enter and leave each segment, the university can protect sensitive data, such as student records and research data, from unauthorized access.

Intrusion detection systems (IDS) play a crucial role in identifying potential breaches. For example, a financial institution may use an IDS to monitor for unusual transaction patterns that could indicate fraudulent activity. If the system detects a high volume of transactions in a short period, it can alert security personnel to investigate potential security threats. IDS work alongside firewalls by monitoring network traffic for suspicious activity and potential threats, effectively acting as the castle's guards. They alert system administrators to any attempted breaches, allowing for quick response to potential threats. Secure coding practices, meanwhile, address vulnerabilities at the software development stage, ensuring that applications are built with security in mind from the ground up. This involves regular testing for vulnerabilities, adherence to security standards, and the implementation of secure design principles.

Secure coding practices are essential for preventing vulnerabilities from being exploited. The case of the SQL injection vulnerability is a prime example. This common

3. Nikita Koselev, "Understanding the Twitter Hack of 2020: A Deep Dive," DEV Community, January 4, 2024, https://dev.to/nikitakoselev/understanding-the-twitter-hack-of-2020-a-deep-dive-2cf4.
4. Zakir Durumeric, Frank Li, James Kasten et al., "The Matter of Heartbleed," in *Proceedings of the 2014 Conference on Internet Measurement Conference*, IMC '14 (Association for Computing Machinery, 2014), 475–88, https://doi.org/10.1145/2663716.2663755.

issue allows attackers to insert malicious SQL code into forms or URLs, manipulating a website's database. By adopting secure coding practices, such as input validation and parameterized queries, developers can prevent these attacks, ensuring the security and integrity of web applications.

Incident Response: Preparing for and Responding to Security Breaches

Despite the best efforts to prevent security breaches, it's crucial to have an incident response plan in place for when breaches occur. This plan outlines the steps an organization should take to detect, respond to, and recover from a security incident. Effective incident response requires coordination across multiple teams within an organization, clear communication channels, and predefined roles and responsibilities.

The importance of a well-prepared incident response plan was highlighted by the response to a major retailer's data breach, where attackers accessed millions of customers' credit card information. The retailer had an incident response team in place that quickly identified and contained the breach, communicated transparently with affected customers, and took steps to enhance their security measures to prevent future incidents.

The initial phase involves detecting and identifying the breach, followed by containment to prevent further damage. This may involve isolating affected systems, revoking access, or taking servers offline. The next steps focus on eradication and recovery, removing the threat from the system and restoring services to normal operation. Finally, a thorough review of the incident and the response to it is conducted to identify lessons learned and improve future security measures. This cycle of preparation, response, and review is essential for building resilience against future attacks.

3.3 Limitations in Data Collection

The principle of purpose limitation is central to ethical data collection, ensuring that data is gathered solely for clear, legitimate purposes and not used in a manner incompatible with those purposes. This principle protects individuals' privacy by restricting the scope of data collection to what is directly relevant and necessary for specified purposes.

For example, when a user signs up for a fitness tracking app, they expect their data to be used to monitor their health and fitness progress, not to be shared with third-party advertisers without their consent. A breach of this expectation, such as the incident where a popular fitness app shared users' data with advertising companies without clear user consent, highlights the importance of adhering to purpose limitation. Such practices not only undermine user trust but can also lead to legal repercussions under data protection laws like the GDPR.

Consent Requirements: The Role of Informed Consent in Data Collection

Informed consent is a foundational element of ethical data collection, requiring that individuals are fully aware of and agree to the collection and use of their data in a specific manner. Consent must be freely given, specific, informed, and unambiguous, with individuals having the right to withdraw consent at any time.

A notable example illustrating the significance of consent is the Cambridge Analytica scandal, where data from millions of social media users was collected without explicit consent for political advertising purposes. This case shed light on the misuse of data under the guise of academic research, sparking global debate on privacy rights and leading to increased scrutiny of consent practices in data collection.

Understanding the Cambridge Analytica Scandal

The Cambridge Analytica scandal, which came to light in early 2018, serves as a watershed moment in the public's understanding of digital privacy.[5] This incident not only highlighted the vulnerabilities in data privacy practices but also spurred a global conversation about the ethics of data collection and usage. At the heart of the scandal was the misuse of personal data from millions of social media users, without their informed consent, to influence voter behavior.

Cambridge Analytica, a British political consulting firm, accessed the data of approximately 87 million social media users. This was achieved through a seemingly harmless personality quiz app named "This Is Your Digital Life." While only about 270,000 people consented to and took the quiz, the app exploited platform policies to also access data from the quiz takers' network of friends, exponentially increasing the scale of data harvested.[6] The information collected included personal details, likes, and online behavior patterns, which Cambridge Analytica then analyzed and used to deliver targeted political advertising aimed at influencing elections, most notably the 2016 United States presidential election.

The scandal's revelation brought to light several critical issues in digital privacy and data protection. First and foremost was the issue of consent. The users whose data was collected were not informed, nor did they consent to their information being used for political profiling and targeted advertising. This blatant disregard for user consent violated not just ethical standards but also highlighted gaps in regulatory frameworks governing data privacy.

Another significant issue was the lack of transparency. Users were unaware of the extent to which their data could be harvested and used, not just by the platforms they

5. Jim Isaak and Mina J Hanna, "User Data Privacy: Facebook, Cambridge Analytica, and Privacy Protection," *Computer* 51, no. 8 (2018): 56–59, https://doi.org/10.1109/mc.2018.3191268; Brian Tarran, "What Can We Learn from the Facebook—Cambridge Analytica Scandal?," *Significance* 15, no. 3 (2018): 4–5, https://doi.org/10.1111/j.1740-9713.2018.01139.x.
6. Tarran, "What Can We Learn from the Facebook—Cambridge Analytica Scandal?"

engaged with but also by third parties like Cambridge Analytica. This incident exposed the complex web of data sharing and usage agreements that often operate behind the scenes, unbeknownst to the average user.

The fallout from the Cambridge Analytica scandal was far-reaching. It prompted a rigorous scrutiny of social media platforms' data practices, leading to calls for stricter data protection regulations worldwide. The EU's GDPR, which came into effect shortly after the scandal broke, was hailed as a timely response to such concerns, setting a new standard for data privacy laws globally. The GDPR emphasizes transparency, informed consent, and users' rights to their data, principles that were starkly violated in the Cambridge Analytica case.

Moreover, the scandal underscored the power of data analytics and the potential for abuse in the absence of stringent data privacy measures. It served as a wake-up call for both users and companies about the importance of protecting personal information in an increasingly data-driven world.

The Cambridge Analytica scandal is more than just a cautionary tale; it's a critical lesson on the importance of ethical data collection, the need for robust privacy protections, and the role of informed consent in the digital age. It reminds us that in the digital world, where data flows freely, the responsibility to safeguard personal information is paramount. This incident continues to influence how data privacy is viewed, regulated, and enforced, marking a pivotal point in the ongoing dialogue about the rights of digital citizens in the age of digital communication.

Transparency: Communicating Openly with Users About Data Collection Practices

Transparency in data collection involves clearly communicating with users about what data is being collected, for what purpose, and how it will be used. This openness is crucial for building trust and ensuring compliance with privacy laws.

An example of transparency done right can be seen with certain open-source projects or services that provide detailed privacy notices explaining their data collection and use practices. These notices often include information on the types of data collected, the purposes of collection, data retention policies, and how users can exercise their rights over their data. By contrast, companies that have faced backlash for opaque data practices, such as unexpected sharing of user data with third parties, underscore the negative impact that a lack of transparency can have on consumer trust and brand reputation.

3.4 Compliance with Data Privacy Laws

In the wake of high-profile data breaches and scandals, such as Cambridge Analytica, there has been a global shift toward strengthening regulations that govern the collection, use, and protection of personal information. Compliance with data privacy laws is not just a legal requirement but also a critical component of building trust with users and maintaining the integrity of digital communications. This section delves into the principles of the GDPR, one of the most comprehensive data protection laws, and explores the importance of data retention policies.

GDPR: Understanding Its Principles

The GDPR, which came into effect in May 2018, represents a landmark in the effort to protect personal data in the EU. However, its impact is global, affecting any organization that deals with the personal data of EU citizens.[7] The GDPR is built around several key principles that underscore the rights of individuals and the obligations of entities processing personal data. These principles include the following:

- Lawfulness, Fairness, and Transparency: Personal data must be processed lawfully, fairly, and in a transparent manner in relation to the data subject.
- Purpose Limitation: Data collected for specified, explicit, and legitimate purposes cannot be used in a way that is incompatible with those purposes.
- Data Minimization: The collection of personal data must be limited to what is necessary in relation to the purposes for which they are processed.
- Accuracy: Personal data must be accurate and, where necessary, kept up-to-date.
- Storage Limitation: Personal data should be kept in a form that permits identification of data subjects for no longer than is necessary for the purposes for which the personal data are processed.
- Integrity and Confidentiality: Personal data must be processed in a manner that ensures appropriate security, including protection against unauthorized or unlawful processing and against accidental loss, destruction, or damage.
- Compliance with the GDPR requires organizations to implement measures that uphold these principles, such as obtaining clear consent for data processing, enabling data subjects to access and control their data, and reporting data breaches within tight deadlines.

While the GDPR has set a high standard for data privacy and protection in the EU, various jurisdictions around the world, including in the United States, have developed their own data privacy laws. These laws reflect growing concerns about privacy in the digital age and the need for regulations to protect personal information. In this expanded section, we will explore key state data privacy laws in the United States, focusing on Cali-

7. Liviu Adrian Stoica and Robert Adrian Candoi Savu, "Risks and Exploits Exposed By GDPR," *Eurasian Journal of Social Sciences* 9, no. 1 (2021): 24–30, https://doi.org/10.15604/ejss.2021.09.01.003; Lilian Mitrou, "The General Data Protection Regulation: A Law for the Digital Age?," in *EU Internet Law*, ed. Tatiana-Eleni Synodinou, Philippe Jougleux, Christiana Markou, and Thalia Prastitou (Springer International Publishing, 2017), 19–58, https://doi.org/10.1007/978-3-319-64955-9.

fornia, Texas, and Virginia, to illustrate the diverse legal landscape of data privacy across the country.

California: The California Consumer Privacy Act (CCPA)

The CCPA, which took effect in January 2020, marked a significant milestone in the United States for data privacy. The CCPA grants California residents new rights regarding their personal information and imposes various obligations on businesses that collect, process, or sell Californians' personal data.[8]

Key provisions of the CCPA include the right to know what personal data is being collected, the right to request the deletion of personal data, the right to opt out of the sale of personal data, and the right to non-discrimination for exercising these rights. The CCPA applies to businesses that meet certain criteria, such as having annual gross revenues exceeding $25 million, buying or selling the personal information of 50,000 or more consumers or households, or deriving 50 percent or more of their annual revenues from selling consumers' personal information.

Texas: The Texas Privacy Protection Act (HB 4390)

While Texas does not have a comprehensive data privacy law akin to the CCPA, it has taken steps to strengthen data protection with the Texas Privacy Protection Act (HB 4390), which amended the Texas Identity Theft Enforcement and Protection Act.[9] Enacted in June 2019, HB 4390 enhances data breach notification requirements for businesses that experience a breach of system security.[10]

Under HB 4390, businesses are required to notify affected Texas residents of a data breach within 60 days of its discovery. Additionally, if a breach affects 250 or more Texas residents, the business must also notify the Texas attorney general. While HB 4390 focuses primarily on breach notification, it represents a step toward greater accountability and protection of personal information in Texas.

8. Danielle Kucera, "CCPA vs. GDPR: Similarities and Differences Explained," Okta, accessed October 24, 2024, https://www.okta.com/blog/2021/04/ccpa-vs-gdpr/; Deloitte US, "A Quick Reference Guide for CCPA Compliance," accessed October 24, 2024, https://www2.deloitte.com/us/en/pages/advisory/articles/ccpa-compliance-readiness.html.
9. Amrit Nagi, "Comparing GDPR Against the United States' Approach to Data Breach Notification by Examining Texas and California and the Feasibility of a Universal Standard," *Cybaris* 15, no. 2 (2024), https://open.mitchellhamline.edu/cybaris/vol15/iss2/14.
10. John C. Domino, *The Right to Privacy in Texas: From Common Law Origins to 21st Century Protections* (Lexington Books, 2024).

Virginia: The Virginia Consumer Data Protection Act (VCDPA)

The VCDPA, set to take effect in January 2023, positions Virginia as another key player in the realm of state-level data privacy legislation in the United States.[11] Similar to the CCPA and the GDPR, the VCDPA provides Virginia residents with several rights over their personal data, including the rights to access, correct, delete their personal data, and the right to opt out of the processing of personal data for targeted advertising, the sale of personal data, or profiling in furtherance of decisions that produce legal or similarly significant effects.[12]

The VCDPA applies to businesses that control or process the personal data of at least 100,000 Virginia residents or derive over 50 percent of their gross revenue from the sale of personal data and process or control personal data of at least 25,000 Virginia residents. This law emphasizes consumer rights, data minimization, and the establishment of data protection assessments for certain types of data processing activities.

Colorado: The Colorado Privacy Act (CPA)

The CPA, signed into law in July 2021 and effective from July 2023, mirrors some aspects of the GDPR and CCPA, positioning Colorado as a leader in state-level data privacy. The CPA grants Colorado residents rights similar to those under the GDPR and CCPA, such as the rights to access, correct, delete their personal data, and opt out of data processing for targeted advertising, the sale of personal data, or profiling in significant decisions.

The CPA applies to entities that conduct business in Colorado or produce products or services targeted to Colorado residents and either control or process the personal data of 100,000 consumers or more in a calendar year; or derive revenue or receive a discount on the price of goods or services from the sale of personal data and process or control the personal data of at least 25,000 consumers. Unlike the CCPA, the CPA does not have a revenue threshold, focusing instead on the scale of data processing and sales.

New York: The New York SHIELD Act

The New York Stop Hacks and Improve Electronic Data Security Act (SHIELD Act), effective from March 2020, focuses on enhancing cybersecurity practices rather than providing consumers with rights over their personal data. The SHIELD Act requires businesses that own or license computerized data, which includes private information of New York

11. Le Cheng, Xiuli Liu, and Chunlei Si, "Identifying Stance in Legislative Discourse: A Corpus-Driven Study of Data Protection Laws," *Humanities and Social Sciences Communications* 11, no. 1 (2024): 1–13, https://doi.org/10.1057/s41599-024-03322-9.
12. Andrew P. Quay, "Desperation for Legislation: The Need for the American Data Privacy and Protection Act," *Wisconsin International Law Journal* 41 (2024): 707.

residents to implement and maintain reasonable safeguards to protect the security, confidentiality, and integrity of the private information.[13]

The SHIELD Act broadens the scope of information covered under the notification requirements to include biometric information and email addresses with their corresponding passwords or security questions and answers. It also updates the definition of a data breach to include unauthorized access to private information, in addition to the acquisition of such information.

Data Retention Policies: Setting Limits on How Long Data Can Be Stored

Data retention policies are a critical aspect of compliance with data privacy laws, including the GDPR. These policies define how long data can be kept and outline procedures for its deletion or anonymization once it is no longer needed for the purposes for which it was collected. The goal is to prevent the indefinite storage of personal data, minimizing the risk of breaches and unauthorized access.

For example, a company might retain customer data for the duration of the customer relationship plus a certain number of years, as required by tax laws or industry regulations. After this period, the data should be reviewed and either deleted or anonymized, depending on the company's data retention policy and legal obligations.

Implementing effective data retention policies involves a thorough understanding of the types of data held, the legal and operational requirements for retaining the data, and the technologies and processes needed to securely delete or anonymize data when it is no longer required. This not only ensures compliance with data privacy laws but also reduces data storage costs and streamlines data management processes.

3.5 Anonymization and Pseudonymization

In the realm of data privacy, anonymization and pseudonymization are critical techniques employed to protect personal information. These methods modify the data in such a way that the identity of data subjects cannot be readily inferred, thereby reducing privacy risks. Understanding these techniques is essential for compliance with data privacy laws, such as the GDPR, which emphasize the importance of protecting individuals' privacy while allowing data to be used for legitimate purposes.

Anonymizing Personal Data: Techniques for Removing Identifying Information

Anonymization irreversibly removes or modifies personal identifiers in datasets, ensuring that individuals cannot be identified, directly or indirectly, by anyone. This process involves more than just removing obvious identifiers like names and Social Security num-

13. Matt Davis, "The Definitive Guide to the New York SHIELD Act," Osano, last updated December 10, 2024, https://www.osano.com/articles/new-york-shield-law.

bers. It also includes managing data attributes that could be combined with other information to identify an individual, known as "quasi-identifiers." Examples of anonymization techniques include data aggregation, where individual entries are combined into summaries, and data perturbation, which involves adding random noise to data points.

Anonymization has profound implications for data privacy because truly anonymized data is no longer considered personal data under laws like the GDPR, thereby exempting it from data protection requirements. However, achieving complete anonymization is challenging due to the increasing amount of publicly available information and advancements in data analytics, which can potentially reidentify individuals from anonymized datasets.

Pseudonymization: Replacing Direct Identifiers with Pseudonyms While Maintaining Usability

Pseudonymization is a data management technique that replaces private identifiers in a dataset with pseudonyms or placeholders, effectively separating the data from direct personal identifiers. Unlike anonymization, pseudonymization is reversible under certain conditions. This means that with additional information, which is kept separately and securely, the process can be reversed, linking pseudonyms back to the individuals they represent.

This technique allows for a balance between data utility and privacy. Pseudonymized data can still be used for data analysis and processing purposes, but the risk of harm from data breaches is significantly reduced since the data cannot be attributed to specific individuals without access to the additional information required for reidentification. Pseudonymization is explicitly recognized under the GDPR, which encourages its use as a measure to enhance the protection of personal data while enabling data analytics and processing activities.

Anonymization Methodologies and Challenges

Anonymization involves several methodologies, each with its own set of challenges:

- **Data Aggregation:** Combining individual data points into larger datasets to prevent identification of individuals. While effective for some uses, this method can limit the granularity and utility of the data for detailed analysis.
- **Data Masking:** Removing or obfuscating specific data elements. For instance, replacing names with random characters or masking parts of addresses. The challenge here lies in ensuring that the data remains useful for analysis without revealing personal identifiers.
- **Randomization:** Introducing random noise into datasets. This method alters the data slightly to prevent identification while preserving its overall structure and utility. The difficulty is in balancing the level of noise: too much can render the data useless, while too little might not sufficiently protect against reidentification.

- **k-Anonymity:** Ensuring that individuals cannot be distinguished from at least k−1*k*−1 individuals within the dataset. The challenge with k*k*-anonymity is the potential loss of data specificity and the risk of homogeneity attacks, where an attacker can deduce personal information if the k*k* individuals in a subset share certain characteristics.

These challenges underscore a fundamental issue with anonymization: maintaining the balance between data utility and privacy protection. As data analysis techniques become more sophisticated, the risk of reidentification increases, raising questions about the long-term effectiveness of anonymization strategies.

Pseudonymization Techniques and Considerations

Pseudonymization, while offering a reversible form of data protection, involves its own techniques and considerations:

- **Tokenization:** Replacing sensitive data elements with nonsensitive equivalents, called tokens, which can be mapped back to the original data through a tokenization system. The security of pseudonymized data heavily relies on the security of the tokenization system and the token mapping.
- **Hashing with Salts:** Applying a hash function to data elements along with a "salt" (a random value) to enhance security. While hashing without salts can be vulnerable to dictionary attacks, salting adds a layer of protection. However, the reversibility of this method depends on the secrecy and integrity of the salts used.
- **Encryption:** Encrypting data elements and treating the encrypted form as a pseudonym. The key management practices become crucial here, as the security of the pseudonymized data is contingent on the encryption keys' security.

The main consideration with pseudonymization is the requirement for additional information (e.g., tokens, salts, keys) to be stored securely, as unauthorized access to this information could allow reidentification of the data subjects. Therefore, while pseudonymization reduces the risk associated with data breaches, it does not eliminate it and necessitates robust security measures to protect the additional information required for reidentification.

Implications for Data Privacy and Protection

Both anonymization and pseudonymization have significant implications for data privacy and protection:

- **Regulatory Compliance:** Anonymized data is generally not considered personal data under regulations like the GDPR, potentially simplifying compliance requirements. However, pseudonymized data is still considered personal data, albeit with reduced risks, and must be handled according to data protection laws.

- **Data Utility Versus Privacy:** Anonymization can significantly reduce the utility of data for certain analytical purposes, while pseudonymization offers a compromise by preserving more of the data's utility while still enhancing privacy protections.
- **Security and Risk Management:** Implementing these techniques requires careful consideration of the security measures protecting the data and any additional information used in the pseudonymization process.

Understanding the methodologies, challenges, and implications of anonymization and pseudonymization is crucial for organizations navigating the complexities of data privacy and protection. These techniques are not panaceas but are valuable components of a comprehensive data protection strategy that includes robust security measures, ethical data handling practices, and compliance with data protection regulations.

3.6 Accuracy of Data

In the digital age, the accuracy of data is paramount, not just for the integrity of analyses and decision-making processes but also for protecting individuals' rights and privacy. Inaccurate data can lead to a range of problems, from minor inconveniences to significant harm, affecting everything from personalized recommendations to credit scores and healthcare decisions. This section explores the importance of data quality, strategies to ensure data accuracy, and the rights of individuals to correct inaccuracies in their personal data.

Data Quality: Ensuring Accurate and Up-to-Date Information

The quality of data collected and processed by organizations is a cornerstone of effective data management and privacy protection. High-quality data is accurate, complete, relevant, and up-to-date. Ensuring the accuracy of data is particularly challenging in dynamic environments where information can quickly become outdated. For example, individuals may change addresses, jobs, or names, and if these changes are not reflected in the data, it can lead to incorrect assumptions or decisions.

Organizations employ various strategies to maintain data accuracy, including the following:

- **Regular Data Audits:** Conducting periodic reviews of data to identify and correct inaccuracies, duplicates, or outdated information.
- **Validation Checks:** Implementing automated checks to validate data at the point of entry, such as verifying email formats or using CAPTCHA to prevent bot submissions.
- **Feedback Mechanisms:** Allowing users to report inaccuracies or changes in their information, providing a direct way to update data.

Despite these efforts, inaccuracies can still occur, underscoring the need for robust mechanisms that allow individuals to review and correct their data.

User Rights**:** Allowing individuals to correct inaccuracies in their personal data

Data privacy regulations, like the GDPR, emphasize the rights of individuals to control their personal data. This includes the right to access data held about them and to have incorrect data corrected. The ability for individuals to rectify inaccuracies is critical for several reasons:

- **Personal Autonomy:** Individuals have a fundamental right to ensure that information about them is accurate and reflective of their true circumstances.
- **Decision Impact:** Decisions made based on inaccurate data can have negative consequences for individuals, affecting their access to services, employment opportunities, and more.
- **Compliance and Trust:** Organizations that facilitate the correction of inaccuracies demonstrate compliance with data protection laws and build trust with their users.

For instance, if a consumer discovers that their credit report contains incorrect information that negatively affects their credit score, they should be able to challenge and correct this information. Financial institutions, credit bureaus, and other entities are required to provide mechanisms for individuals to dispute and rectify inaccuracies.

Implementing Corrective Measures

To comply with data protection laws and uphold individuals' rights, organizations should do the following:

- **Provide Easy Access:** Ensure individuals can easily access their data and understand the process for requesting corrections.
- **Act Promptly:** Respond to correction requests in a timely manner, updating information as quickly as possible.
- **Verify Changes:** Implement procedures to verify the accuracy of the new data before making corrections, ensuring that changes are legitimate and not fraudulent.

3.7 Data Storage Limits

The management of how long personal data is stored—often referred to as data retention—is a critical aspect of data privacy and protection. Proper data storage limits are not only a requirement under various data protection laws but also a best practice for minimizing potential risks to privacy. This section delves into defining storage duration, the balance between archiving and deletion, and the implications of these practices for data privacy.

Storage Duration: Defining How Long Data Should Be Retained

Data storage limits are determined by a variety of factors, including legal requirements, operational needs, and individual consent. The principle of storage limitation, as underscored by regulations like the GDPR, mandates that personal data should not be kept in a form that permits identification of data subjects for longer than is necessary for the purposes for which the personal data are processed.

For example, a business may retain customer data for as long as the customer maintains an account with the business, plus a certain period after account closure to comply with financial reporting requirements or to address potential disputes. However, the specific duration for which data should be retained must be justified based on the purpose of data processing and legal obligations, such as tax laws or statutes of limitations for legal claims.

Archiving Versus Deletion: Balancing the need for historical records with privacy concerns

The decision between archiving data for long-term preservation and deleting data that is no longer necessary involves a delicate balance. Archiving may be appropriate for data that has historical, research, or legal value, but it should be done in a way that continues to protect the privacy of individuals involved.

1. **Archiving*:*** When data is archived, it should be anonymized or pseudonymized to protect individuals' identities, ensuring that personal information is not accessible for general processing or analysis. Access to archived data should be restricted and monitored, with clear policies governing its use.
2. **Deletion*:*** Deleting data that is no longer necessary for its original purpose is a clear way to reduce risks to data privacy. Deletion should be complete and irreversible, ensuring that personal data cannot be reconstructed or retrieved.

Implementing effective data storage limits requires organizations to have policies and procedures in place for data classification, retention, archiving, and deletion. This includes regular reviews of stored data to determine whether it should be kept, archived, or deleted, based on legal requirements and operational needs.

Implementing Data Storage Limits

To effectively implement data storage limits, organizations should do the following:

- **Develop Clear Policies:** Establish and document data retention and deletion policies that outline how long different types of data are stored, the criteria for archiving, and the procedures for deletion.
- **Automate Retention Schedules:** Use automated tools to help manage the life cycle of data, ensuring that data is deleted or archived according to the organization's policies.

- **Regular Audits:** Conduct periodic audits of data storage practices to ensure compliance with policies and legal requirements, identifying any data that should be archived or deleted.

Understanding Data Storage Limits Through Narrative

Imagine a small, bustling café named "Java Journeys," located in the heart of a busy city. The café is known for its cozy atmosphere, excellent coffee, and a loyalty program that rewards customers for their frequent visits. As part of joining the loyalty program, customers provide their names, email addresses, and birthday months to receive personalized offers and birthday discounts. The owner, Alex, aware of the importance of data privacy, is committed to ensuring customers' personal information is protected and handled responsibly.

The Journey of Customer Data

When a customer—let's call them Maggie—signs up for the Java Journeys loyalty program, their information begins a journey through the café's data management system. Alex, having recently attended a seminar on data privacy, understands the significance of setting appropriate storage limits for customer data.

1. **Initial Data Collection:** The customer fills out a form on a digital tablet, joining the loyalty program. The form clearly states the purpose of data collection: to administer loyalty rewards and provide monthly offers.
2. **Data Storage and Use:** The information is stored in a secure, encrypted database. Access is restricted to Alex and two trusted employees, who use the data to send out monthly offers and birthday discounts. The data is also used to analyze general customer trends, helping Alex make informed decisions about the café's menu and promotions.

Implementing Data Storage Limits

Alex knows that keeping customer data indefinitely is unnecessary and increases the risk of privacy breaches. To address this, Alex implements a clear data storage policy:

- **Retention Period:** Customer data is retained for as long as the individual remains a member of the loyalty program. If a customer hasn't made a purchase at Java Journeys for two years, their data is flagged for review.
- **Review and Deletion:** Alex periodically reviews the flagged data. Customers who have been inactive for over two years receive an email asking if they wish to remain in the loyalty program. If there's no response within a month, their data is securely deleted from the system.

- **Archiving:** In a few cases, data is archived instead of deleted. For example, transaction records are anonymized and kept for financial analysis and reporting, but personal identifiers are removed to ensure privacy.

Balancing Archiving and Deletion

Alex is mindful of the balance between archiving and deletion. Financial records, stripped of personal details but retaining transaction data, are archived for seven years to comply with tax regulations. This ensures that Java Journeys can respond to any legal or financial inquiries without retaining unnecessary personal information.

Lessons Learned

Through this narrative of Java Journeys, students can see the practical application of data storage limits and the balance between data utility and privacy:

- Proactive Data Management: Alex's approach demonstrates the importance of proactive data management, ensuring customer data is only kept as long as necessary and used responsibly.
- Compliance and Trust: By implementing clear data storage policies, Java Journeys not only complies with data protection regulations but also builds trust with its customers. Patrons feel secure knowing their information is handled with care and respect for their privacy.
- The Importance of Regular Reviews: The regular review process for data retention emphasizes the dynamic nature of data management. It's not enough to set policies; ongoing vigilance is required to adapt to changes in customer behavior and legal requirements.

Through the story of Java Journeys, we see how data storage limits are a crucial component of data privacy, blending regulatory compliance with ethical considerations to protect individuals' privacy rights while enabling businesses to operate effectively and responsibly.

3.8 Integrity and Confidentiality

In our increasingly digital world, the principles of data integrity and confidentiality are cornerstone elements of robust data privacy and protection strategies. These principles ensure that personal information is not only protected from unauthorized access but also remains accurate and unaltered throughout its life cycle. This nuanced approach to data management underscores the critical balance between safeguarding sensitive information and maintaining its fidelity, ensuring that the data serves its intended purpose without compromising individual privacy.

Data Integrity: Preventing Unauthorized Modifications or Corruption

Data integrity focuses on maintaining the accuracy and consistency of data across all stages of its life cycle. Ensuring data integrity means that the information remains reliable and unaltered, except by authorized actions. This is crucial for decision-making processes, where the authenticity of data can significantly impact outcomes. Whether it's for personal health records, financial transactions, or legal documents, the integrity of data underpins the trust and confidence individuals place in digital systems.

To uphold data integrity, organizations adopt several key strategies. Access controls are fundamental, restricting data access to authorized personnel and minimizing the risk of unauthorized data alterations. Implementing rigorous data validation processes at the point of entry helps ensure that incoming data meets predefined quality standards, reducing errors and inconsistencies. Additionally, maintaining comprehensive audit trails provides a transparent record of all interactions with the data, enabling accountability and facilitating the detection and correction of any unauthorized changes.

Confidentiality Measures: Safeguarding Sensitive Information from Unauthorized Disclosure

The confidentiality of data pertains to its protection from unauthorized access and disclosure. In the digital age, where personal information traverses global networks, confidentiality measures are vital for securing sensitive data against exposure and misuse. This protection covers a broad spectrum of information, from personal identifiers and financial details to health records and private communications. Ensuring confidentiality is not just a matter of privacy; it's a safeguard against identity theft, financial fraud, and other forms of cybercrime that thrive on unauthorized access to personal data.

Organizations protect data confidentiality through various mechanisms. Encryption stands out as a critical tool, transforming sensitive information into unreadable formats for anyone without the decryption key, thus securing data both in storage and during transmission. Secure authentication methods, including multifactor authentication, ensure that only authorized individuals can access the data, providing a robust defense against unauthorized entry. For situations where full data detail isn't necessary, data masking techniques can be employed, allowing for the safe use of data in testing or training environments by obscuring sensitive details.

Balancing Integrity and Confidentiality with Usability

The pursuit of data integrity and confidentiality, while essential, must be carefully balanced with the need for data usability. Overly stringent security measures can impede legitimate access and use of data, affecting operational efficiency and innovation. Organizations face the challenge of implementing security measures that robustly protect personal information without unduly restricting its availability for legitimate purposes. This balance is critical in environments where data not only needs to be secure but also accessible and useful for analysis, decision-making, and day-to-day operations.

The Role of Integrity and Confidentiality in Data Privacy

Integrity and confidentiality are not just operational or technical issues; they are fundamental to the ethical and legal aspects of data privacy. These principles support the trust that individuals place in organizations to handle their personal information responsibly. Regulations such as the GDPR highlight the legal imperatives for data integrity and confidentiality, requiring organizations to adopt measures that prevent unauthorized data processing activities and ensure the protection of personal information against security breaches. By adhering to these principles, organizations can navigate the complexities of data privacy, ensuring compliance while fostering a culture of trust and respect for individual privacy.

Ensuring data integrity and confidentiality is a multifaceted endeavor, requiring a strategic approach to security, legal compliance, and ethical data handling. As we navigate the evolving landscape of digital privacy, these principles serve as guiding lights, ensuring that our digital futures are built on a foundation of trust, security, and respect for personal privacy.

Chapter Conclusion: Navigating Data Privacy in the Digital Age

As we conclude this exploration of the fundamental concepts of data privacy, it's clear that the landscape of digital communication presents both challenges and opportunities. The principles of data confidentiality, security, accuracy, storage limits, integrity, and confidentiality form the bedrock of responsible data management practices. Each concept, as discussed in this chapter, plays a crucial role in safeguarding personal information against the myriad threats that pervade our interconnected world, while also ensuring that data remains a powerful tool for innovation and progress.

The Importance of a Multifaceted Approach

Navigating data privacy in the digital age requires a multifaceted approach. Organizations must not only adopt technical measures such as encryption and access controls but also embrace ethical practices that prioritize the rights and dignity of individuals. Laws and regulations like the GDPR, CCPA, and others around the globe provide a legal framework for data protection, but true privacy protection goes beyond mere compliance. It involves cultivating a culture of privacy that values data minimization, transparency, and accountability at all levels of operation.

The Role of Education and Awareness

For undergraduate communications students, understanding these fundamental concepts is not just about navigating potential future workplaces. It's also about recognizing the importance of privacy in their personal lives, as digital citizens who share and consume information daily. Education and awareness are key to empowering individuals to make informed decisions about their data, question practices that may infringe on their privacy, and advocate for stronger protections.

Looking Forward

The dynamics of data privacy are constantly evolving, driven by technological advancements, emerging threats, and shifting societal norms. What remains constant, however, is the need for vigilance, adaptability, and a proactive stance toward privacy protection. As future professionals and informed citizens, understanding the nuances of data privacy will enable you to contribute positively to the discourse on digital rights and participate actively in shaping the landscape of digital communication.

We invite you, the reader, to view data privacy not just as a set of legal obligations or technical challenges but as a fundamental human right that underpins the trust and integrity of all digital interactions. As you move forward, whether in your studies, your careers, or your personal lives, carry with you the principles discussed in this chapter. Advocate for strong data protection measures, practice responsible data management, and continue to educate yourself and others about the importance of data privacy.

In the age of digital communication, protecting data privacy is a shared responsibility—one that requires the collective effort of individuals, organizations, and governments worldwide. By embracing the concepts outlined in this chapter and advocating for their application in the digital realm, we can all contribute to a more secure, private, and trustworthy digital future.

This chapter has laid the foundation for understanding the critical importance of data privacy. As we move forward in this textbook, we'll explore more specialized topics, each building on the knowledge you've gained here, to provide you with a comprehensive understanding of cybersecurity in the context of digital communication.

Key Takeaways

- Data confidentiality ensures personal information is kept secure from unauthorized access or disclosure, protecting individuals' privacy.
- Data security involves measures to protect data from threats and vulnerabilities, including the use of firewalls, encryption, and secure coding practices.
- Limitations in data collection emphasize the importance of collecting data only for specific, legitimate purposes, with informed consent, and transparency about collection practices.

- Compliance with data privacy laws such as the GDPR, CCPA, and others, requires organizations to adhere to principles that safeguard personal data, including lawfulness, fairness, transparency, and accountability.
- Anonymization and pseudonymization are techniques used to protect individuals' privacy by removing or altering personal identifiers in datasets, making it difficult to link data back to specific individuals.
- Accuracy of data is crucial for ensuring that decisions made based on data are correct and fair, and individuals have the right to correct inaccuracies in their personal data.
- Data storage limits dictate that personal data should not be retained longer than necessary, with organizations needing to balance between archiving for historical/legal purposes and deleting data to protect privacy.
- Integrity and confidentiality of data are essential for preventing unauthorized access and ensuring that data remains accurate and unaltered, upholding the trust and confidence in digital systems.

Chapter Review Questions

Question 1: What is the significance of data confidentiality in the context of data privacy, and how can it be achieved?

Answer: Data confidentiality is significant because it protects personal information from unauthorized access or disclosure, thereby safeguarding individuals' privacy. It can be achieved through measures such as encryption, access controls, and secure authentication mechanisms, ensuring that only authorized individuals can access sensitive information.

Question 2: Explain the difference between anonymization and pseudonymization. Why are these techniques important for data privacy?

Answer: Anonymization involves altering personal data in such a way that the individual cannot be identified by anyone, and this process is irreversible. Pseudonymization replaces personal identifiers with pseudonyms, making it difficult to attribute the data to a specific individual without additional information, which is kept separately; this process can be reversed under certain conditions. These techniques are important for data privacy because they allow data to be used for analysis and other legitimate purposes while reducing the risk of compromising individuals' privacy.

Question 3: What are the key principles underlying compliance with data privacy laws like the GDPR, and how do they impact organizational practices?

Answer: The key principles include lawfulness, fairness, transparency, purpose limitation, data minimization, accuracy, storage limitation, and integrity and confidentiality. These principles impact organizational practices by requiring businesses to collect and process personal data in a transparent and secure manner, only for specified purposes, and to retain data only as long as necessary. Organizations must also ensure the accuracy of data and provide individuals with the ability to access, correct, or delete their personal information, thereby fostering accountability and promoting trust.

Chapter 4

Encryption and Data Protection

Tiffany Ceasor, PhD; ed. Shane McNeil, PhD

Learning Outcomes

- Understand the Fundamentals of Encryption:
  - Explain the purpose and basic mechanisms of encryption, including the differences between encryption in transit and end-to-end encryption (E2EE).
  - Describe how encryption protects data and communications from unauthorized access.
- Differentiate Between Encryption Types:
  - Identify the key differences between encryption in transit and end-to-end encryption.
  - Recognize the strengths and weaknesses of various encryption protocols, such as AES-256.
- Assess the Practical Applications of Encryption:
  - Understand how encryption is applied in personal communications, commercial interactions, and governmental systems.
  - Evaluate real-world use cases, such as HTTPS, VPNs, Wi-Fi encryption, and local device encryption.
- Analyze the Advantages and Disadvantages of Encryption:
  - Discuss the benefits of encryption, including privacy, trust, and data security.
  - Critically evaluate the drawbacks, such as latency, convenience challenges, and potential misuse by bad actors.
- Explore the Implications of Quantum Computing:

- Understand how quantum computing could compromise current encryption standards.
- Discuss the ongoing development of quantum-resistant encryption algorithms and their importance for future security.

Key Terms

- **Encryption:** The process of converting information into a coded format to prevent unauthorized access.
- **Decryption:** The process of converting encrypted data back into its original readable form using a key or algorithm.
- **AES-256 (Advanced Encryption Standard 256-bit):** A widely recognized encryption standard that uses a 256-bit key length for secure data encryption.
- **End-to-End Encryption (E2EE):** A type of encryption that secures data at every stage of its life cycle—on the sender's device, during transmission, and on the recipient's device.
- **Encryption in Transit:** The practice of encrypting data while it is being transmitted between two points, such as over a network.
- **HTTPS (HyperText Transfer Protocol Secure):** A protocol used to secure communication over the internet by encrypting data in transit.
- **VPN (Virtual Private Network):** A technology that creates a secure, encrypted connection over a less secure network, protecting user identity and activity.
- **Quantum Computing:** A type of computing that leverages quantum mechanics to perform complex calculations at speeds far beyond traditional computers.
- **Quantum-Resistant Algorithms:** Encryption algorithms designed to withstand attacks from quantum computers.
- **Ciphertext:** Data that has been encrypted and is unreadable without a decryption key.
- **Metadata:** Data that provides information about other data, such as timestamps or file sizes, which can sometimes be used to infer patterns or behaviors.
- **Cryptography:** The study and practice of securing communication and data through encryption techniques.
- **Latency:** The delay between the transmission of a message and its receipt, often influenced by the complexity of encryption processes.
- **GDPR (General Data Protection Regulation):** A legal framework in the European Union for data privacy and protection, emphasizing user control over personal data.
- **Post-Quantum Cryptography:** Cryptographic methods and algorithms designed to be secure against quantum computing attacks.

Introduction

The concept of encryption isn't new; in fact, it's actually very old. When we think about the first instances of encryption, we might recall spy movies. These stories often depict one person trying to send a secret message to someone else without it being intercepted. The message contains important or private information that the sender doesn't want anyone else to know—except the intended recipient.

Now, in the modern day, most of us aren't spies. So how does encryption relate to us? Well, we see it everywhere. It's in our passwords, our emails, and our messages. Whenever we handle private information or documents—like medical records—we use encryption to ensure that it stays private. We want this information to be available only to ourselves or the intended recipient.

So, what is encryption? Encryption is when you have a message, like "Hello, World," and you don't want anyone else to understand it until it reaches the intended recipient. Instead of sending "Hello, World" directly, you might use an algorithm—a complex sequence of actions that both you and the recipient know. This algorithm transforms the message into a scrambled format, such as "Jgnnq, Yqtnf."

Here's how it works: suppose the rule of the algorithm is to shift each letter two spaces forward in the alphabet. The letter H becomes J, E becomes G, and so on. The resulting encrypted message looks strange to anyone who doesn't know the rule. When the recipient gets the message, they know to shift each letter two spaces backward to decode it, revealing the original message: "Hello, World."

This is the essence of encryption—a process that allows us to protect sensitive information, ensuring that only the intended recipient can understand it.

4.1 Understanding Encryption

When we think about encryption, let's start with a simple example. Imagine you have a string of characters that makes up a message, such as "hello." Each letter—H, E, L, L, and O—represents a separate character in computer science terms. Encryption is the process of transforming these characters so that the message becomes unreadable to anyone except the intended recipient.

A basic way to think about this is by shifting each letter in the message by a specific number of spaces in the alphabet. For example, if you shift each letter two spaces forward, H becomes J, E becomes G, and so on. The encrypted version of "hello" now looks like "jgnnq." This scrambled text makes the message appear meaningless to anyone who doesn't know the shifting rule.

On the recipient's side, decryption is the reverse process. If they know the rule used to encrypt the message—shifting letters by two spaces—they can simply shift the characters back by two spaces to reveal the original message, "hello." This process of encryption and decryption ensures privacy, allowing only those with the correct key or knowledge of the algorithm to understand the message.

In modern terms, encryption works like placing a valuable gift in a locked box. Without the key, no one can open the box or use its contents. But if the recipient has the key, they can unlock the box and access the item inside, keeping its contents secure from anyone else.

Simple and Modern Encryption Methods

The example above describes a basic substitution cipher, which was once a popular way to encode messages. However, because such methods are easy to figure out, encryption today is far more sophisticated. Modern encryption uses complex algorithms, such as **AES-256 (Advanced Encryption Standard with 256-bit keys)**, which is the current standard recognized by the National Institute of Standards and Technology (NIST).[1]

Here's how it works:

Instead of shifting all characters the same way, each character in the message has 256 possible outcomes based on a unique combination of transformations.

For example, in "hello," the H could transform into any one of 256 possibilities, the E into another 256 possibilities, and so on for each character. The total number of combinations is astronomically large, making it virtually impossible to crack the encryption using current computational power.

To put this into perspective, brute-forcing an AES-256 encrypted message—trying every possible combination to decrypt it—would take trillions of years with today's computers. This makes it more practical for hackers to attempt to steal passwords rather than try to break the encryption directly.

However, as computing technology advances, particularly with faster processing speeds, this "trillions of years" timeframe could shrink to hundreds or even fewer years. This is why encryption standards must continually evolve to stay ahead of technological advancements.

Examples of Encryption in Practice

1. **HTTPS Encryption:** HTTPS is a protocol used to secure data transferred over the internet. When you type "https://" into a browser, you're ensuring that the communication between your device and the website is encrypted. This encryption prevents others on the network from seeing sensitive information, such as login credentials or financial details, as it travels from your device to the website's server.
2. **Local Device Encryption:** Data stored locally on devices, such as computers or smartphones, is often encrypted. For example, files or private photos on your device may be protected with a password or encryption key, ensuring that even if

1. National Institute of Standards and Technology (NIST), "Advanced Encryption Standard (AES)," November 26, 2001, https://nvlpubs.nist.gov/nistpubs/FIPS/NIST.FIPS.197-upd1.pdf

someone gains physical access to your device, they cannot read the data without the key.

3. **Wi-Fi Encryption:** When multiple people share the same Wi-Fi network, encryption prevents users on the network from viewing each other's activities. For instance, if a family of five shares a Wi-Fi connection, encryption ensures that no one can intercept private communications, such as messages or sensitive browsing activity, from other devices on the network.

Encryption is everywhere, from securing online communications to protecting data stored on devices. By understanding the principles behind encryption, we can better appreciate its importance in safeguarding our privacy in the digital age.

4.2 Encryption in Transit Versus End-to-End Encryption

Encryption in transit is exactly what it sounds like—it protects a message or data while it is being transferred from one owner to the next or from one location to another. For example, let's say you have files or photos stored on your computer. You don't need a password to view them locally because they're just sitting in your folder. But if you want to send an email containing sensitive information, such as a birth certificate or Social Security number, over a network where unauthorized people could access it, you'd want to make sure it's securely "locked up" so that only the intended recipient can access it.[2]

Encryption in transit works similarly to sending a package. If you were mailing a package with personal data from Seattle to Washington, DC, you'd ensure it was well-packaged or even placed in a lockbox. While the package is in your house, you may not think it needs extra security because it's within your private space. However, during transit, others could intercept it, so you use a lockbox to secure it. Only the recipient has the key to open the box once it arrives, but once they've unlocked it, the data is no longer protected.

This highlights a key characteristic of encryption in transit: the data is only encrypted while it is being transferred. It is a less computationally expensive process and is commonly used for data that isn't considered extremely sensitive. Once the data is "at rest" with either the sender or recipient, it is not encrypted unless additional measures are taken.

2. National Academies of Sciences, Engineering, and Medicine. "2 Introduction to Encryption," in Cryptography and the Intelligence Community: The Future of Encryption, ed. National Academies of Sciences, Engineering, and Medicine (The National Academies Press, 2022), 16–17, https://doi.org/10.17226/26168.

End-to-End Encryption

In contrast, **end-to-end encryption (E2EE)** encrypts the data throughout its entire life cycle. This means the data is scrambled and protected even when it is at rest on the sender's device, during transit, and on the recipient's device after it is received. E2EE uses advanced algorithms, such as AES-256, to ensure data remains inaccessible to anyone without the correct decryption key.[3]

For example, if you're sending a message from your phone, it's encrypted on your device before it leaves. It remains encrypted while being transmitted and is still encrypted when it reaches the recipient's phone. Only the sender and recipient have the keys to decrypt the message. This ensures that even if someone intercepts the data, they cannot understand its contents.

While E2EE is more secure, it is also more computationally intensive because it requires encryption at every stage. It provides a higher level of privacy because the data is never exposed, not even to the platform facilitating the transmission.

Why Use E2EE?

We often trust that our data is safe without taking extra precautions. For instance, many people assume that their phones, computers, or networks are secure enough to prevent unauthorized access. However, this assumption leaves room for vulnerabilities. Hackers or malicious actors could exploit these gaps, and once your unencrypted data is accessed, it can be read, used, or manipulated.

E2EE helps address this by ensuring data remains encrypted even when you aren't actively monitoring it. It is the digital equivalent of locking your private documents in a safe, even when you're at home. This level of security is vital because you never know who might be watching, even within your personal or trusted spaces.

Historically, people recognized the importance of securing data long before digital encryption existed. During wars, for example, generals would write messages in code to prevent enemy spies from understanding their plans, even if the messages were intercepted. Similarly, encryption today protects your data from being read or misused by unauthorized individuals, even if they gain access to your device or network.

Encryption in transit and E2EE both play crucial roles in protecting data. Encryption in transit offers a practical, efficient way to secure information during transfer, while E2EE provides comprehensive protection for data throughout its entire life cycle. Given the increasing risks of data breaches and cyberattacks, E2EE is often the preferred choice for ensuring privacy and security, even when your data is seemingly at rest in a secure environment.

3. Britta Hale and Chelsea Komlo, "On End-to-End Encryption," International Association for Cryptologic Research (IACR), 2022, https://eprint.iacr.org/2022/449.pdf.

4.3 Examples of Encryption

Encryption plays a significant role in our daily digital interactions. Below are several practical examples that demonstrate how encryption works and why it is essential for protecting our data.

HTTPS Encryption

When you type a web address into your browser and see "HTTPS://" at the beginning, the "S" stands for secure. This indicates that the website uses encryption to protect the data being transmitted between your device and the site. HTTPS is an example of **encryption in transit**, meaning the data is encrypted only while it is being sent. Once it reaches the recipient or is at rest, it may not remain encrypted unless additional measures are in place.

For instance, imagine setting up automatic payments for a car loan through your bank's website. When you log in to your account, the data you send, such as your username and password, is encrypted during its journey from your device to the bank's server. Similarly, the bank encrypts the financial data it sends back to you, like account balances and payment schedules. This ensures that any sensitive information is protected from eavesdroppers who might be monitoring the network.

Even though HTTPS primarily focuses on encryption in transit, combining it with E2EE ensures the data remains secure at both the sender's and recipient's ends, offering a more comprehensive layer of protection.

VPNs for Anonymity

A **Virtual Private Network (VPN)** is another tool that leverages encryption to safeguard data and protect user identities. When you connect to the internet through a VPN, it masks your device's identity, ensuring that your activity cannot be traced back to you.[4]

For example, in countries where certain websites or apps are restricted, individuals often use VPNs to access these sites anonymously. Instead of your device appearing as "Tiffany's iPhone" to a website, a VPN assigns a pseudonym like "XYZ123's Device." This makes it difficult for anyone to link your browsing activity to you personally. VPNs essentially wrap your identity in a protective layer, ensuring privacy and anonymity.

Wi-Fi Encryption

Wi-Fi encryption secures data transmitted over shared networks, ensuring that users cannot view each other's activity. For instance, in a household where five people share the

4. Antonio Francesco Gentile, Peppino Fazio, and Giuseppe Miceli, "A Survey on the Implementation and Management of Secure Virtual Private Networks (VPNs) and Virtual LANs (VLANs) in Static and Mobile Scenarios," *Telecom* 2, no. 4 (2021): 430–45. https://doi.org/10.3390/telecom2040025.

same Wi-Fi connection, encryption prevents one user from intercepting another's private messages or browsing data.

Imagine sending a private message using the shared Wi-Fi in your home. Without encryption, other devices on the same network could potentially access that message. Wi-Fi encryption ensures that while everyone can use the shared connection, their data remains private and unreadable to others on the network.

Local Device Encryption

Local device encryption protects the data stored directly on a device, such as a smartphone, tablet, or laptop. This becomes particularly critical if the device is lost or stolen. For instance, if someone misplaces their smartphone, which contains personal emails, financial details, and private photos, local device encryption ensures that even if the device is physically accessed, the data remains scrambled and unreadable.

Here's how it works: encrypted devices store data in a format called **ciphertext**, which is unreadable without the correct decryption key. Even if a thief extracts the data from the device, they cannot decipher its contents without the proper credentials. This provides a critical safeguard for data stored locally, complementing the protection offered by cloud storage providers, which typically have their own encryption measures.[5]

Encryption, whether applied in transit, for anonymity, over shared networks, or on local devices, is an indispensable tool for securing digital information. These examples highlight how encryption protects us in various aspects of our online and offline lives, ensuring our data remains private and secure even in challenging situations.

4.4 How End-to-End Encryption Works

To understand how E2EE works, it helps to think about computer networks as systems that communicate through a central hub. This central hub, or **server**, acts as the system's "source of truth," similar to how the brain functions in the human body. Just as the brain processes and transmits information to different parts of the body to perform actions, the server manages and relays information to connected devices, or **clients**.

The Server and Client Relationship

In a network, clients represent devices such as your phone or computer. When you want to access information, your device communicates with the server to request it. The server processes the request and, if authorized, sends the data back to your device. This interaction involves **access controls**, which determine what data a client can retrieve based on their role. For example, an administrator may have broader access to data than a regular user.

5. National Academies of Sciences, Engineering, and Medicine. "2 Introduction to Encryption," 16–17.

For a client to retrieve data, it must provide valid credentials, such as a password or access key. The server checks these credentials to ensure the client is authorized to view the requested information. If the data belongs to another user, the server denies access, maintaining the privacy and integrity of the information.

The Role of Encryption

The server holds all the information in a network, making it the "source of truth." Protecting this central hub is critical to ensure unauthorized users cannot access sensitive data. Encryption plays a key role here. The server encrypts its stored information, ensuring that even if someone tries to access it without proper authorization, they cannot decipher the data.

Additionally, when a client requests data, encryption ensures that only the client with the correct decryption key can access and view the information. For example, if a client sends a request for information belonging to another user, the server won't provide it because the client doesn't have the proper key. This guarantees that each user can access only their own data.

How E2EE Differs

E2EE goes a step further by encrypting data at every stage of its life cycle—on the sender's device, during transit, and on the recipient's device. With E2EE, even the server acting as the intermediary cannot decrypt or view the data.

Here's how it works:

1. **Encryption at the Sender's End:** Data is encrypted on the sender's device before being transmitted. For example, if you send a message, your device encrypts the content so that it appears as unreadable scrambled text to anyone without the decryption key.
2. **Encryption During Transit:** As the encrypted message travels through the server, it remains in its scrambled state. The server acts only as a relay, forwarding the message to the recipient without being able to decrypt it.
3. **Decryption at the Recipient's End:** When the recipient receives the message, their device uses a decryption key to restore the original content. Only the intended recipient, with the correct key, can view the message.

This process ensures that the data remains secure at all times, preventing unauthorized access even if the server itself is compromised.

The Importance of Protecting the Server

While E2EE protects the content of communications, the server still plays a crucial role in managing data requests. It's essential to encrypt the server to safeguard against unauthorized access attempts. For instance, if hackers target the server, encryption ensures they cannot decipher the stored data without the appropriate keys.

Servers also manage requests from multiple clients simultaneously. Without encryption, the server might inadvertently expose one user's information to another. Proper encryption protocols ensure that data requests are processed securely and that each client accesses only the information they are authorized to view.

End-to-end encryption provides comprehensive security by protecting data throughout its life cycle. By encrypting data at rest, in transit, and at the recipient's end, E2EE ensures that sensitive information remains private and accessible only to authorized users. This layered approach to encryption helps maintain trust and security in today's interconnected digital systems

4.5 Use Cases for E2EE

E2EE has diverse applications across personal, commercial, and hybrid scenarios. This section explores these use cases, emphasizing how E2EE secures data, fosters trust, and protects sensitive information.

Personal Use Cases

Personal data encompasses the messages, photos, and other sensitive content we share daily through platforms like iMessage, Instagram, Snapchat, and TikTok. This information is private, and we value keeping it secure from prying eyes—whether they belong to hackers, malicious actors, or unauthorized individuals.

For example, when you send a text message from your phone to a friend's device, you might assume it is private. However, platforms often retain ownership of the data being transmitted. If your message passes through a server owned by the platform, the platform itself has access to its contents, even though other users cannot see it. This means your personal data is not truly private.

In some cases, platforms or governments may choose to monitor user communications. Without E2EE, entities like social media companies or messaging platforms can view, store, and even share your private messages. This is particularly concerning in cases of mass surveillance or when sensitive personal data, such as financial or legal information, is transmitted. E2EE prevents these risks by ensuring that only the sender and recipient can decrypt and access the data.

Examples of E2EE in Personal Use:

- **Signal and ProtonMail:** Platforms like Signal provide E2EE for messaging, ensuring that even the platform itself cannot read the messages. Similarly, ProtonMail encrypts emails at rest and in transit, protecting sensitive communications.[6]
- **Apple iMessage:** E2EE is applied when messages are sent between Apple devices, making it impossible for Apple to decrypt the messages.[7]

Without E2EE, users are left vulnerable to breaches, misuse of data by platform owners, or unauthorized surveillance.

Intersection of Personal and Commercial Use

When personal data intersects with commercial systems, such as in banking or health care, E2EE becomes even more critical. Users regularly share sensitive details—like Social Security numbers, financial records, or medical information—with businesses or institutions. These interactions require a higher level of security to ensure privacy.

For instance, when creating a bank account, your personal data (e.g., credit history and date of birth) is stored in the bank's systems. If the bank's data is not encrypted end-to-end, hackers could access it during a breach. E2EE ensures that even if the bank's systems are compromised, the stolen data remains indecipherable.

Examples of Personal-Commercial Intersection Use:

- **Online Banking:** When you log into your bank account or make a transaction, E2EE ensures that both your credentials and financial data are encrypted at all times.
- **Health-Care Data:** Telemedicine platforms and electronic health records often use E2EE to comply with privacy regulations like Health Insurance Portability and Accountability Act (HIPAA), protecting patient data from unauthorized access.

E2EE minimizes the risks associated with data breaches, safeguarding both the user's data and the institution's reputation.

Commercial Applications

For businesses and government organizations, E2EE is vital to protecting sensitive data, internal communications, and customer trust. Large-scale hacks and breaches often target these sectors, putting critical information at risk.

6. Venafi, "What You Need to Know About the Signal E2EE Protocol," July 12, 2021, https://venafi.com/blog/what-you-need-know-about-signal-e2ee-protocol/; Proton, "Proton Mail Encryption Explained," https://proton.me/support/proton-mail-encryption-explained.
7. Dan Goodin, "iMessage gets a major makeover that puts it on equal footing with Signal," *Ars Technica*, February 21, 2024. https://arstechnica.com/security/2024/02/imessage-gets-a-major-makeover-that-puts-it-on-equal-footing-with-signal/.

1. **Internal Communication Security:** Companies often manage sensitive internal data, such as employee records, trade secrets, or strategic plans. E2EE ensures that only authorized parties within the organization can access this data, even if it is transmitted across networks. For example, encrypted emails or messaging platforms can secure discussions about confidential projects.
2. **Customer Data Protection:** Businesses handling customer data, such as retail companies or technology platforms, must ensure this data is secure at every stage of its life cycle. Without E2EE, breaches could expose sensitive customer details, resulting in loss of trust and severe financial penalties.
3. **Regulatory Compliance:** Many industries face strict data privacy regulations, such as GDPR in Europe. E2EE enables organizations to meet these compliance requirements by encrypting customer and business data end-to-end, ensuring privacy and avoiding hefty fines.

    a. Example: If a hacker infiltrates a company's network, E2EE limits the damage by ensuring that stolen data is encrypted and unusable. This protects the company's reputation while preventing further harm.

4. **Device-to-Device Security:** Even within a single company network, devices should not implicitly trust one another. By implementing E2EE, businesses ensure that if one device is compromised, the breach does not cascade across the network. For example, a compromised employee laptop would not provide access to other users' devices or sensitive company data.

End-to-end encryption protects sensitive data in personal, commercial, and hybrid contexts. It ensures privacy, secures communications, and safeguards data even in the event of a breach. Whether protecting personal messages, interacting with commercial platforms, or securing organizational communications, E2EE is an indispensable tool in today's digital world.

4.6 Advantages and Disadvantages of Encryption

Disadvantages of Encryption

While the advantages of E2EE are significant, it's important to start by addressing its disadvantages. One of the primary reasons users avoid E2EE is its inconvenience. Remembering multiple passwords or using additional applications that require passcodes can feel burdensome. For example, if you want to send an encrypted message, both you and the recipient need to use the same application and follow the same protocols, including entering passwords. Many people prefer the simplicity of opening their phone, clicking a message, and sending it without these extra steps.

This inconvenience can deter users, especially those who do not fully understand the risks of data privacy breaches or the implications of unauthorized access to their information. Maintaining and managing multiple passwords or encryption keys for various platforms is often perceived as tedious. As a result, people might either use the same password across all applications or forego encryption entirely, opting for convenience over security.

Another significant disadvantage of E2EE is its potential to hinder law enforcement and national security efforts. For example, bad actors, such as cybercriminals or terrorists, may use encryption to conceal their activities. The "dark web," often associated with anonymity and hidden activities, operates similarly to E2EE. These individuals can hide their identities and communications in encrypted "packages" that are unreadable without the decryption key. This poses challenges for agencies like the FBI or other organizations that need access to this data to prevent harmful events. Even with a warrant, encrypted data often appears as scrambled text—unreadable and indecipherable.

This limitation creates a societal-level challenge: While encryption protects individual privacy, it can also shield those with malicious intent. Governments and law enforcement agencies may struggle to track communications and prevent tragic events, as encryption ensures that even intercepted messages remain incomprehensible.

A third disadvantage of E2EE is latency. Encryption involves additional computational steps, such as scrambling data into ciphertext and decrypting it at the recipient's end. While sending an unencrypted message may take only a second, an encrypted message might take several seconds to process. Although this delay is minimal, it can still frustrate users who prioritize speed and efficiency. For many, the trade-off between privacy and a slight delay can feel unnecessary, especially in noncritical communications.

Finally, E2EE can create a false sense of security. Users may believe their communications are entirely untraceable, but metadata—such as timestamps, file sizes, and usage patterns—can still be analyzed. For example, even if law enforcement cannot read encrypted messages, they can infer relationships and behaviors based on message frequency, timing, and patterns. Similarly, hackers could use metadata to deduce communication details or target specific users.

In summary, the disadvantages of E2EE include its inconvenience, potential to hinder national security, latency, and the possibility of creating a false sense of security. These challenges highlight why some users and institutions may hesitate to adopt it.

Advantages of Encryption

Despite its drawbacks, the advantages of E2EE are profound and far-reaching. At its core, E2EE protects trust, privacy, and security—fundamental principles for safeguarding personal and societal data.

One of the primary benefits is that E2EE ensures true privacy. If an entity, such as a platform or service provider, can access and read your messages, your data isn't truly private. For example, if you use TikTok, Snapchat, or other platforms that lack end-to-end encryption, those companies can theoretically access all your messages, photos, and other shared content. This exposes users to significant risks, including unauthorized data sharing or breaches.

E2EE eliminates this concern by ensuring that no one—not even the platform—can access your messages without your permission. This level of security protects against bad actors who might seek to steal or misuse your information, such as passwords or financial details. For instance, if a hacker obtains your banking credentials, they could potentially transfer funds or access sensitive accounts. However, with additional encryption layers like multifactor authentication (MFA), your data remains secure. MFA, often used by banks, requires a secondary verification step (e.g., a text message code) to confirm your identity, further strengthening encryption.

Beyond personal protection, E2EE safeguards society as a whole. When data is left unprotected, it can be manipulated or weaponized, giving malicious individuals or groups undue influence over public systems or individuals. Encryption ensures that sensitive data is secure, preventing scenarios where stolen information could lead to identity theft, blackmail, or broader societal harm.

E2EE also empowers users to take control of their data. In a world where trust in corporations and governments can waver, encryption provides a tangible way to ensure that your data remains yours. By encrypting data, you reduce your reliance on external entities to protect your privacy, acknowledging that their interests may not always align with your own.

Finally, E2EE is a proactive measure. It may add a few seconds to message transmission or require the use of passwords, but it protects against future risks and consequences that could arise from unencrypted data being intercepted or exposed.

The advantages and disadvantages of E2EE demonstrate its complexities. While it adds inconvenience, latency, and challenges for law enforcement, it also provides unparalleled privacy, security, and trust. In a world where digital data is constantly at risk, E2EE ensures that individuals and institutions can safeguard their most sensitive information, protecting themselves and others from harm. Its adoption reflects a commitment to prioritizing privacy and security in an increasingly interconnected world.

4.7 Encryption and Quantum Computing

In this final section, we'll explore a groundbreaking, innovative, and potentially risky technological advancement: quantum computing. The question is, how does quantum computing affect encryption? To answer this, let's revisit the concept of encryption, specifically AES-256, the longest and most secure encryption standard currently in use.

How Quantum Computing Challenges Encryption

AES-256 encryption works by assigning each character in a message a unique combination from 256 possible options. This means every character in an encrypted message could theoretically represent one of 256 combinations. The result is an encryption process so robust that it would take trillions of years for traditional computers to try every possible combination and decrypt the message. This is why most hackers focus on stealing passwords or exploiting vulnerabilities rather than attempting to brute-force an encrypted message.

The security of AES-256 hinges on the speed and capability of current computers. Even with a small number of possible combinations, decrypting a message using traditional methods would take an impractical amount of time. For example, with only three possible combinations for each character, a human or standard computer would need about an hour to test all the iterations.

Enter Quantum Computing

Unlike traditional computers, quantum computers can process vast amounts of data simultaneously, exponentially increasing their speed and computational power. With quantum computing, the ability to compute and test combinations has advanced so significantly that decrypting AES-256 encryption is no longer unfeasible. A quantum computer can potentially iterate over all combinations for every character in a message within a realistic time frame, effectively breaking the encryption.[8]

Implications of Quantum Computing on Current Encryption Standards

The development of quantum computing poses a significant risk to our current encryption methods. The AES-256 standard, widely accepted by organizations like NIST and considered unbreakable with traditional technology, could soon become vulnerable. Quantum computers, with their extraordinary processing power, can efficiently trial combinations until they find the correct one to decrypt a message.

If quantum computing becomes more advanced and accessible, our existing encryption systems could be rendered obsolete. This scenario presents a potential crisis for data security and privacy, as the encryption methods that currently protect sensitive information—like financial transactions, government communications, and personal data—might no longer provide sufficient protection.

The Race for Quantum-Proof Algorithms

The rise of quantum computing has sparked a race in the cryptography sector to develop quantum-resistant algorithms. These algorithms aim to secure data, even against the immense processing power of quantum computers. The goal is to create encryption methods so complex that even a quantum computer would require an impractical amount of time—years, decades, or even centuries—to decrypt the message.

8. Yaser Baseri, Vikas Chouhan, and Ali Ghorbani, "Cybersecurity in the Quantum Era: Assessing the Impact of Quantum Computing on Infrastructure," arXiv, 2024. https://arxiv.org/pdf/2404.10659.

Quantum-resistant cryptography, also known as post-quantum cryptography, is a rapidly evolving field. Researchers and technology companies are working on innovative encryption methods that will not only withstand current computational capabilities but also remain secure in the quantum era. These advancements are critical to ensuring the continued privacy and security of our data in the face of emerging quantum technologies.

The Future of Encryption

Quantum computing represents a significant leap forward in technology, but it also poses challenges that could fundamentally reshape the landscape of data security. While current encryption standards like AES-256 provide robust protection, they are at risk of becoming obsolete as quantum computing advances.

The race to develop quantum-proof encryption methods highlights the importance of staying ahead of technological breakthroughs to protect sensitive information. At the same time, quantum computing opens up exciting possibilities for innovation in fields like artificial intelligence, material science, and medicine, demonstrating its dual-edged potential.

As we look to the future, one thing is clear: the evolution of quantum computing will not only redefine the limits of computation but also inspire groundbreaking advancements in encryption and cryptography, ensuring that data security keeps pace with technological progress. This is an exciting and pivotal moment in the history of cybersecurity.

Discussion Questions

1. **The Balance of Privacy and Security:** How can governments and organizations balance the need for privacy provided by end-to-end encryption with the need to prevent misuse by bad actors? Should there be limits to encryption in certain scenarios, such as national security investigations? Why or why not?
2. **Quantum Computing and Encryption**: With the advent of quantum computing, current encryption standards like AES-256 may become vulnerable. How should organizations and individuals prepare for this potential threat? What steps can be taken to ensure long-term data security in a post-quantum world?
3. **Personal Responsibility in Data Security**: Many people avoid using end-to-end encryption due to perceived inconvenience, such as managing multiple passwords. Do you think individuals have a responsibility to prioritize their own data security, even if it requires extra effort? How can companies encourage better encryption adoption without sacrificing usability?

Chapter 5

Types of Digital Communication

Shane McNeil, PhD

Learning Outcomes

- Understand Various Digital Communication Methods: Identify and describe different types of digital communication tools and their specific uses, including email, instant messaging, video conferencing, social media, mobile texting, Voice over Internet Protocol (VoIP), web chats, forums, blogs, and podcasts.
- Recognize the Applications and Advantages of Each Tool: Evaluate the unique features, benefits, and appropriate contexts for using each type of digital communication platform.
- Appreciate the Role of Digital Communication in Modern Society: Discuss the impact of digital communication tools on personal and professional interactions, highlighting their role in enhancing connectivity and collaboration.
- Understand Data Privacy Implications: Analyze the data privacy and security considerations associated with each type of digital communication, understanding best practices for protecting personal and sensitive information.
- Apply Best Practices for Secure Communication: Implement strategies to maintain data privacy and security when using various digital communication tools, ensuring safe and effective exchanges.

Key Terms

- **Email:** A method of exchanging digital messages over the internet, widely used for both personal and professional communication.
- **Instant Messaging (IM):** A form of real-time text communication between two or more people over the internet.
- **Video Conferencing:** Technology that allows users in different locations to hold face-to-face meetings without having to move to a single location.
- **Social Media:** Online platforms that enable users to create content, share information, and interact with others.

- **Short Message Service (SMS):** A text messaging service component of most telephone, internet, and mobile device systems.
- **Voice over Internet Protocol (VoIP):** A technology that allows users to make voice calls using a broadband internet connection instead of a regular phone line.
- **Web Chats:** Online communication platforms where users can engage in text-based conversations in real time.
- **Forums:** Online discussion sites where people can hold conversations in the form of posted messages.
- **Blogs:** Websites or web pages that are regularly updated with new content, often written in an informal or conversational style.
- **Podcasts:** Digital audio files available on the internet for downloading, typically as part of a themed series.
- **Data Privacy:** The protection of personal information from unauthorized access and misuse.
- **Encryption:** The process of converting information or data into a code to prevent unauthorized access.
- **Authentication:** The process of verifying the identity of a user or device, often as a prerequisite to allowing access to resources in an information system.
- **Multifactor Authentication (MFA):** A security system that requires more than one method of authentication from independent categories of credentials to verify the user's identity.
- **Role-Based Access Control (RBAC):** A method of regulating access to computer or network resources based on the roles of individual users within an enterprise.

In today's interconnected world, digital communication has become an integral part of daily life, transforming how we interact, share information, and collaborate. The variety of digital communication methods available allows for diverse and dynamic exchanges, catering to both personal and professional needs. This chapter explores the different types of digital communication tools and platforms, each with its unique features and applications.

The evolution of digital communication has significantly influenced modern society, enhancing our ability to connect instantly across vast distances. This transformation has brought about unprecedented convenience and efficiency, enabling seamless interactions that transcend geographical barriers. Whether it's through emails, instant messaging (IM), video conferencing, or social media, digital communication tools have reshaped the way we live and work.

Email, one of the earliest forms of digital communication, remains a cornerstone for exchanging written messages electronically. Its versatility makes it suitable for various purposes, from formal business correspondence to casual personal interactions. IM platforms, such as Jabber, Slack, and Microsoft Teams, offer real-time chat capabilities that facilitate quick and efficient communication, making them indispensable in both professional and personal contexts.

Video conferencing has revolutionized remote collaboration, providing a virtual space for real-time visual and auditory interactions. This technology has become essential for business meetings, webinars, and online classes, bridging the gap between physical and virtual presence. Social media platforms like Facebook, Twitter, and Instagram enable global connectivity, allowing users to share content, engage with others, and build online communities.

Mobile texting, or Short Message Service (SMS), provides a straightforward and concise method of communication, ideal for brief updates and alerts. VoIP technology allows users to make voice calls via the internet, offering a cost-efficient alternative to traditional phone services. Web chats and forums, such as Reddit and various online communities, facilitate interactions on specific topics, fostering discussions and knowledge sharing among like-minded individuals.

Blogs and podcasts have emerged as powerful tools for content creation and audience engagement. These platforms allow individuals to share their thoughts, information, and stories with a broad audience, building a following through regular updates and engaging content. Each of these digital communication methods has unique advantages and is suited to different contexts, making them invaluable in our daily lives.

While digital communication offers numerous benefits, it also presents challenges, particularly concerning data privacy and security. The widespread use of these tools necessitates a thorough understanding of how to protect personal information and maintain confidentiality. This chapter will address these concerns, providing insights into the best practices for using digital communication tools securely.

Understanding the nuances of these communication types is essential for leveraging their full potential while maintaining data privacy and security. By examining these tools, we aim to equip readers with the knowledge to choose and use the right communication method for their needs, ensuring effective and secure exchanges in the digital age.

The subsequent sections will delve into various digital communication methods, providing an overview of their functionalities, common uses, and implications for data privacy. By exploring these different types of digital communication, we can appreciate their significance in modern society and understand how to use them responsibly and effectively. This knowledge will empower readers to navigate the digital landscape with confidence, optimizing their communication strategies for personal and professional success.

Applying Digital Communication Tools in a Professional Setting

Imagine you are a newly hired project manager at a midsized tech company. Your role involves coordinating a team spread across different cities, managing project timelines, and ensuring seamless communication among team members. As you settle into your new position, you quickly realize the importance of choosing the right digital communication tools to foster collaboration and maintain productivity. Here's how you apply the information from Chapter 5 to your daily work:

Email for Formal Communication

Your first task is to send a welcome email to your team, introducing yourself and outlining your initial plans for the project. Email, a ubiquitous method for exchanging written messages electronically, is the perfect tool for this purpose. It allows you to compose a detailed message, attach relevant documents, and ensure that everyone on the team receives the information. Throughout the project, you continue to use email for formal communications, such as sending meeting agendas, summarizing decisions, and documenting important discussions.

Instant Messaging for Quick Updates

As you move through your day, you often need to get quick updates or provide immediate feedback to your team members. IM platforms like Slack or Microsoft Teams become invaluable for real-time chat. For instance, when you notice a minor issue in a project report, you send a quick message to the responsible team member via Slack. The instant response allows you to address the issue promptly without disrupting your workflow. These platforms also support group chats, enabling spontaneous brainstorming sessions and fostering a collaborative environment.

Video Conferencing for Remote Meetings

Given that your team is geographically dispersed, regular face-to-face meetings are impractical. Instead, you rely on video conferencing tools such as Zoom or Microsoft Teams for your weekly project meetings. These virtual meetings allow you to engage with team members in real time, share screens to review documents, and discuss project progress as if you were all in the same room. Video conferencing proves essential for maintaining a personal connection with your team and ensuring that everyone is aligned on project goals.

Social Media for Broader Engagement

Your company encourages employees to share project milestones and successes on social media platforms like LinkedIn. By doing so, you can engage with a broader audience, including clients, partners, and potential new hires. You post updates about the project's progress, celebrate team achievements, and share industry-related insights. This not only promotes the project externally but also enhances your team's visibility and morale.

Mobile Texting for Urgent Alerts

Occasionally, urgent issues arise that require immediate attention, such as last-minute changes to a client meeting or a critical system outage. For these situations, you use SMS to send brief and direct updates to your team members' mobile phones. SMS ensures that your message is received and read quickly, regardless of whether the recipients are actively checking their email or IM apps.

VoIP for Cost-Efficient Calls

Sometimes, you need to have detailed discussions that are best handled over a voice call. Instead of using traditional phone lines, you opt for VoIP services like Skype or Zoom Phone. VoIP allows you to make high-quality calls over the internet, significantly reducing costs, especially for international communications. This tool is particularly useful when you need to have in-depth conversations with clients or partners located in different countries.

Web Chats and Forums for Community Building

To foster a sense of community and knowledge sharing among your team, you set up a web chat group and encourage participation in relevant online forums. Platforms like Reddit or specific professional forums related to your industry allow team members to share ideas, ask questions, and learn from others' experiences. This approach helps in building a supportive and collaborative team environment, where everyone can contribute and grow.

Blogs and Podcasts for Thought Leadership

To position your company as a thought leader in the industry, you initiate a project blog and podcast series. These platforms enable you to share insights, project updates, and expert opinions with a wider audience. By regularly updating the blog and podcast, you build a following and engage with stakeholders, clients, and industry peers. This not only enhances your company's reputation but also provides a platform for team members to showcase their expertise.

Through the strategic use of these diverse digital communication tools, you effectively manage your team, enhance productivity, and foster a collaborative and engaging work environment. Understanding and applying the right communication methods for different contexts ensure that you maintain strong connections, protect data privacy, and drive your projects to success.

5.1 Email

Email stands as one of the most ubiquitous and enduring methods of digital communication. Since its inception, email has transformed how individuals and organizations exchange written messages electronically. Its versatility, reliability, and wide acceptance make it a cornerstone in both personal and professional communication landscapes.

Usage: Business Communication

In the business world, email is the primary mode of formal communication. It is used for sending memos, reports, meeting agendas, and official correspondences. Email's ability to attach documents and provide a written record of communications makes it invaluable for professional interactions. It allows for clear, concise, and documented exchanges that can be referenced later, aiding in accountability and clarity.

Project managers, for example, use email to communicate project plans, updates, and deadlines to their teams. They send meeting invites with detailed agendas to ensure all participants are informed and prepared. Follow-up emails summarize meeting outcomes and assign tasks, providing a clear record of discussions and decisions.

Moreover, email is crucial for external business communication. Companies use email to interact with clients, vendors, and partners. A well-crafted email can help secure business deals, respond to customer inquiries, or handle complaints professionally. Marketing teams use email for campaigns, sending promotional materials, newsletters, and personalized offers to engage customers and drive sales.

Usage: Personal Correspondence

On a personal level, email remains a vital communication tool. It allows individuals to stay connected with friends and family, share news, and coordinate plans. The ability to send and receive messages asynchronously (not requiring both parties to be online simultaneously) makes email convenient for people with different schedules and time zones.

Personal emails can range from simple "catch-up" messages to more significant communications like sending invitations, sharing travel itineraries, or even exchanging holiday greetings. The ease of attaching photos and documents makes email a preferred choice for sharing memories and important information.

Email Security and Privacy Considerations

While email is a powerful communication tool, it is not without its risks. Email security and privacy are critical concerns, especially given the sensitive nature of many communications. Ensuring the confidentiality, integrity, and availability of email communications is paramount.

Encryption: One of the primary methods to ensure email security is encryption. Email encryption converts the contents of an email into a code that can only be deciphered by the intended recipient. This process protects the email's content from being read by unauthorized parties during transmission. There are two main types of email encryption: transport-level encryption (like TLS) and end-to-end encryption (E2EE). Transport-level encryption secures the email while it's being sent over the network, whereas E2EE ensures that the email remains encrypted from the sender's device to the recipient's device.

Popular encrypted email services include ProtonMail and Tutanota. ProtonMail offers E2EE and is based in Switzerland, known for its strong privacy laws. Tutanota, similarly, provides E2EE and includes secure calendar and contact features, enhancing overall privacy. These services automatically encrypt emails, ensuring that only the intended recipients can read the messages.[1]

Anonymous Email Providers: For users who need additional privacy, anonymous email providers like Guerrilla Mail and Mailinator offer solutions. These services allow users to send and receive emails without revealing their identity.[2] Guerrilla Mail provides disposable email addresses that expire after a certain period, while Mailinator offers public email addresses for receiving emails without creating an account. These services are useful for situations where privacy is paramount, such as signing up for online services or sending sensitive information without revealing personal details.

One-time use email services, such as Sharklasers (a service provided by Guerrilla Mail), offer temporary email addresses that self-destruct after a single use. These emails are ideal for signing up for websites, newsletters, or services that require email verification but may lead to spam or unwanted communication. By using a one-time email, users can protect their primary email address from potential spam and reduce the risk of phishing attacks.

Spam and Phishing: Spam and phishing emails pose significant threats to email users. Spam refers to unsolicited and often irrelevant messages sent in bulk, typically for advertising purposes. Phishing emails, on the other hand, are malicious attempts to trick recipients into divulging sensitive information, such as passwords or credit card details. These emails often appear to come from trusted sources and may contain links to fraudulent websites or malicious attachments.

To combat these threats, email service providers implement various security measures, such as spam filters, which use algorithms to identify and block unwanted emails. Users are also encouraged to adopt safe email practices, such as not clicking on links or downloading attachments from unknown senders and using MFA for their email accounts.

Legal and Compliance Issues

Email communication also intersects with various legal and compliance issues. Organizations must adhere to regulations governing the storage, retrieval, and transmission of

1. UMATechnology, "ProtonMail vs. Tutanota: Which Is the Best Secure Email Provider?," *UMA Technology* (blog), December 21, 2024, https://umatechnology.org/protonmail-vs-tutanota-which-is-the-best-secure-email-provider/.
2. Hang Hu, Peng Peng, and Gang Wang, "Characterizing Pixel Tracking through the Lens of Disposable Email Services," paper presented at *2019 IEEE Symposium on Security and Privacy (SP)*, San Francisco, CA, USA, 2019, 365–79, https://doi.org/10.1109/SP.2019.00033.

email data. Laws such as the General Data Protection Regulation (GDPR) in the European Union and the California Consumer Privacy Act (CCPA) in the United States impose stringent requirements on how personal data, including emails, is handled.[3]

Compliance with these regulations involves implementing data protection measures, obtaining consent for data collection, and providing users with rights over their data, such as the right to access and delete their information. Organizations must also ensure that their email practices comply with industry standards and internal policies to avoid legal repercussions and maintain trust with stakeholders.

Email Etiquette

Effective email communication also requires adherence to certain etiquette rules. Email etiquette refers to the set of guidelines and best practices for composing and sending emails professionally and respectfully. Key aspects of email etiquette include the following:

- **Clear Subject Lines:** A concise and descriptive subject line helps the recipient understand the email's purpose at a glance.
- **Professional Tone:** The tone of the email should be appropriate for the context, whether formal for business communications or casual for personal messages.
- **Brevity and Clarity:** Emails should be succinct and to the point, avoiding unnecessary jargon or lengthy explanations.
- **Proper Greetings and Signatures:** Using appropriate salutations and closing remarks adds a touch of professionalism to the email. Including a signature with contact information ensures the recipient knows who sent the email and how to reach them.
- **Proofreading:** Reviewing the email for spelling and grammatical errors before sending ensures that the message is clear and professional.

The Future of Email

As technology continues to evolve, so does the landscape of email communication. Innovations such as artificial intelligence (AI) and machine learning are being integrated into email systems to enhance functionality and user experience. For example, AI-powered email assistants can help draft emails, schedule meetings, and sort incoming messages based on priority.

Additionally, the rise of collaborative platforms is changing how email fits into the broader communication ecosystem. Tools like Slack and Microsoft Teams, which combine

3. Danielle Kucera, "CCPA vs. GDPR: Similarities and Differences Explained," Okta, accessed October 24, 2024, https://www.okta.com/blog/2021/04/ccpa-vs-gdpr/; Deloitte US, "A Quick Reference Guide for CCPA Compliance," accessed October 24, 2024, https://www2.deloitte.com/us/en/pages/advisory/articles/ccpa-compliance-readiness.html.

IM, file sharing, and project management features, are becoming increasingly popular in professional settings.[4] While these tools offer new ways to collaborate, email remains a critical component of digital communication, valued for its versatility and reliability.

Section Summary

Email is a foundational tool in digital communication, essential for both personal and professional interactions. Its ability to facilitate detailed, documented exchanges makes it invaluable in business settings, while its convenience and flexibility ensure its continued use in personal correspondence. As email continues to evolve, understanding its functionalities, security considerations, legal implications, and best practices for effective use will remain crucial for leveraging its full potential in the digital age. This comprehensive understanding of email will enable individuals and organizations to communicate more effectively, securely, and professionally in an increasingly interconnected world.

5.2 Instant Messaging

IM holds a significant place in the history of digital communication, tracing its roots back to the earliest days of the public internet. As one of the original methods for online interaction, IM revolutionized how people communicated in real time. Platforms like ICQ, AIM (AOL Instant Messenger), and MSN Messenger became immensely popular in the late 1990s and early 2000s, offering users a way to chat instantly, share files, and express themselves through text, emojis, and status updates.[5]

In its heyday, IM was a staple of online communication, particularly among younger users and early internet adopters. It provided a quick and efficient alternative to email, which was more formal and slower by comparison. The immediacy of IM allowed for spontaneous conversations and fostered a sense of community among users. However, with the advent of social media and the rise of mobile messaging apps like WhatsApp and Facebook Messenger, traditional IM platforms saw a significant decline in user engagement.[6]

Despite this decline in the consumer market, IM has found a renewed purpose and continued relevance in professional settings. The need for efficient, real-time communication in the workplace has ensured that IM remains a vital tool for businesses. Modern IM platforms have evolved to meet the demands of professional environments, offering enhanced features and integrations that support collaboration and productivity.

4. Jacqueline N. Lane, Paul M. Leonardi, Noshir S. Contractor, and Leslie A. DeChurch, "Teams in the Digital Workplace: Technology's Role for Communication, Collaboration, and Performance," *Small Group Research* 55, no. 1 (2024): 139–83, https://doi.org/10.1177/10464964231200015.
5. Anirudh Krishnan, "History and Statistics," OCF Berkeley, 2005, https://www.ocf.berkeley.edu/~anirudh/history.html.
6. Arun Kumar Tarofder, Ahasanul Haque, Nishad Nawaz et al., "Determinants of Instant Messenger (IM) Adoption and Its Effect on Team Performance: Mediating Role of Knowledge Creation and Quality Communication," *PLOS One* 18, no. 11 (2023): e0289168, https://doi.org/10.1371/journal.pone.0289168.

Examples: Jabber, Slack, Microsoft Teams

Several IM platforms have become integral to workplace communication, each offering unique features tailored to professional use. Among the most widely used are Jabber, Slack, and Microsoft Teams.

Jabber: Jabber, based on the Extensible Messaging and Presence Protocol (XMPP), was one of the early IM technologies that transitioned into professional use. It supports real-time text messaging, presence information (indicating whether a user is online, offline, or away), and file transfers. Its flexibility and open-source nature make it adaptable to various organizational needs, ensuring secure and customizable communication.[7]

Slack: Slack has become synonymous with team communication and collaboration in the modern workplace. Initially launched as a messaging app for businesses, Slack has evolved into a comprehensive platform that integrates with a wide range of tools and services. Beyond real-time messaging, Slack offers features such as channels (organized spaces for conversations), direct messaging, file sharing, and integrations with applications like Google Drive, Trello, and GitHub. Its user-friendly interface and powerful search functionality make it easy to find information and keep track of conversations, fostering efficient team collaboration.[8]

Microsoft Teams: Part of the Microsoft 365 suite, Microsoft Teams is a robust collaboration platform that combines IM, video conferencing, file storage, and application integration. Teams allows users to create channels for different projects or departments, facilitating organized and focused discussions. Integration with other Microsoft 365 applications, such as Word, Excel, and SharePoint, enhances productivity by enabling seamless collaboration and document sharing. Microsoft Teams also offers advanced security and compliance features, making it a preferred choice for organizations with stringent data protection requirements.[9]

Usage: Professional and Personal Contexts

Professional Contexts: In the workplace, IM is used for a variety of purposes, from quick questions and status updates to in-depth discussions and collaborative brainstorming sessions. The ability to create group chats or channels for specific teams or projects ensures that communication is organized and relevant. For example, a marketing team might have a dedicated channel for discussing campaign strategies, while a product development team could use IM to coordinate tasks and share progress updates.

7. Chris Olsen, "Implementing Cisco Collaboration Applications (CAPPS) Foundation Learning Guide," *Cisco Press*, n.d., https://ptgmedia.pearsoncmg.com/images/9781587144479/samplepages/9781587144479.pdf.
8. Dakuo Wang, Haoyu Wang, Mo Yu, Zahra Ashtorab, and Ming Tan, "Group Chat Ecology in Enterprise Instant Messaging: How Employees Collaborate Through Multi-User Chat Channels on Slack," *Proceedings of the ACM on Human-Computer Interaction* 6, no. 94 (2022): 1–14, https://doi.org/10.1145/3512941.
9. Lane et al., "Teams in the Digital Workplace."

IM also enhances remote work by providing a platform for virtual communication that mimics the immediacy of in-person interactions. Employees can quickly check in with their colleagues, share files, and even conduct video meetings, all within a single application. This helps maintain productivity and engagement, even when team members are not physically present in the same location.

Personal Contexts: On a personal level, IM allows individuals to stay connected with friends and family in real time. The convenience of IM makes it easy to share updates, plan events, and engage in casual conversations. Many IM platforms also support multimedia sharing, enabling users to send photos, videos, and voice messages, enhancing the richness of their interactions.

Additionally, IM platforms often include features such as emojis, stickers, and GIFs, allowing users to express themselves creatively and add a fun element to their conversations. This informal and interactive nature of IM makes it a popular choice for personal communication.

Security and Privacy Considerations

While IM offers numerous benefits, it also presents certain security and privacy challenges that users must be aware of and address.

Encryption: To ensure the confidentiality of messages, many IM platforms use E2EE. This means that messages are encrypted on the sender's device and can only be decrypted by the intended recipient. E2EE protects messages from being intercepted or accessed by unauthorized parties, including the service provider. However, not all IM platforms offer E2EE, so users should choose platforms that prioritize this security feature.[10]

Authentication and Access Controls: Implementing strong authentication measures, such as MFA, helps protect IM accounts from unauthorized access. Additionally, organizations should establish access controls to ensure that only authorized personnel can join specific channels or groups, minimizing the risk of data breaches and insider threats.[11]

Compliance and Data Protection: Organizations must also consider compliance with data protection regulations, such as the GDPR and the CCPA. This involves implementing policies and practices to safeguard personal data and ensure that IM communications are stored, accessed, and shared in compliance with legal requirements.

10. Ksenia Ermoshina, Francesca Musiani, and Harry Halpin, "End-to-End Encrypted Messaging Protocols: An Overview," in *Internet Science*, ed. Franco Bagnoli et al. (Springer International Publishing, 2016), 244–54, https://doi.org/10.1007/978-3-319-45982-0_22.
11. Jason Garbis and Jerry W. Chapman, "Identity and Access Management," in *Zero Trust Security: An Enterprise Guide*, eds. Jason Garbis and Jerry W. Chapman (Apress, 2021), 71–91, https://doi.org/10.1007/978-1-4842-6702-8_5.

Best Practices for Using IM

To maximize the benefits of IM while minimizing potential risks, users should follow best practices for secure and effective communication.

Define Clear Communication Policies: Organizations should establish clear guidelines for using IM, including appropriate use, response times, and escalation procedures. This ensures that IM is used effectively and professionally.

Regularly Update Software: Keeping IM applications up to date is crucial for maintaining security. Software updates often include patches for vulnerabilities and enhancements to encryption protocols.

Educate Users: Providing training on secure IM practices, such as recognizing phishing attempts and managing privacy settings, empowers users to protect their information and use IM responsibly.

Monitor and Audit: Regular monitoring and auditing of IM communications help identify and address potential security issues. Organizations should implement tools and processes to track usage and detect anomalies.

Balance Informal and Formal Communication: While IM is suited for informal and quick exchanges, it's important to balance it with more formal communication methods when necessary. Sensitive or complex topics may be better addressed through email or face-to-face meetings to ensure clarity and documentation.

Section Summary

IM has a storied history as one of the original forms of online communication and, despite its decline in the consumer market, remains a vital tool in professional settings. Platforms like Jabber, Slack, and Microsoft Teams have adapted to meet the needs of modern workplaces, providing features that enhance productivity and collaboration.

Understanding the benefits and challenges of IM, along with implementing best practices for security and privacy, ensures that users can leverage this powerful tool effectively. As digital communication continues to evolve, IM will remain a cornerstone of our interconnected world, bridging distances and fostering collaboration in real time.

5.3 Encrypted Chat Applications

With growing concerns about data privacy and security, encrypted chat applications have emerged as essential tools for secure communication. These applications provide E2EE, ensuring that only the intended recipients can read the messages. This section explores the significance of encrypted chat apps in maintaining privacy and security in digital communication, highlighting popular platforms like Signal, Wickr, Wire, and WhatsApp.

Importance of Encrypted Chat Applications

In an era where digital surveillance and data breaches are prevalent, encrypted chat applications play a critical role in protecting sensitive information. E2EE ensures that messages are encrypted on the sender's device and can only be decrypted by the recipient's device, preventing unauthorized access during transmission. This level of security is particularly important for individuals and organizations that need to protect confidential communications from potential eavesdroppers, including service providers, hackers, and even government agencies.

Encrypted chat applications not only safeguard personal conversations but also enhance the security of professional and business communications. For businesses dealing with sensitive information, such as legal, financial, or health-care data, using encrypted chat apps helps ensure compliance with data protection regulations and mitigates the risk of data breaches.

Examples: Signal, Wickr, Wire, WhatsApp

Signal: Signal is widely regarded as one of the most secure messaging apps available. It offers E2EE for messages, voice calls, video calls, and file transfers. Signal's encryption protocol is open-source, allowing security experts to review and verify its security. The app also includes features like disappearing messages and screen security, which prevent screenshots of conversations. Signal's commitment to privacy is further demonstrated by its minimal data collection practices; it only retains information necessary for the service to function.[12]

Wickr: Wickr, now owned by Amazon, is another robust encrypted messaging platform designed for both personal and enterprise use. It offers E2EE for text messages, voice and video calls, and file sharing. Wickr also includes features like self-destructing messages, secure file shredding, and ephemeral messaging, which ensure that data is not stored longer than necessary. Wickr's enterprise version provides additional security and compliance features, making it suitable for businesses with stringent data protection needs.[13]

Wire: Wire is an encrypted messaging app known for its strong security features and user-friendly interface. It offers E2EE for messages, voice calls, video calls, and file sharing. Wire's security protocol is open-source, and the app undergoes regular security audits to maintain its high security standards. Wire is suitable for both personal and professional use, providing features like secure group chats, screen sharing, and collaboration tools for business environments.[14]

12. Ermoshina et al., "End-to-End Encrypted Messaging Protocols."
13. Amazon Web Services, "Secure Messaging and Collaboration—AWS Wickr," Amazon Web Services, Inc., accessed December 24, 2024, https://aws.amazon.com/wickr/.
14. Wire, "Security & Privacy with Wire," accessed December 24, 2024, https://wire.com/en/security.

WhatsApp: WhatsApp, owned by Facebook, is one of the most popular messaging apps globally, with over two billion users. WhatsApp uses the Signal Protocol for E2EE, ensuring that messages, calls, and media shared on the platform are secure. Despite its widespread use and robust encryption, WhatsApp has faced scrutiny over its data sharing practices with Facebook. However, its E2EE ensures that the content of communications remains private and secure from third parties.[15]

Usage: Personal and Professional Contexts

Personal Contexts: Encrypted chat applications are widely used in personal contexts to protect private conversations from prying eyes. Users can communicate with confidence, knowing that their messages are secure and cannot be intercepted. Features like disappearing messages and self-destructing media add an extra layer of privacy, allowing users to control how long their information is accessible.

Professional Contexts: In professional settings, encrypted chat applications are invaluable for maintaining the confidentiality of business communications. Organizations use these apps to discuss sensitive topics, share confidential documents, and conduct secure voice and video calls. Encrypted chat apps are particularly beneficial for industries that handle sensitive information, such as legal firms, health-care providers, financial institutions, and government agencies.

For example, a legal firm might use Signal to discuss case details and share legal documents securely with clients and colleagues. A health-care provider could use Wire to communicate patient information securely, ensuring compliance with data protection regulations like Health Insurance Portability and Accountability Act (HIPAA). Financial institutions might use Wickr to share sensitive financial data and conduct secure meetings with clients and partners.

Security and Privacy Considerations

While encrypted chat applications provide strong security features, users must still be aware of potential risks and best practices to maximize their privacy.

Trust and Verification: Even with E2EE, users should verify the identities of their contacts to prevent man-in-the-middle attacks. Many encrypted chat apps provide verification methods, such as scanning a QR code or comparing security codes with the contact.

Regular Updates: Keeping the app updated is crucial for maintaining security. Updates often include patches for vulnerabilities and enhancements to encryption protocols.

15. Gareth T. Davies et al., "Security Analysis of the WhatsApp End-to-End Encrypted Backup Protocol," in *Advances in Cryptology – CRYPTO 2023*, eds. Helena Handschuh and Anna Lysyanskaya (Springer Nature Switzerland, 2023), 330–61, https://doi.org/10.1007/978-3-031-38551-3_11.

Awareness of Metadata: While encrypted chat apps secure the content of messages, they may still collect metadata, such as the time and date of communication, the sender and recipient information, and the duration of calls. Users should be aware of the app's data collection practices and choose platforms that minimize metadata collection.

Device Security: The security of the app also depends on the security of the device. Users should ensure that their devices are protected with strong passwords, biometric authentication, and regular security updates.

Best Practices for Using Encrypted Chat Applications

To ensure secure and effective use of encrypted chat applications, users should follow these best practices:

Choose Reputable Apps: Select encrypted chat apps with a strong track record of security and privacy. Open-source apps that undergo regular security audits provide additional assurance.

Enable Security Features: Utilize built-in security features, such as disappearing messages, screen security, and MFA, to enhance privacy.

Educate Users: Organizations should provide training on the importance of encrypted communication and how to use encrypted chat apps securely. This includes recognizing phishing attempts and avoiding sharing sensitive information over unsecured channels.

Monitor Compliance: For businesses, regular audits and monitoring of encrypted communication practices ensure compliance with data protection regulations and internal security policies.

Section Summary

Encrypted chat applications have become essential tools for ensuring privacy and security in digital communication. Platforms like Signal, Wickr, Wire, and Sudo provide robust E2EE, making them suitable for both personal and professional use. By understanding the benefits and limitations of these apps, and following best practices for secure communication, users can protect their sensitive information and communicate confidently in an increasingly digital world.

5.4 Video Conferencing

Video conferencing has revolutionized the way individuals and organizations communicate, particularly in an era where remote work and virtual collaboration have become increasingly prevalent. This technology allows people to conduct face-to-face meetings in real time, regardless of geographical barriers, enhancing the ability to collaborate effectively and maintain personal connections.

Usage: Business Meetings

In the business world, video conferencing is an indispensable tool for conducting meetings, interviews, training sessions, and webinars. The ability to see and hear participants in real time fosters a more engaging and interactive environment compared to traditional phone calls or emails. It allows for non-verbal communication cues, such as facial expressions and body language, which are crucial for understanding and engagement.

For instance, project managers can use video conferencing to hold regular team meetings, discuss project updates, and address any issues promptly. This real-time interaction helps ensure that all team members are on the same page and can contribute effectively to discussions. Video conferencing also facilitates cross-departmental collaboration, allowing employees from different parts of the organization to work together seamlessly.

Moreover, video conferencing is essential for client meetings and presentations. It enables businesses to connect with clients worldwide, present proposals, and discuss projects without the need for travel. This not only saves time and costs associated with travel but also allows for more frequent and flexible meetings.

Usage: Webinars and Online Classes

Beyond business meetings, video conferencing is widely used for webinars and online classes. Webinars allow organizations to share knowledge, conduct training sessions, and engage with a large audience in a structured format. Participants can join from anywhere in the world, making it an effective way to reach a broad audience. Features such as screen sharing, live polls, and Q&A sessions enhance the interactive experience, making webinars a powerful tool for education and marketing.

In the educational sector, video conferencing has become a cornerstone of remote learning. Schools, colleges, and universities use video conferencing platforms to conduct virtual classes, allowing students to continue their education from home. This technology supports various teaching methods, including lectures, group discussions, and one-on-one tutoring. It also enables educators to share multimedia content, conduct virtual labs, and assess student performance in real time.

Applications: Popular Video Conferencing Platforms

Several video conferencing platforms have gained popularity for their robust features and ease of use. Among the most widely used are Zoom, Microsoft Teams, and Google Meet.[16]

16. Gadjo Sevilla, "Zoom vs. Microsoft Teams vs. Google Meet: Which Top Videoconferencing App Is Best?," *PC Magazine*, April 15, 2020, https://dalesaki.opened.ca/wp-content/uploads/sites/723/2021/03/200415-PC-Magazine-Zoom-vs-Meet-vs-Teams.pdf.

Zoom: Zoom has become synonymous with video conferencing, offering a wide range of features that cater to both personal and professional needs. It supports high-definition video and audio, screen sharing, virtual backgrounds, breakout rooms, and recording capabilities. Zoom's user-friendly interface and reliable performance have made it a preferred choice for businesses, educational institutions, and social gatherings.[17]

Microsoft Teams: Part of the Microsoft 365 suite, Microsoft Teams integrates video conferencing with IM, file sharing, and collaborative tools. Teams allows users to schedule and join meetings directly from their calendar, share documents, and collaborate on projects in real time. The platform's integration with other Microsoft 365 applications, such as Word, Excel, and PowerPoint, enhances productivity and streamlines workflows.[18]

Google Meet: Google Meet is a video conferencing tool that integrates seamlessly with Google Workspace (formerly G Suite). It offers features such as high-definition video and audio, screen sharing, real-time captions, and recording capabilities. Google Meet is accessible directly from Google Calendar, making it easy to schedule and join meetings. Its integration with other Google services, such as Gmail and Google Drive, makes it a convenient choice for users who rely on the Google ecosystem.[19]

Security and Privacy Considerations

While video conferencing offers numerous benefits, it also presents security and privacy challenges that users must address to protect their communications.

Encryption: Many video conferencing platforms use encryption to protect data during transmission. E2EE is the most secure form, ensuring that only the meeting participants can access the content. However, not all platforms offer E2EE, so users should choose services that prioritize this level of security for sensitive meetings.[20]

Meeting Controls: Implementing meeting controls helps prevent unauthorized access and disruptions. Features such as password protection, waiting rooms, and the ability to mute or remove participants enhance the security of virtual meetings. Hosts should also be vigilant about sharing meeting links publicly and use unique meeting IDs for each session.

Compliance and Data Protection: Organizations must ensure that their use of video conferencing complies with data protection regulations, such as GDPR and CCPA. This involves understanding how the platform handles data storage, access, and sharing.

17. Karolina Balogova and Duncan Brumby, "How Do You Zoom?: A Survey Study of How Users Configure Video-Conference Tools for Online Meetings," in *Proceedings of the 1st Annual Meeting of the Symposium on Human-Computer Interaction for Work*, CHIWORK '22 (Association for Computing Machinery, 2022), 1–7, https://doi.org/10.1145/3533406.3533408.
18. Lane et al., "Teams in the Digital Workplace."
19. Sevilla, "Zoom vs. Microsoft Teams vs. Google Meet."
20. Ermoshina et al., "End-to-End Encrypted Messaging Protocols"; Davies et al., "Security Analysis."

Choosing platforms that adhere to industry standards and provide transparency about their data practices is essential for maintaining compliance.

Best Practices for Video Conferencing

To maximize the effectiveness and security of video conferencing, users should follow best practices for setup, usage, and etiquette.

Prepare for Meetings: Before a video conference, ensure that all technical aspects are set up correctly. This includes testing the internet connection, video and audio equipment, and ensuring that necessary software updates are installed. Preparing an agenda and sharing it with participants in advance helps keep the meeting focused and productive.

Maintain Professionalism: Although video conferencing often takes place in a more casual setting, maintaining professionalism is important. This includes dressing appropriately, using a clean and clutter-free background, and minimizing distractions. Using virtual backgrounds can help create a professional appearance, especially in home office environments.

Engage Participants: Keeping participants engaged can be challenging in virtual meetings. Using features like screen sharing, polls, and breakout rooms can make the meeting more interactive. Encouraging participants to turn on their cameras and actively participate in discussions fosters a sense of presence and collaboration.

Secure Your Meetings: Implementing security measures, such as using strong passwords, enabling waiting rooms, and controlling screen sharing, helps protect meetings from unauthorized access. Regularly reviewing and updating security settings ensures that the platform remains secure.

Record and Share Responsibly: Recording meetings can be useful for future reference, but it's important to do so responsibly. Informing participants that the meeting is being recorded and obtaining their consent is essential. Ensuring that recorded content is stored securely and shared only with authorized individuals helps maintain privacy and confidentiality.

Section Summary

Video conferencing has become an essential tool for real-time communication, enabling virtual meetings, webinars, and online classes. Platforms like Zoom, Microsoft Teams, and Google Meet offer a range of features that enhance collaboration and productivity. Understanding the benefits and challenges of video conferencing, along with implementing best practices for security and professionalism, ensures that users can leverage this powerful tool effectively. As remote work and virtual collaboration continue to grow, video conferencing will remain a cornerstone of digital communication, connecting people and fostering collaboration across the globe.

5.5 Social Media

Social media has revolutionized how we communicate, connect, and share information globally. Platforms like Facebook, Twitter, and Instagram have become integral to daily life, enabling users to interact with friends, family, and even strangers across the world. Social media's ability to foster connections and facilitate the exchange of ideas makes it a powerful tool for both personal and professional communication.

Usage: Personal Interactions

For students who have grown up with social media, these platforms are second nature. They provide a space to share experiences, express opinions, and stay connected with their peers. Facebook allows users to create detailed profiles, connect with friends, join groups, and participate in discussions. Twitter, with its concise 280-character limit, encourages brief and frequent updates, fostering real-time conversations and engagement.

Instagram focuses on visual content, allowing users to share photos and videos with their followers. Features like stories, live videos, and direct messaging enhance the interactive experience, enabling users to communicate in diverse ways. Social media also supports multimedia posts, such as sharing articles, videos, and music, enriching the communication landscape.

While students may be adept at using these platforms, understanding how to stay safe and secure is crucial. Social media can expose users to various risks, including privacy breaches, cyberbullying, and misinformation. It's important to be aware of these risks and know how to protect oneself while enjoying the benefits of social media.

Usage: Professional Interactions

Beyond personal use, social media has become a crucial tool for professional networking and career development. LinkedIn, for example, is tailored for professional use, allowing users to build their résumés, connect with colleagues, and search for job opportunities. Companies use LinkedIn to share updates, publish articles, and engage with industry professionals, enhancing their online presence and reputation.

Businesses leverage social media platforms like Facebook, Twitter, and Instagram to market their products and services, engage with customers, and build brand loyalty. By creating compelling content and interacting with their audience, companies can reach a broader audience and drive sales. Social media advertising, which targets users based on their interests and behaviors, further amplifies marketing efforts.

For students entering the workforce, using social media professionally can enhance career prospects. Building a professional online presence, networking with industry professionals, and staying updated on industry trends are key benefits of professional social media use. However, it's essential to recognize that inappropriate or unprofessional use of social media, even in personal interactions, can lead to negative professional repercussions.

Security and Privacy Considerations

While social media offers numerous benefits, it also presents significant security and privacy challenges. Users must be vigilant about protecting their personal information and maintaining privacy.

Data Privacy: Social media platforms collect vast amounts of personal data, including profile information, activity logs, and interaction histories. This data can be used for targeted advertising, content personalization, and even sold to third parties. To protect their privacy, users should review and adjust their privacy settings, limiting the information shared publicly and with third parties.

Account Security: Ensuring the security of social media accounts is crucial. Users should employ strong, unique passwords for each platform and enable MFA to add an extra layer of security. Being cautious about phishing attempts and suspicious links can prevent unauthorized access to accounts.

Content Management: Users should be mindful of the content they share on social media, considering the potential long-term implications. Once posted, content can be difficult to remove and may be accessed by unintended audiences. Using privacy controls to restrict who can view and interact with posts helps manage content visibility and privacy.

Professional Repercussions of Social Media Use

It's important to understand that social media activity can have significant professional repercussions. Inappropriate or unprofessional behavior online can impact one's reputation and career prospects. Employers and potential employers often review social media profiles to gain insights into candidates' personalities and professionalism. Offensive comments, inappropriate photos, or controversial opinions can harm one's professional image and lead to job rejections or disciplinary actions.

For instance, a seemingly harmless tweet or Facebook post might be perceived negatively by a future employer, affecting their hiring decision. Likewise, sharing confidential information or expressing unprofessional behavior on social media can lead to disciplinary actions, including termination. Therefore, maintaining a professional demeanor on social media, even in personal interactions, is essential for safeguarding one's career.

Best Practices for Using Social Media

To maximize the benefits of social media while minimizing risks, users should follow best practices for secure and effective communication.

Understand Platform Policies: Each social media platform has its own policies regarding data usage, privacy, and content moderation. Familiarizing oneself with these policies helps users make informed decisions about their online activities and privacy settings.

Regularly Update Privacy Settings: Social media platforms frequently update their privacy settings and features. Users should regularly review and adjust their settings to ensure they align with their privacy preferences and security needs.

Be Mindful of Sharing Personal Information: Sharing too much personal information on social media can lead to privacy risks. Users should be cautious about sharing details like their location, contact information, and daily routines. Using discretion when posting about personal activities helps protect privacy.

Engage Responsibly: Social media is a public forum where interactions can have far-reaching consequences. Engaging responsibly, respecting others' opinions, and avoiding contentious or harmful behavior fosters a positive online environment. Users should also be aware of the potential for their posts to be taken out of context or misunderstood.

Use Secure Connections: Accessing social media platforms over secure connections, such as using HTTPS and avoiding public Wi-Fi, helps protect data from being intercepted by malicious actors. Using a virtual private network (VPN) adds an additional layer of security, especially when accessing social media from unfamiliar networks.

Professional Use of Social Media

For professionals and students entering the workforce, leveraging social media effectively can enhance career opportunities and professional growth. LinkedIn is the premier platform for professional networking, allowing users to showcase their skills, experience, and accomplishments. Engaging with industry groups, sharing professional content, and participating in discussions can help build a professional reputation and expand one's network.

Professionals can also use platforms like Twitter to share industry insights, engage with thought leaders, and stay informed about the latest trends and developments. Creating and sharing high-quality content, such as blog posts, articles, and videos, can establish individuals as experts in their field and attract opportunities for collaboration and career advancement.

Social Media for Businesses

Businesses can harness the power of social media to achieve various goals, from brand awareness and customer engagement to lead generation and sales. Creating a comprehensive social media strategy involves identifying target audiences, choosing the right platforms, and developing compelling content that resonates with users.

Engaging with customers on social media provides valuable insights into their preferences, behaviors, and feedback. Companies can use this information to refine their products, services, and marketing strategies. Social media also offers opportunities for real-time customer support, allowing businesses to address inquiries and resolve issues promptly, enhancing customer satisfaction.

Measuring Social Media Success

To gauge the effectiveness of social media efforts, businesses and individuals can use various metrics and analytics tools. Key performance indicators (KPIs) such as engagement rates, follower growth, website traffic, and conversion rates provide insights into the impact of social media activities. Analyzing these metrics helps identify successful strategies and areas for improvement, enabling continuous optimization of social media efforts.

Section Summary

Social media has transformed how we connect, communicate, and share information on a global scale. Platforms like Facebook, Twitter, Instagram, and LinkedIn offer diverse opportunities for personal interaction, professional networking, and business growth. Understanding the benefits and challenges of social media, along with implementing best practices for security and privacy, ensures that users can leverage these powerful tools effectively. Additionally, recognizing the potential professional repercussions of inappropriate social media use underscores the importance of maintaining a professional demeanor online. As social media continues to evolve, it will remain a cornerstone of digital communication, connecting people and fostering engagement across the world.

5.6 Mobile Texting (SMS)

SMS, commonly known as mobile texting, is one of the oldest and most widely used digital communication methods. Introduced in the early 1990s, SMS allows users to send brief text messages of up to 160 characters between mobile phones. Despite the advent of more advanced messaging platforms, SMS remains a fundamental tool for quick, concise communication.[21]

Usage: Personal Communication

Mobile texting is a convenient and straightforward method for staying in touch with friends and family. Its simplicity and ubiquity make it accessible to almost everyone with a mobile phone, regardless of the device's capabilities or the availability of internet access. SMS is particularly useful for sending brief updates, reminders, and alerts. For instance, a quick "I'm on my way" or "Let's meet at 5 p.m." text can efficiently convey essential information without the need for a phone call or a lengthy email.

One of the key advantages of SMS is its reliability. Text messages can be sent and received even in areas with weak or no internet connection, ensuring that important mes-

21. Friedhelm Hillebrand, Finn Trosby, Kevin Holley, and Ian Harris, *Short Message Service (SMS): The Creation of Personal Global Text Messaging* (Wiley, 2010).

sages get through. This makes SMS an essential tool for emergency communications, where timely and reliable delivery is crucial.

Usage: Professional Communication

In professional settings, SMS is often used for internal communications, marketing, and customer service. Businesses use SMS to send appointment reminders, order confirmations, delivery updates, and other time-sensitive information. The high open rate of text messages—often cited as being over 90 percent—makes SMS an effective channel for ensuring that important messages are seen promptly.

For example, a health-care provider might use SMS to remind patients of upcoming appointments, reducing no-show rates and improving service efficiency. Retail businesses can send promotional offers and discounts to customers, driving engagement and sales. Customer service teams can use SMS to provide quick responses to customer inquiries, enhancing the overall customer experience.

SMS Versus iMessage and Other Services

While SMS remains widely used, many users have transitioned to more advanced messaging services like iMessage, WhatsApp, and other similar applications. These services offer several advantages over traditional SMS, particularly in terms of security, functionality, and user experience.

iMessage: iMessage, available on Apple devices, is a messaging service that offers E2EE, ensuring that messages are secure and can only be read by the intended recipients. In addition to text messaging, iMessage supports multimedia messages, stickers, and a range of interactive features, providing a richer communication experience. Unlike SMS, iMessage requires an internet connection, either through Wi-Fi or cellular data.

WhatsApp and Similar Apps: WhatsApp, Signal, and Sudo are examples of messaging apps that provide encrypted communication, offering greater security than traditional SMS. These apps support a variety of features, including voice and video calls, group chats, file sharing, and more. The use of E2EE ensures that messages, calls, and shared media are protected from unauthorized access.

Security and Privacy Considerations

While SMS is convenient and widely used, it also presents certain security and privacy challenges. Unlike more modern messaging platforms, standard SMS does not provide E2EE, making it vulnerable to interception by third parties. Users must be aware of these limitations and take steps to protect their information when using SMS.

Encryption: One of the primary distinctions between SMS and modern messaging apps like iMessage and WhatsApp is the presence of E2EE in the latter. E2EE ensures that only the sender and recipient can read the messages, protecting the content from being accessed by service providers, hackers, or other third parties. In contrast, SMS messages are typically encrypted only during transmission between the phone and the cellular tower, but they can be accessed by the mobile carrier and are vulnerable to interception.

Phishing and Smishing: Phishing attacks via SMS, known as "smishing," are a significant threat. Smishing involves sending fraudulent text messages that appear to be from legitimate sources, such as banks or service providers, to trick recipients into revealing personal information or clicking on malicious links. Users should be cautious of unsolicited messages, especially those requesting sensitive information or prompting urgent action.

Spam and Unsolicited Messages: Spam messages can clutter inboxes and pose security risks. Many mobile carriers offer tools to block spam, but users should also be vigilant about not sharing their mobile numbers unnecessarily and reporting suspicious messages.

Privacy: Users should be mindful of the personal information they share via SMS. Given the lack of encryption, sensitive data should be communicated through more secure channels when possible. Additionally, users can enable features like read receipts and delivery reports to ensure messages are sent and received as intended.

One-Time Passwords (OTPs) and Two-Factor Authentication (2FA): SMS is commonly used to deliver one-time passwords and two-factor authentication codes, adding an extra layer of security to online accounts. While this method enhances security compared to single-factor authentication, it's important to be aware of potential vulnerabilities, such as SIM swapping attacks, where attackers take control of a victim's phone number to intercept authentication codes. Using app-based authenticators or hardware tokens can provide a more secure alternative.

Best Practices for Using SMS

To maximize the benefits of SMS while minimizing risks, users should follow best practices for secure and effective communication.

Verify Senders: Always verify the sender's identity before responding to messages requesting personal information. If in doubt, contact the organization directly using known contact details rather than replying to the message.

Use Secure Alternatives When Needed: For sensitive communications, consider using secure messaging apps that offer E2EE. While SMS is convenient, it should not be used for sharing confidential information.

Be Cautious with Links: Avoid clicking on links in unsolicited text messages. These links can lead to phishing websites or downloading malicious software. If a message appears to be from a legitimate source, navigate to the website directly using a browser or official app.

Manage Message Storage: Regularly review and delete unnecessary messages from your device. Keeping your inbox organized helps you quickly identify suspicious messages and reduces the risk of exposing sensitive information if your phone is lost or stolen.

Enable Security Features: Use any available security features offered by your mobile carrier or device, such as spam filters and message blocking, to protect against unwanted messages and potential threats.

Section Summary

Mobile texting via SMS remains a fundamental tool for quick and reliable communication. Its simplicity and accessibility make it indispensable for personal and professional interactions. However, users must be aware of the security and privacy limitations of SMS and take steps to protect their information. By following best practices for secure communication and leveraging the strengths of SMS while mitigating its risks, users can effectively utilize this enduring method of digital communication in a safe and efficient manner. Understanding the advantages of more secure alternatives like iMessage and WhatsApp can further enhance their communication strategies in an increasingly digital world.

5.7 Voice over Internet Protocol

VoIP technology has revolutionized the way we make voice calls by allowing them to be transmitted over the internet rather than traditional telephone lines. This shift has brought numerous benefits, including cost savings, flexibility, and a wide range of advanced features that enhance communication.

Usage: Personal Communication

VoIP has become an integral part of personal communication, providing a cost-effective alternative to traditional phone calls. Applications like Skype, WhatsApp, and Viber allow users to make voice and video calls to anyone in the world, often at little to no cost. These services leverage the internet to bypass traditional phone networks, making international calls much more affordable and accessible.

For instance, families separated by long distances can use VoIP services to stay connected through regular voice and video calls without worrying about high international calling rates. Additionally, VoIP services often include features such as messaging, file sharing, and group calls, offering a comprehensive communication solution.

Usage: Professional Communication

In professional settings, VoIP has become a cornerstone of business communication. Companies use VoIP services for internal communication, customer service, and conferencing. The flexibility of VoIP allows businesses to integrate voice communication with other digital services, enhancing overall efficiency and collaboration.

Internal Communication: VoIP systems enable employees to communicate seamlessly, regardless of their location. This is particularly valuable for remote teams and organizations with multiple offices. Employees can make and receive calls using their computers, smartphones, or dedicated VoIP phones, ensuring they remain connected wherever they are.

Customer Service: VoIP is widely used in customer service operations due to its cost-effectiveness and advanced features. Call centers can handle large volumes of calls efficiently, and features like call forwarding, voicemail, and automated attendants improve customer service quality. Additionally, VoIP systems can integrate with customer relationship management (CRM) software, providing agents with valuable customer information during calls.

Conferencing: VoIP facilitates audio and video conferencing, enabling businesses to conduct meetings with participants from different locations. Services like Zoom, Microsoft Teams, and Google Meet offer robust conferencing solutions with features such as screen sharing, recording, and virtual backgrounds. These capabilities enhance collaboration and allow teams to work together effectively, regardless of physical distance.

Cost-Efficient Communication

One of the most significant advantages of VoIP is its cost-efficiency. Traditional phone systems require substantial investments in hardware, maintenance, and long-distance call charges. In contrast, VoIP utilizes existing internet infrastructure, reducing the need for dedicated phone lines and minimizing costs associated with long-distance and international calls.

For businesses, switching to VoIP can result in significant savings on communication expenses. VoIP providers typically offer flexible pricing plans, allowing companies to choose packages that suit their needs and scale up or down as required. Additionally, the integration of VoIP with other digital tools can streamline workflows and reduce operational costs.

Secure VoIP Options

As with any digital communication method, security is a crucial consideration for VoIP. While traditional VoIP services offer many benefits, secure VoIP options like MySudo provide enhanced privacy and security features that protect users' communications and data.

MySudo: MySudo is a secure communication platform that offers VoIP services along with other secure options such as SMS, email, and web browsing. MySudo allows users to create multiple "Sudos," or identities, each with its own phone number, email address, and browser. This separation of identities helps protect privacy and keeps personal information secure. MySudo uses E2EE for all communications, ensuring that only the intended recipients can access the content.[22]

MySudo's features make it an excellent choice for users who prioritize privacy and security. By using MySudo, individuals can communicate securely without worrying about their data being intercepted or accessed by unauthorized parties.

Security and Privacy Considerations

While VoIP offers numerous benefits, it also introduces specific security and privacy challenges that users must address to ensure safe and secure communication.

Encryption: Ensuring that VoIP calls are encrypted is crucial for protecting sensitive information from being intercepted. Many VoIP services offer encryption, but users should verify that their provider uses strong encryption protocols to safeguard their communications.

Network Security: VoIP systems are susceptible to various network-based attacks, such as denial-of-service (DoS) attacks, eavesdropping, and phishing. Implementing robust network security measures, such as firewalls, intrusion detection systems, and secure routers, helps protect VoIP infrastructure from these threats.

Authentication and Access Controls: Strong authentication methods, such as MFA, are essential for securing VoIP accounts and preventing unauthorized access. Additionally, implementing access controls to restrict who can access certain features or information helps mitigate the risk of internal threats.

Compliance and Data Protection: Organizations using VoIP must ensure compliance with data protection regulations, such as GDPR and CCPA. This involves implementing policies and practices to protect personal data during VoIP communications and ensuring that providers adhere to regulatory requirements.

Best Practices for Using VoIP

To maximize the benefits of VoIP while minimizing risks, users should follow best practices for secure and effective communication.

Choose Reputable Providers: Select VoIP providers with a strong track record of security and reliability. Look for providers that offer encryption, robust network security, and compliance with data protection regulations.

Regularly Update Software: Keeping VoIP software and devices up to date is crucial for maintaining security. Software updates often include patches for vulnerabilities and enhancements to encryption protocols.

22. Michael Bazzell, "Privacy & Security: Breaking It Down By Threat Model," IntelTechniques, 2020, https://inteltechniques.com/data/je/privacy.pdf; Tytti Katariina Rintamäki, "GDPR's Reflection in Privacy-Enhancing Technologies: Implications for AI Data Protection" (Thesis, European University Institute, 2023), https://doi.org/10.2870/4790569.

Implement Network Security Measures: Use firewalls, secure routers, and intrusion detection systems to protect VoIP infrastructure from network-based attacks. Regularly monitor network traffic for suspicious activity.

Educate Users: Provide training on secure VoIP practices, such as recognizing phishing attempts, managing privacy settings, and using strong passwords. Educating users helps them understand the importance of security and how to protect their communications.

Monitor and Audit: Regular monitoring and auditing of VoIP communications help identify and address potential security issues. Implement tools and processes to track usage, detect anomalies, and ensure compliance with security policies.

Section Summary

VoIP technology has transformed voice communication by enabling calls to be made over the internet, offering cost savings, flexibility, and advanced features. It is widely used for personal and professional communication, enhancing connectivity and collaboration. However, users must be aware of the security and privacy challenges associated with VoIP and take steps to protect their information. By following best practices for secure communication and leveraging the strengths of VoIP, including secure options like MySudo, users can effectively utilize this powerful technology to enhance their communication strategies in the digital age.

5.8 Web Chats and Forums

Web chats and forums are foundational elements of online communication, providing platforms where individuals can discuss specific topics, share knowledge, and build communities. These platforms foster interactive dialogues and create spaces for users to connect based on shared interests, whether they are related to hobbies, professional pursuits, or support groups.

Usage: Personal and Professional Interactions

Web chats and forums cater to both personal and professional needs, offering environments where users can seek advice, share experiences, and engage in discussions.

Personal Contexts: For many individuals, web chats and forums are vital for finding communities that share their interests. Sites like Reddit and specialized forums cater to virtually every hobby and interest imaginable. Whether it's a forum dedicated to gardening, video games, or fitness, these platforms enable users to exchange tips, share their progress, and seek advice from like-minded individuals.

For example, a hobbyist photographer might join a photography forum to discuss techniques, get feedback on their work, and learn about the latest equipment. Similarly, a fitness enthusiast could participate in a fitness forum to find workout routines, share their fitness journey, and stay motivated through community support.

Professional Contexts: In professional settings, web chats and forums provide invaluable resources for networking, learning, and collaboration. Platforms like Stack Overflow allow developers to ask questions, share code snippets, and solve programming challenges collectively. Industry-specific forums and LinkedIn groups offer spaces where professionals can discuss trends, share job opportunities, and collaborate on projects.

For instance, a marketing professional might join a digital marketing forum to stay updated on the latest strategies, tools, and case studies. These professional forums are excellent for continuous learning and career development, as they provide access to a wealth of knowledge and the collective expertise of the community.

Examples: Reddit, Stack Overflow, Specialized Forums

Reddit: Reddit is one of the most popular online forums, comprising thousands of subreddits dedicated to specific topics. Users can join these subreddits to participate in discussions, share content, and vote on posts. The platform's diverse range of communities makes it a go-to resource for information on virtually any subject.

Stack Overflow: Stack Overflow is a well-known forum for programmers and developers. It provides a platform for users to ask technical questions, share knowledge, and find solutions to coding problems. The community-driven nature of Stack Overflow ensures that users receive accurate and reliable answers from experienced developers.

Specialized Forums: Numerous specialized forums cater to specific interests and professions. For example, forums like GardenWeb for gardening enthusiasts, AVForums for home theater and audio equipment, and Behance for creative professionals provide focused environments where users can delve deeply into their particular areas of interest.

Professional Ramifications of Engaging in Certain Online Communities

While many web chats and forums are beneficial, engaging in certain online communities can have serious professional repercussions. For instance, participating in forums associated with extremist ideologies, hate speech, or illegal activities can harm one's professional reputation and career prospects. Sites like 4Chan have been known for their association with controversial and sometimes extremist content. Future professionals must consider the impact of their online activities on their careers.

4Chan and Similar Platforms**:** Forums like 4Chan, while popular for their anonymity and freedom of speech, have also been criticized for hosting content related to extremist ideologies, harassment, and illegal activities. Engaging in or being associated with such platforms can reflect poorly on an individual's character and judgment, potentially affecting job opportunities and professional relationships.

Employers often conduct online background checks on potential hires, including reviewing their social media profiles and online activities. Associations with controversial or extremist forums can raise red flags and lead to negative perceptions, even if the individual's participation was innocuous. Future professionals should be mindful of how their online behavior might be perceived and avoid engaging in platforms that could tarnish their professional image.

Security and Privacy Considerations

While web chats and forums offer valuable opportunities for interaction and learning, they also present certain security and privacy risks. Users must be cautious about the information they share and be aware of the potential for misuse or exploitation.

Personal Information: Users should avoid sharing sensitive personal information on public forums. Details such as full names, addresses, phone numbers, and financial information can be exploited by malicious actors. It's advisable to use pseudonyms and limit the sharing of personal details to protect privacy.

Phishing and Scams: Forums can be targets for phishing attacks and scams. Malicious users may post links to fraudulent websites or attempt to solicit personal information under false pretenses. Users should be skeptical of unsolicited messages and links, especially those that promise unrealistic rewards or require sensitive information.

Community Guidelines and Moderation: Reputable forums typically have community guidelines and active moderation to ensure a safe and respectful environment. Users should familiarize themselves with these guidelines and report any suspicious or inappropriate behavior to the moderators. Participating in well-moderated communities can significantly reduce the risk of encountering harmful content or interactions.

Anonymity and Accountability: While anonymity can provide a layer of privacy, it can also lead to irresponsible behavior. Users should strive to maintain a balance between protecting their identity and contributing positively to the community. Adhering to forum rules and engaging respectfully with others fosters a healthier and more productive environment.

Best Practices for Using Web Chats and Forums

To maximize the benefits of web chats and forums while minimizing risks, users should follow best practices for secure and effective participation.

Use Pseudonyms: To protect personal privacy, use pseudonyms instead of real names. This helps prevent unwanted attention and protects your identity.

Be Skeptical of Links: Avoid clicking on links from unverified sources. If a link appears suspicious, it's safer to navigate to the website directly through a trusted search engine.

Report Suspicious Activity: Report any suspicious behavior, phishing attempts, or inappropriate content to forum moderators. Active moderation helps maintain a safe community environment.

Respect Community Guidelines: Adhere to the community guidelines of each forum. Respectful and constructive participation enhances the quality of discussions and fosters a positive atmosphere.

Limit Sharing of Personal Information: Avoid sharing sensitive personal information publicly. If necessary, use private messaging for more secure communication, but still exercise caution.

Engage Responsibly: Contribute positively to discussions by providing helpful, accurate, and respectful responses. Avoid engaging in arguments or spreading misinformation.

Consider Professional Repercussions: Be mindful of how participation in certain forums might be perceived professionally. Avoid engaging in communities that could negatively impact your career prospects or professional reputation.

Section Summary

Web chats and forums are valuable tools for personal and professional communication, enabling users to connect with like-minded individuals and engage in meaningful discussions. Platforms like Reddit, Stack Overflow, and specialized forums offer diverse opportunities for learning, networking, and community building. However, users must be aware of the security and privacy challenges associated with these platforms and take steps to protect their information. Additionally, recognizing the potential professional repercussions of engaging in certain online communities underscores the importance of maintaining a responsible and mindful online presence. By following best practices for secure participation and engaging responsibly, users can maximize the benefits of web chats and forums while maintaining their privacy and security.

5.9 Blogs and Podcasts

Blogs and podcasts have emerged as powerful tools for content creation and audience engagement. They allow individuals and organizations to share their thoughts, information, and stories with a wide audience, building a following through regular updates and engaging content. These platforms cater to diverse interests and provide a unique opportunity to establish expertise, foster community, and influence public opinion.

Usage: Personal and Professional Contexts

Blogs and podcasts serve both personal and professional purposes, offering flexibility in how content is created and consumed.

Personal Contexts: For many individuals, blogs and podcasts are a way to express personal interests, share experiences, and connect with others. Personal blogs can cover a wide range of topics, from travel and lifestyle to cooking and personal development. Similarly, personal podcasts can explore hobbies, discuss life experiences, or provide commentary on current events.

For example, a travel enthusiast might create a blog to document their adventures, share travel tips, and recommend destinations. This blog can become a valuable resource for fellow travelers and a platform for the blogger to showcase their writing and photography skills. Podcasts, with their conversational format, allow creators to delve into topics more deeply, engage in storytelling, and interview guests, creating a rich and immersive experience for listeners.

Professional Contexts: In professional settings, blogs and podcasts are used to share industry insights, promote expertise, and engage with clients and stakeholders. Companies use blogs to publish articles on relevant topics, share case studies, and announce product updates. This content helps establish the company as a thought leader in its industry, drives website traffic, and improves search engine rankings.

Professionals use blogs and podcasts to build their personal brand, showcase their knowledge, and network with peers. For instance, a marketing consultant might maintain a blog that offers tips on digital marketing strategies, analyzes industry trends, and reviews marketing tools. A podcast hosted by the same consultant could feature interviews with industry experts, providing valuable insights and building credibility.

Examples: WordPress, Medium, Anchor, and Spotify

WordPress: WordPress is one of the most popular blogging platforms, offering extensive customization options and a user-friendly interface. It supports both personal and professional blogs, allowing users to create and manage content easily. WordPress's robust ecosystem includes themes, plugins, and search engine optimization (SEO) tools, making it a versatile choice for bloggers of all levels.

Medium: Medium is a blogging platform known for its clean design and focus on quality content. It allows writers to publish articles and reach a large audience through Medium's built-in readership and recommendation system. Medium is particularly popular among professionals and thought leaders who want to share insights and engage with a community of readers.

Anchor: Anchor is a comprehensive podcast creation platform that simplifies the process of recording, editing, and distributing podcasts. It offers tools for creating high-quality audio content, adding background music, and incorporating listener messages. Anchor also helps podcasters distribute their episodes to major platforms like Spotify, Apple Podcasts, and Google Podcasts.

Spotify: Spotify, originally a music streaming service, has become a major platform for podcasts. It offers extensive features for podcasters, including analytics, monetization options, and audience engagement tools. Spotify's vast user base provides podcasters with a significant opportunity to reach new listeners and grow their audience.

Security and Privacy Considerations

While blogs and podcasts offer numerous benefits, they also present specific security and privacy challenges that content creators must address to protect their work and personal information.

Content Ownership: Ensuring that you retain ownership of your content is crucial. Platforms like WordPress and Medium allow creators to retain ownership of their work, but it's important to read the terms of service and understand any rights you may be granting to the platform.

Personal Information: Be mindful of the personal information you share in your content. Avoid disclosing sensitive details that could compromise your privacy or security. Using pseudonyms and maintaining a separation between your personal and professional identities can help protect your privacy.

Copyright and Intellectual Property: Respecting copyright and intellectual property laws is essential when creating content. Ensure that any images, music, or other media you use in your blog or podcast are either your own, in the public domain, or licensed for your use. Giving proper credit to sources and avoiding plagiarism is crucial for maintaining your credibility and legal compliance.

Platform Security: Use strong passwords and enable MFA to protect your accounts on blogging and podcasting platforms. Regularly update your software and be cautious of phishing attempts that could compromise your account security.

Best Practices for Creating and Maintaining Blogs and Podcasts

To maximize the impact of your blog or podcast while minimizing risks, follow these best practices for secure and effective content creation.

Plan Your Content: Develop a content plan that outlines your topics, publication schedule, and goals. Consistency is key to building an audience, so aim to publish new content regularly.

Engage with Your Audience: Respond to comments, messages, and feedback from your audience. Engaging with your readers and listeners fosters a sense of community and loyalty.

Optimize for SEO: Use SEO techniques to improve the visibility of your blog. This includes using relevant keywords, optimizing your meta descriptions, and ensuring your site is mobile-friendly.

Promote Your Content: Use social media, email newsletters, and other channels to promote your blog or podcast. Collaborating with other creators and participating in relevant communities can also help you reach a wider audience.

Monitor Analytics: Use analytics tools to track the performance of your blog or podcast. Understanding your audience's behavior and preferences can help you refine your content strategy and improve engagement.

Maintain Professionalism: Whether you're creating content for personal or professional purposes, maintaining a high standard of quality and professionalism is essential. This includes proofreading your work, using high-quality audio equipment, and adhering to ethical standards in your content.

Section Summary

Blogs and podcasts are powerful tools for sharing information, telling stories, and engaging with audiences. Platforms like WordPress, Medium, Anchor, and Spotify provide the tools and reach needed to build a successful blog or podcast. However, creators must be mindful of security and privacy considerations, ensuring that their content and personal information are protected. By following best practices for content creation and engagement, bloggers and podcasters can build a loyal audience, establish their expertise, and make a meaningful impact in their chosen fields.

5.10 Conclusion

In this chapter, we have explored various types of digital communication technologies and the essential measures to ensure privacy and security while using them. Understanding and effectively utilizing these tools is critical for both personal and professional communication in the digital age.

Email remains a cornerstone of digital communication, essential for both formal and informal exchanges. While it offers unparalleled convenience and reliability, it also requires robust security measures. Using encrypted email services, anonymous email providers, and one-time use emails can significantly enhance email privacy and security. Encrypting emails ensures that only the intended recipients can access the content, protecting sensitive information from unauthorized access.

IM, one of the original online communication methods, continues to play a crucial role, particularly in professional settings. Platforms like Slack and Microsoft Teams have revolutionized workplace communication by providing real-time chat capabilities, facilitating quick decision-making, and fostering collaboration. However, users must be aware of the security challenges, such as the lack of E2EE in some services, and opt for secure alternatives where necessary.

Encrypted chat applications such as Signal, Wickr, and MySudo offer robust security features, including E2EE, ensuring that messages remain private. These applications are essential for maintaining secure communications, particularly in environments where confidentiality is paramount. Understanding the importance of encryption and choosing reputable, open-source apps with strong security protocols is vital for protecting sensitive information.

Video Conferencing has become indispensable for remote collaboration, enabling virtual meetings, webinars, and online classes. Platforms like Zoom, Microsoft Teams, and Google Meet offer extensive features that enhance productivity and engagement. However, ensuring the security of video conferencing sessions through encryption, strong authentication methods, and careful management of meeting settings is crucial to prevent unauthorized access and data breaches.

Social Media platforms like Facebook, Twitter, and LinkedIn facilitate global connections and content sharing. While these platforms offer significant benefits for personal interaction and professional networking, they also pose security and privacy risks. Users must be cautious about the information they share, engage responsibly, and be aware of the potential professional repercussions of their online activities. Maintaining a professional demeanor and adhering to best practices for privacy and security can help protect one's reputation and career prospects.

Mobile Texting (SMS) remains a fundamental tool for quick communication. However, it lacks the security features of more advanced messaging services. Users should be aware of the inherent vulnerabilities of SMS and consider secure alternatives like iMessage and WhatsApp, which offer E2EE. Protecting mobile communications from phishing attacks and unauthorized access through strong passwords and MFA is essential.

VoIP technology has transformed voice communication by enabling calls over the internet. VoIP services like Skype and WhatsApp provide cost-effective and flexible communication solutions. Secure VoIP options like MySudo offer enhanced privacy features, including E2EE and multiple identities for added security. Implementing robust network security measures and choosing reputable VoIP providers are key to safeguarding voice communications.

Web chats and forums offer valuable opportunities for interaction and learning. Platforms like Reddit and Stack Overflow provide spaces for sharing knowledge and building communities. However, users must be cautious about the information they share and be aware of the professional repercussions of engaging in certain online communities. Avoiding forums associated with extremist ideologies and adhering to community guidelines can help maintain a positive online presence.

Blogs and Podcasts are powerful tools for content creation and audience engagement. Platforms like WordPress, Medium, Anchor, and Spotify enable users to share their thoughts, information, and stories with a wide audience. Ensuring content ownership, respecting copyright laws, and maintaining a high standard of quality and professionalism are essential for successful content creation.

By understanding and applying the principles of digital communication privacy and security discussed in this chapter, users can navigate the complexities of the digital age more effectively. Implementing best practices, choosing secure platforms, and staying informed about emerging threats are crucial steps in protecting personal and professional information in an increasingly interconnected world.

Key Takeaways

- Email Security: Email remains a critical communication tool for both personal and professional use. Enhancing email privacy and security through encrypted email services, anonymous email providers, and one-time use emails is essential to protect sensitive information from unauthorized access.
- Instant Messaging: IM continues to play a vital role in professional communication, especially for real-time collaboration. Understanding the security limitations of some IM services and opting for secure alternatives is crucial for maintaining privacy.

- Encrypted Chat Applications: Apps like Signal, Wickr, and MySudo provide robust E2EE, ensuring secure communication. Choosing reputable, open-source apps with strong security protocols is important for protecting sensitive information.
- Video Conferencing: Video conferencing platforms like Zoom, Microsoft Teams, and Google Meet facilitate remote collaboration. Ensuring the security of these sessions through encryption and strong authentication methods is necessary to prevent unauthorized access.
- Social Media: Social media platforms offer significant benefits for personal interaction and professional networking. However, users must be cautious about the information they share and aware of the potential professional repercussions of their online activities.
- Mobile Texting (SMS): While SMS is a fundamental communication tool, it lacks the security features of more advanced messaging services. Users should consider alternatives like iMessage and WhatsApp for more secure communications.
- VoIP: VoIP technology has revolutionized voice communication. Secure VoIP options like MySudo offer enhanced privacy features, and implementing robust network security measures is key to safeguarding voice communications.
- Web Chats and Forums: These platforms provide valuable opportunities for interaction and learning. Users should be cautious about the information they share and avoid forums associated with extremist ideologies to maintain a positive online presence.
- Blogs and Podcasts: These are powerful tools for content creation and audience engagement. Ensuring content ownership, respecting copyright laws, and maintaining high standards of quality and professionalism are essential for successful content creation.

Chapter Review Questions

1. Why is it important to use encrypted email services, and what are some examples of such services?

    - **Answer:** Encrypted email services are important because they protect the content of emails from being accessed by unauthorized parties during transmission. This ensures that sensitive information remains confidential. Examples of encrypted email services include ProtonMail and Tutanota, which provide E2EE for emails.

2. What are the primary differences between SMS and secure messaging apps like Signal or WhatsApp in terms of security?

    - **Answer:** The primary differences between SMS and secure messaging apps like Signal or WhatsApp are related to encryption and privacy. SMS does not provide E2EE, making it vulnerable to interception and unauthorized access. In contrast, Signal and WhatsApp use E2EE, ensuring that only the intended recipients can read the messages, thus providing a higher level of security and privacy.

3. What are some best practices for maintaining security and privacy when using web chats and forums?

    - **Answer:** Best practices for maintaining security and privacy when using web chats and forums include the following:

        - Using pseudonyms to protect personal identity.
        - Being skeptical of unsolicited messages and links to avoid phishing and scams.
        - Reporting suspicious or inappropriate behavior to forum moderators.
        - Respecting community guidelines to foster a positive environment.
        - Limiting the sharing of sensitive personal information publicly.
        - Being mindful of the potential professional repercussions of engaging in certain online communities, such as those associated with extremist ideologies.

Chapter 6

Cyber Privacy and Ethical Considerations

Shane McNeil, PhD

Learning Outcomes

- **Define digital ethics** and explain its foundational principles, including autonomy, justice, transparency, and accountability, as they apply to data privacy and technology use.
- **Analyze the ethical dilemmas** associated with data collection during emergencies, such as the COVID-19 pandemic, and evaluate the trade-offs between public benefit and individual privacy.
- **Distinguish between compliance and ethical responsibility**, identifying how organizations can move beyond legal requirements to implement ethical data practices.
- **Evaluate the challenges of social media regulation**, including content moderation, algorithmic amplification, and balancing free speech with harm reduction.
- **Explain the role of privacy-enhancing technologies**, such as anonymization, pseudonymization, differential privacy, and federated learning, in addressing ethical concerns.
- **Identify best practices for empowering consumers**, including the use of privacy tools, education initiatives, and simplified privacy policies.
- **Discuss the ethical implications of emerging technologies**, including artificial intelligence, blockchain, and the Internet of Things (IoT), and propose strategies for mitigating associated risks.
- **Apply ethical decision-making frameworks** to real-world scenarios, demonstrating the ability to assess the impact of data practices on individuals and society.

Key Terms

- **Digital Ethics:** The study of moral principles governing the responsible use of technology and data.
- **Autonomy:** The right of individuals to control their personal data and make informed decisions about its use.

- **Transparency:** Clear and accessible communication about how data is collected, stored, and used, fostering trust and accountability.
- **Accountability:** The obligation of organizations and individuals to take responsibility for their actions and data practices.
- **Proportionality:** Ensuring that data collection practices are appropriate to the goals they aim to achieve, particularly during emergencies.
- **Privacy-Enhancing Technologies (PETs):** Tools and techniques, such as encryption and anonymization, that protect user privacy while enabling data analysis.
- **Anonymization:** The process of removing personally identifiable information from datasets to protect individual identities.
- **Pseudonymization:** Replacing direct identifiers in a dataset with pseudonyms to protect privacy while maintaining usability for analysis.
- **Differential Privacy:** A statistical technique that adds noise to datasets, preventing the identification of individuals while preserving overall trends.
- **Federated Learning:** A method of training machine learning models on decentralized datasets without transferring raw data, enhancing privacy.
- **Privacy-by-Design:** A framework for embedding privacy considerations into every stage of product or system development.
- **Content Moderation:** The process of monitoring and managing user-generated content on social media platforms to ensure compliance with policies and reduce harm.
- **Algorithmic Amplification:** The process by which social media algorithms prioritize certain content, often based on engagement metrics, which can unintentionally amplify harmful or polarizing posts.
- **Sunset Clauses:** Policies that mandate the expiration or deletion of data collected during emergencies to prevent long-term misuse.
- **Ethical AI:** The practice of designing artificial intelligence systems that prioritize fairness, transparency, and accountability.
- **Blockchain:** A decentralized ledger technology that enables secure and transparent data storage and transactions, raising both opportunities and ethical challenges.
- **Internet of Things (IoT):** A network of interconnected devices that collect and exchange data, often raising privacy and security concerns.
- **Free Speech Versus Harm Reduction:** The ethical dilemma of balancing the right to free expression with the need to protect users from harmful content on digital platforms.

Introduction

In the digital age, data has become one of the most valuable resources on the planet. Every interaction we have—whether it's sending an email, posting on social media, or using a GPS app—generates information that can be collected, analyzed, and monetized.

This data is the backbone of technological innovation, driving progress in sectors ranging from healthcare to education to global commerce. Yet, as our digital footprint grows, so too does the ethical complexity surrounding how this information is collected, used, and protected.

At its core, the challenge of cyber privacy isn't just about protecting personal information. It's about ensuring that technology serves humanity ethically and responsibly. Data can be a force for good, empowering medical breakthroughs and global connectivity, but it can also be exploited to manipulate behavior, erode trust, and compromise individual freedoms. Striking the right balance between these possibilities requires not only robust technical safeguards but also clear ethical guidelines.

Consider the case of pandemic contact-tracing apps. These tools played a critical role in mitigating the spread of COVID-19 by identifying individuals who may have been exposed to the virus. But they also raised significant concerns about mass surveillance, data retention, and the potential misuse of sensitive health information. This tension—between collective good and individual privacy—lies at the heart of many digital ethics debates. Who decides how much privacy should be sacrificed for the greater good? What mechanisms ensure that temporary surveillance measures don't become permanent? And how can trust be built when the stakes are so high?

These questions are not limited to public health crises. Social media platforms wrestle with similar issues, navigating the fine line between moderating harmful content and preserving free speech. Companies face dilemmas about how much data they should collect to improve their services versus respecting user autonomy. Governments weigh the benefits of surveillance technologies against their potential to infringe on civil liberties. In every case, the answers are rarely clear-cut, and the solutions often demand compromises that leave no one fully satisfied.

At the same time, the rise of privacy-preserving technologies like encryption, anonymization, and virtual private networks (VPNs) offers hope. These tools empower individuals to reclaim control over their data, but their effectiveness hinges on awareness and adoption. Education plays a crucial role here—not just for the engineers and policymakers building these systems but also for the students and future professionals who will navigate an increasingly data-driven world.

This chapter dives deep into the ethical landscape of cyber privacy. It begins by exploring the foundational principles of digital ethics and their application to data governance. It then examines the real-world challenges of data collection, particularly during crises like the COVID-19 pandemic, and the shift from legal compliance to ethical responsibility. The chapter also addresses the regulation of social media platforms, where debates about free speech, harm reduction, and corporate accountability are particularly fraught. Finally, it offers practical solutions for navigating the privacy minefield, emphasizing the need for transparency, trust, and proactive decision-making.

By understanding the complexities of cyber privacy and the ethical considerations that accompany it, students will be better equipped to engage thoughtfully in the digital age. Whether as future professionals, consumers, or citizens, their decisions will shape how technology evolves and whether it becomes a tool for empowerment or exploitation. This chapter seeks to provide not just a theoretical framework but also the practical tools needed to make those decisions with confidence and integrity.

6.1 Digital Ethics and Privacy

Digital ethics refers to the moral principles and guidelines governing the use of technology and data. As our lives become increasingly digital, the ethical dilemmas surrounding data privacy, security, and governance are becoming more complex and pervasive. Unlike legal frameworks, which establish baseline protections, digital ethics asks deeper, more fundamental questions: What is the right thing to do? How can technology be used to enhance society while respecting individual rights? And who bears responsibility for the unintended consequences of innovation?

At its core, digital ethics emphasizes autonomy, or the right of individuals to control their personal data. It challenges the notion that technology companies should collect and use data simply because they can. For example, consider the design of social media platforms. Many are engineered to collect as much user data as possible to refine algorithms and drive advertising revenue. While this practice is legal, it raises ethical concerns about user manipulation and the erosion of privacy.

Another pillar of digital ethics is justice, which ensures that the benefits and burdens of technology are distributed equitably. This principle highlights disparities in access to privacy tools and the disproportionate impact of data exploitation on marginalized communities. For example, low-income individuals may rely on free digital services that monetize their data, while wealthier users can afford premium privacy-focused alternatives. Addressing such inequities is a key ethical challenge.

Lastly, digital ethics demands accountability, ensuring that organizations and individuals take responsibility for their actions. This is particularly critical when dealing with emerging technologies whose long-term implications may be unclear. Ethical organizations not only comply with laws but also anticipate potential risks and take proactive steps to mitigate harm.

Ethical Principles in Data Privacy

The application of ethical principles to data privacy can be illustrated through three main concepts: consent, transparency, and fairness.

Consent is a cornerstone of ethical data practices. Users should have the ability to make informed decisions about how their data is collected, used, and shared. However, achieving true informed consent is often difficult in practice. Many companies use opaque language in their privacy policies or bury important details in lengthy terms of service agreements. For example, a 2018 Deloitte survey found that over 90 percent of people accept terms and conditions without reading them.[1] This raises the ethical question: Can consent be truly informed if users don't understand what they're agreeing to?

Transparency builds trust between organizations and their users. Companies should clearly communicate how they handle data and provide users with easy access to their own information. Ethical practices go beyond simply stating "we use your data" to explaining why the data is collected, how it will be used, and what safeguards are in place. Apple's App Tracking Transparency (ATT) feature is a prime example of how transparency can empower users, giving them the choice to opt out of tracking.[2]

Fairness ensures that data practices do not disproportionately harm certain individuals or groups. Biased algorithms, for instance, can perpetuate discrimination in hiring, credit scoring, or law enforcement. Ethical data governance requires organizations to audit their systems regularly, identify potential biases, and implement corrective measures.

Real-World Examples of Ethical Dilemmas

The importance of digital ethics can be seen in both the successes and failures of organizations to handle user data responsibly. Two illustrative examples are Facebook's Cambridge Analytica scandal and Apple's privacy initiatives.

The Facebook–Cambridge Analytica Scandal: In 2018, it was revealed that Cambridge Analytica had harvested the personal data of millions of Facebook users without their consent. This data was used to influence voter behavior during the 2016 US presidential election. While Facebook had technically complied with its terms of service, its lack of oversight allowed third-party developers to misuse user data. The scandal led to widespread criticism, lawsuits, and a significant loss of trust. Ethically, Facebook failed to prioritize user autonomy and accountability, illustrating the dangers of a compliance-only mindset.

Apple's Privacy Initiatives: In contrast, Apple has positioned itself as a leader in ethical data practices. Its ATT feature, introduced in 2021, requires apps to obtain explicit user permission before tracking their activity across other apps and websites. By prioritizing user autonomy and transparency, Apple has demonstrated that ethical data practices can also be a competitive advantage. However, even Apple faces challenges in balancing privacy with innovation, as seen in debates about its plans to scan devices for illegal content.

1. Caroline Cakebread, "You're Not Alone, No One Reads Terms of Service Agreements," *Yahoo Finance*, November 15, 2017, https://finance.yahoo.com/news/apos-not-alone-no-one-123000652.html; Jonathan A. Obar and Anne Oeldorf-Hirsch, "The Biggest Lie on the Internet: Ignoring the Privacy Policies and Terms of Service Policies of Social Networking Services," *Information, Communication & Society* (2018): 1–20, https://doi.org/10.2139/ssrn.2757465.
2. Anthony Ha, "What You Need to Know about Apple App Tracking Transparency," *TechCrunch* (blog), April 26, 2021, https://techcrunch.com/2021/04/26/apples-app-tracking-transparency-feature-has-arrived-heres-what-you-need-to-know/.

Tools and Technologies for Ethical Data Practices

Advances in privacy-preserving technologies provide tangible solutions to many ethical challenges. These tools empower individuals to protect their data while enabling organizations to analyze information responsibly.

Encryption: Encryption ensures that data is accessible only to authorized parties, protecting sensitive information during transmission and storage. Tools like Signal, Sudo, and Proton use end-to-end encryption to secure communications, making it nearly impossible for unauthorized entities to intercept messages.

Differential Privacy: This technique allows organizations to analyze datasets while safeguarding individual anonymity. For example, Apple uses differential privacy to collect usage data for product improvement without exposing personal details. By adding statistical noise to the data, differential privacy ensures that no single individual can be identified.

Privacy-by-Design: This framework incorporates privacy considerations into every stage of product development. Instead of treating privacy as an afterthought, organizations prioritize it from the outset, building tools that minimize data collection, provide clear user controls, and use secure architectures.

Virtual Private Networks (VPNs) and **Anonymous Browsers:** VPNs encrypt internet traffic and mask users' IP addresses, while anonymous browsers like Tor allow individuals to access the web without leaving identifiable traces. These tools are especially valuable for protecting privacy in regions with restrictive internet policies.

While these technologies are powerful, their success depends on widespread adoption and user education. Ethical organizations should invest not only in developing these tools but also in teaching users how to use them effectively.

Digital ethics and privacy are not abstract concepts: They are the foundation of trust in an increasingly interconnected world. By adhering to ethical principles such as autonomy, justice, and accountability, organizations can ensure that their data practices respect individual rights and contribute to the greater good. At the same time, users must be empowered with tools and knowledge to take control of their own privacy. This interplay between technology, ethics, and education will shape the future of digital communication and data governance.

6.2 Data Collection in the Pandemic Era

The Role of Technology in Pandemic Response

The COVID-19 pandemic demonstrated how technology could be mobilized to address a global crisis. Governments, health-care organizations, and private companies used digital tools to track infections, monitor symptoms, enforce quarantines, and disseminate public health information. One of the most significant technological developments was the introduction of contact-tracing apps, which leveraged location and proximity data to notify individuals who had been exposed to the virus.

Contact-tracing apps, such as those implemented in South Korea, Singapore, and several US states, relied on Bluetooth and GPS technology to identify individuals who were near confirmed COVID-19 cases. For instance, Singapore's TraceTogether app used Bluetooth signals to record close contacts and sent exposure alerts directly to users.[3] These tools provided public health officials with valuable data to make informed decisions, such as where to allocate medical resources or when to impose targeted lockdowns.

However, the success of these apps was often contingent on widespread adoption and public trust. In countries like South Korea, a combination of mandatory data-sharing and robust government communication led to high adoption rates. Conversely, in the United States, concerns about privacy and data misuse led to resistance, limiting the effectiveness of similar tools.

Privacy Versus Public Health: An Ethical Dilemma

The use of data during the pandemic sparked significant debates about the balance between public health and individual privacy. On one hand, sharing sensitive health and location data helped slow the spread of the virus and saved lives. On the other, it raised ethical concerns about consent, data security, and the potential for long-term surveillance.

One critical issue was the scope of data collection. While some apps collected only proximity data, others gathered detailed information such as GPS location, personal identifiers, and medical history. For example, in China, the Health Code app not only tracked users' movements but also assigned a color-coded health status that determined their access to public spaces. While effective in curbing the virus, this system sparked fears of authoritarian overreach and misuse of personal data.[4]

A related concern was data retention and reuse. In some cases, governments initially assured citizens that the data collected would be used exclusively for public health purposes. However, as seen in Singapore, law enforcement agencies later accessed contact-tracing data for criminal investigations, eroding public trust.[5] Such incidents highlighted the importance of setting clear boundaries and adhering to promises about data usage.

3. Vanessa Ong, "Everything About TraceTogether, an App Developed by the Gov That Helps in Contact Tracing," Goody Feed, March 21, 2020, https://goodyfeed.com/tracetogether/.
4. James Gregory, "China Deactivates National Covid Tracking App," *BBC News*, December 12, 2022, https://www.bbc.com/news/world-asia-china-63941512; "As Chinese Authorities Expand Use of Health Tracking Apps, Privacy Concerns Grow," NBC News, May 26, 2020, https://www.nbcnews.com/tech/tech-news/chinese-authorities-expand-use-health-tracking-apps-privacy-concerns-grow-n1214626.
5. Mia Sato, "Singapore's Police Now Have Access to Contact Tracing Data," *MIT Technology Review*, January 5, 2021, https://www.technologyreview.com/2021/01/05/1015734/singapore-contact-tracing-police-data-covid/.

Ethical frameworks for navigating this tension emphasize the principles of proportionality and necessity. Data collection should be limited to what is strictly necessary for achieving public health goals, and privacy protections should be embedded into the design of these tools. Furthermore, transparency about how data is collected, stored, and shared is essential for maintaining public trust.

Case Study: South Korea Versus the United States

South Korea's approach to data collection during the pandemic offers a stark contrast to that of the United States. In South Korea, the government implemented aggressive contact tracing by combining smartphone data, credit card records, and surveillance footage.[6] This comprehensive approach allowed authorities to quickly identify and isolate outbreaks, contributing to the country's relatively low infection rates.

While effective, South Korea's strategy raised concerns about the potential for abuse. Critics argued that such extensive surveillance could set a dangerous precedent for privacy violations in noncrisis situations.[7] To address these concerns, South Korea established a system of strict oversight, including sunset clauses that required the deletion of collected data after a specified period.

In the United States, the decentralized nature of governance led to a fragmented response. Contact-tracing apps developed by state governments and private companies often lacked interoperability, limiting their effectiveness. Moreover, the American public's skepticism of government surveillance, fueled by past controversies like the National Security Agency's mass data collection program, hindered adoption rates. Ethical missteps—such as unclear privacy policies or inadequate security measures—further eroded trust.

These contrasting approaches highlight the importance of balancing efficacy with ethical safeguards. While South Korea's system demonstrated the power of comprehensive data collection, it also underscored the need for transparency and accountability. The US experience, on the other hand, illustrated the challenges of gaining public trust in a fragmented and historically skeptical environment.

6. Juliette Schwak, "Korea's Exemplary Response to the COVID-19 Pandemic: Successes and Challenges," National Defense University Press, February 24, 2022, https://ndupress.ndu.edu/Media/News/News-Article-View/Article/2944861/koreas-exemplary-response-to-the-covid-19-pandemic-successes-and-challenges/https://ndupress.ndu.edu/Media/News/News-Article-View/Article/2944861/koreas-exemplary-response-to-the-covid-19-pandemic-successes-and-challenges/.
7. Helen Chan, "Pervasive Personal Data Collection at the Heart of South Korea's COVID-19 Success May Not Translate," Thomson Reuters Institute, March 26, 2020, https://www.thomsonreuters.com/en-us/posts/news-and-media/south-korea-covid-19-data-privacy/.

Assurances of Anonymity

One way to address privacy concerns during data collection is through anonymization techniques, which remove or obscure personal identifiers to protect individual identities. Anonymization can involve methods such as the following:

- Generalization*:* Reducing the precision of data, such as reporting only approximate locations or age ranges instead of exact details.
- Aggregation*:* Combining individual data points into broader categories, such as overall movement trends rather than specific user paths.
- Tokenization*:* Replacing personal identifiers with random strings of characters, ensuring that raw data cannot directly identify individuals.

For example, Google and Apple implemented anonymization in their COVID-19 Exposure Notification framework.[8] The system used Bluetooth to detect proximity without recording GPS locations or other personal data. Additionally, it relied on decentralized storage, meaning that data was stored on users' devices rather than a central server, reducing the risk of mass breaches.

However, anonymization is not a perfect solution. Researchers have shown that anonymized datasets can often be de-anonymized by cross-referencing them with other publicly available information. For instance, if anonymized location data is combined with social media posts that reveal an individual's movements, their identity can potentially be reconstructed. This underscores the need for ongoing vigilance and innovation in anonymization techniques.

Lessons Learned and Future Implications

The pandemic highlighted both the potential and the pitfalls of data collection during emergencies. Key takeaways include:

- Transparency Builds Trust: Clear communication about the purpose, scope, and limitations of data collection is essential for public buy-in. Users are more likely to adopt technologies when they understand how their data will be used and protected.
- Ethics by Design: Privacy and ethical considerations should be embedded into the development of data collection tools from the outset. This includes incorporating features like anonymization, limited data retention, and decentralized storage.

8. Apple Inc, "Exposure Notification," Apple Developer, accessed December 23, 2024, https://developer.apple.com/exposure-notification/; Google, "Exposure-Notification-FAQ-v1.2," Exposure Notifications: Frequently Asked Questions, September 2020, https://static.googleusercontent.com/media/www.google.com/en//covid19/exposurenotifications/pdfs/Exposure-Notification-FAQ-v1.2.pdf.

- Oversight and Accountability: Independent oversight bodies can help ensure that data collection practices adhere to ethical standards. Regular audits and sunset clauses can prevent the misuse of data after the crisis has passed.
- Global Collaboration: Future crises will require a coordinated international response. Sharing best practices and aligning ethical frameworks across countries can enhance both effectiveness and equity.

As we look ahead, the lessons of the pandemic offer a road map for navigating similar challenges in the future. By prioritizing ethics and privacy alongside innovation, we can ensure that technology serves as a force for good in times of crisis.

6.3 Shifting from Privacy to Ethics

Compliance Versus Ethics: The Next Frontier

In recent years, regulations such as the **General Data Protection Regulation (GDPR)** in Europe and the **California Consumer Privacy Act (CCPA)** in the United States have established legal frameworks to protect user privacy. These laws set standards for data collection, storage, and usage, holding organizations accountable for violations. However, compliance with legal requirements is not the same as acting ethically. Ethical practices go beyond the minimum legal obligations to consider the broader societal impact of data handling.

For example, a company might legally track user behavior across websites to optimize advertising strategies, but this practice can still feel invasive to users. Ethical decision-making in this scenario would involve asking whether the benefits to the company outweigh the potential harm to user trust and autonomy. While compliance is mandatory, ethics are often self-imposed, driven by organizational culture and leadership.

The Ethical "Should" Versus the Legal "Can"

The distinction between "can" and "should" is critical in this context. Legally, companies may be allowed to collect extensive amounts of user data, provided they inform users through privacy policies. But ethically, companies should minimize data collection, prioritizing user consent and transparency over profit motives. This ethical restraint fosters trust and sets companies apart in an increasingly privacy-conscious market.

For example, companies like Apple have adopted privacy-focused approaches, introducing features such as **App Tracking Transparency (ATT)**. This tool forces apps to request user permission before tracking data, even though this level of transparency is not legally required in most jurisdictions.[9] By going beyond compliance, Apple demon-

9. Apple Inc, "App Tracking Transparency," Apple Developer Documentation, 2024, https://developer.apple.com/documentation/apptrackingtransparency.

strates how ethical decision-making can align with both user interests and long-term brand loyalty.

Ethical Decision-Making Frameworks

Making ethical decisions in data management requires a structured approach. Organizations can adopt frameworks to evaluate the implications of their practices and ensure that they align with ethical principles. One widely used approach is the three-part ethical framework:

- **Purpose:** What is the intended purpose of the data collection? Organizations must define clear, specific objectives for using data and ensure they align with user expectations. For example, a health app collecting step counts for fitness tracking should not sell that data to advertisers without explicit user consent.
- **Proportionality:** Is the scope of data collection proportional to its purpose? Companies should collect only the data necessary to achieve their stated objectives. For instance, a navigation app may need location data to provide accurate directions, but it does not need access to a user's contact list.
- **Accountability:** Who is responsible for safeguarding this data and ensuring ethical use? Organizations must assign clear roles and responsibilities for data protection, with oversight mechanisms to address potential abuses. Regular audits and transparency reports can reinforce accountability.

This framework helps organizations navigate complex ethical dilemmas, ensuring that their practices are not only legally sound but also morally responsible.

Building Trust Through Transparency

Trust is a cornerstone of ethical data practices. Users are more likely to engage with platforms and services when they feel confident that their data is being handled responsibly. Transparency plays a crucial role in building and maintaining this trust. Yet, transparency is often misunderstood as simply providing information. True transparency involves making information accessible, understandable, and actionable.

- **Accessibility and Clarity:** Transparency begins with clear communication. Privacy policies and terms of service, often criticized for being dense and unreadable, should be rewritten in plain language. For example, Google's "Your Data in Search" page simplifies its privacy practices, breaking down how data is collected and used in an easy-to-read format.[10] By doing so, Google empowers users to make informed decisions about their data.

10. Google, "Your Data in Search," 2024, https://myaccount.google.com/yourdata/search.

- **User Empowerment:** Transparency should also give users control over their data. Features such as data dashboards, where users can view, edit, or delete their information, demonstrate ethical accountability. Companies like Facebook and LinkedIn have implemented tools that allow users to download their data, fostering a sense of ownership.

However, transparency is not without challenges. Overloading users with too much information can lead to decision fatigue, where users ignore privacy settings or fail to exercise their rights. Ethical transparency involves striking a balance: providing enough information for informed consent without overwhelming users.

Case Study: Facebook and the Cambridge Analytica Scandal

The 2018 Facebook–Cambridge Analytica scandal remains a cautionary tale about the consequences of prioritizing profit over ethical responsibility. Cambridge Analytica, a political consulting firm, harvested data from millions of Facebook users without their explicit consent. This data was then used to create psychographic profiles for targeted political advertising, influencing elections in the United States and the United Kingdom.[11]

While Facebook had technically complied with its terms of service, its lack of oversight allowed a third-party app to exploit user data. The ethical failure lay in Facebook's failure to prioritize user trust over business partnerships. The fallout was severe: Facebook faced lawsuits, public backlash, and a $5 billion fine from the US Federal Trade Commission (FTC).[12]

This scandal underscored the importance of moving beyond compliance. Ethical practices could have prevented such a breach of trust, protecting both users and the company's reputation. Lessons from this case emphasize the need for accountability, transparency, and proactive governance.

Ethical Innovation: Apple's Privacy Leadership

In contrast to Facebook's missteps, Apple has emerged as a leader in ethical data practices. By embedding privacy into its core business model, Apple has set a benchmark for transparency and user empowerment. Its ATT feature, introduced in 2021, requires apps to obtain user permission before tracking their activity across other apps and websites. This initiative not only aligns with ethical principles but also reflects Apple's commitment to user autonomy.[13]

11. Brian Tarran, "What Can We Learn from the Facebook—Cambridge Analytica Scandal?," *Significance* 15, no. 3 (2018): 4–5, https://doi.org/10.1111/j.1740-9713.2018.01139.x.
12. Axel Bruns, "Facebook Shuts the Gate after the Horse Has Bolted, and Hurts Real Research in the Process," *Internet Policy Review*, April 25, 2018, https://policyreview.info/articles/news/facebook-shuts-gate-after-horse-has-bolted-and-hurts-real-research-process/786.
13. Apple Inc, "App Tracking Transparency."

Apple's success demonstrates that ethical innovation can be a competitive advantage. By prioritizing privacy, the company has cultivated a loyal user base and differentiated itself in a crowded tech market. However, even Apple faces ethical dilemmas, such as balancing privacy with public safety. Its controversial plan to scan iCloud photos for illegal content sparked debates about the trade-offs between individual rights and collective security.

Trust and Transparency in Action

Trust and transparency are more than abstract ideals—they are practical strategies that drive ethical decision-making and long-term success. Companies that prioritize these values build stronger relationships with their users, reduce regulatory risks, and position themselves as industry leaders.

Practical Steps for Building Trust:

1. **Simplify Privacy Practices:** Make privacy policies and settings user-friendly and easy to understand.
2. **Empower Users:** Provide tools that allow users to control their data, such as opt-out mechanisms and data management dashboards.
3. **Be Proactive:** Address potential ethical issues before they become scandals by conducting regular audits and engaging with privacy advocates.
4. **Engage in Dialogue:** Actively seek feedback from users and stakeholders to align practices with community values.

As technology continues to evolve, ethical data practices will become increasingly important. Companies that embrace transparency and trust will not only navigate the challenges of today but also lead the way in shaping a more ethical digital future.

6.4 Social Media Regulation

The Role of Social Media in Society

Social media platforms have transformed the way individuals interact, share information, and build communities. With billions of users worldwide, platforms like Facebook, Twitter, Instagram, and TikTok have become essential for everything from personal expression to political activism.[14] Social media allows users to connect globally, amplify their voices, and access real-time news. However, this influence comes with significant ethical and regulatory challenges.

The open nature of social media has made it a breeding ground for harmful content, including hate speech, misinformation, and extremist ideologies. While these platforms

14. While Twitter has been renamed "X," most of the information in this chapter applies to when it was still called "Twitter" so that name will be used in this chapter.

often position themselves as neutral spaces for free expression, their algorithms and moderation policies can shape public discourse in profound ways. The ethical question at the heart of social media regulation is this: How do we balance the right to free speech with the need to protect users from harm?

Content Moderation Challenges

Content moderation is one of the most contentious aspects of social media regulation. Platforms employ a combination of human moderators, artificial intelligence (AI), and user reporting mechanisms to monitor and manage content. While these efforts aim to create safer environments, they are far from perfect.

AI Moderation: Pros and Cons

AI tools are widely used for detecting and removing harmful content at scale. For instance, Facebook uses machine learning algorithms to flag posts containing hate speech or graphic violence. These tools can process vast amounts of data quickly, making them indispensable for platforms with millions of daily users.

However, AI moderation has its limitations. Algorithms often struggle to understand context, leading to errors such as flagging benign content or failing to catch subtle forms of harmful speech. For example, satire or cultural references might be misinterpreted as offensive, while coded language used by extremist groups can go undetected. These shortcomings highlight the need for human oversight in moderation processes.

Human Moderation: Ethical Dilemmas

Human moderators play a crucial role in handling cases that require nuanced judgment. However, this work comes with significant ethical and psychological costs. Moderators are often exposed to graphic and disturbing content, leading to high rates of burnout and mental health issues. Additionally, moderators must navigate complex cultural and legal contexts, making consistent decision-making difficult.

For example, a post that is acceptable in one cultural context might be considered offensive in another. Platforms must develop moderation policies that account for these differences while maintaining global standards. This challenge underscores the ethical complexity of content moderation and the need for robust support systems for moderators.

Free Speech Versus Harm Reduction

One of the central ethical dilemmas in social media regulation is balancing free speech with harm reduction. Social media platforms often position themselves as champions of free expression, but this commitment is tested when harmful content spreads on their platforms. Misinformation about public health, hate speech, and calls to violence can have real-world consequences, from undermining vaccination efforts to inciting riots.

Case Study: Twitter's Ban on Political Ads

In 2019, Twitter announced a ban on political advertising, citing concerns about misinformation and the potential for undue influence. While the decision was praised by some as a proactive step toward harm reduction, others criticized it as an infringement on free speech. Critics argued that banning political ads disproportionately impacts smaller campaigns and grassroots movements that rely on social media to reach voters.[15]

This case illustrates the trade-offs inherent in social media regulation. While the ban addressed one type of harm, it also raised questions about fairness and access. Ethical regulation requires a careful evaluation of such trade-offs, ensuring that policies are both effective and equitable.

The Problem of Algorithmic Amplification

Another challenge is the role of algorithms in amplifying harmful content. Social media platforms prioritize engagement, often surfacing sensational or polarizing posts to keep users online longer. This has the unintended consequence of amplifying misinformation, divisive rhetoric, and extremist views.

For example, during the 2020 US presidential election, platforms like Facebook and YouTube were criticized for allowing false claims about voter fraud to go viral.[16] These claims, amplified by algorithms, contributed to widespread mistrust in the electoral process. Ethical regulation must address not only what content is allowed but also how algorithms influence their visibility.

Global Perspectives on Social Media Regulation

Social media regulation varies widely across countries, reflecting different cultural values, legal traditions, and political systems. Understanding these global perspectives provides valuable insights into the ethical challenges of regulating a borderless digital space.

The European Union: A Rights-Based Approach

The European Union (EU) has taken a proactive approach to social media regulation, focusing on protecting user rights. The EU's **Digital Services Act (DSA)**, introduced in 2022, aims to increase transparency and accountability for platforms. It requires companies to disclose how their algorithms work, remove illegal content promptly, and provide mechanisms for users to appeal moderation decisions.

15. Katie Snyder, "Twitter's Decision to Ban Political Ads: Violation of First Amendment Rights?," *Richmond Journal of Law and Technology*, November 20, 2019, https://jolt.richmond.edu/2019/11/19/twitters-decision-to-ban-political-ads-violation-of-first-amendment-rights/.
16. Gordon Pennycook and David G. Rand, "Research Note: Examining False Beliefs about Voter Fraud in the Wake of the 2020 Presidential Election," *Harvard Kennedy School Misinformation Review*, January 11, 2021, https://doi.org/10.37016/mr-2020-51.

The DSA reflects the EU's commitment to balancing free speech with harm reduction while safeguarding individual rights. However, critics argue that the act places a significant burden on smaller platforms that may lack the resources to comply.

The United States: A Focus on Free Speech

In the United States, social media regulation is heavily influenced by the First Amendment, which protects free speech. Platforms are granted broad immunity under Section 230 of the Communications Decency Act, which shields them from liability for user-generated content.[17] While this framework has allowed platforms to flourish, it has also led to a hands-off approach to moderation.

Recent debates about Section 230 have highlighted the need for reform. Advocates for change argue that platforms should be held accountable for harmful content, while opponents warn that stricter regulations could stifle innovation and free expression.

China: State-Controlled Regulation

In China, social media regulation is tightly controlled by the government, with platforms required to censor content that contradicts state narratives. This approach prioritizes social stability and state interests over individual rights, raising significant ethical concerns. While effective in curbing misinformation, such stringent regulation often leads to the suppression of dissent and free speech.

These global differences underscore the complexity of social media regulation. Platforms operating across multiple jurisdictions must navigate conflicting legal and cultural expectations, making ethical decision-making even more challenging.

Future Directions in Social Media Regulation

As social media continues to evolve, so too must the frameworks for regulating it. Emerging technologies like blockchain and decentralized platforms offer new opportunities for transparency and user control. For instance, blockchain-based social networks could give users ownership over their data and greater say in moderation policies.

At the same time, policymakers and technologists must work together to address pressing challenges, such as misinformation, algorithmic bias, and data privacy. Collaborative efforts like the Christchurch Call, which brings together governments and tech companies to combat online extremism, demonstrate the potential for collective action.

Social media regulation is a complex and evolving field, requiring platforms to balance competing priorities of free speech, harm reduction, and global compliance. Content moderation, algorithmic amplification, and the trade-offs between user rights and

17. Joel R. Reidenberg et al., "Section 230 of the Communications Decency Act: A Survey of the Legal Literature and Reform Proposals," *Fordham Law Legal Studies Research Paper* no. 2046230 (2012), https://doi.org/10.2139/ssrn.2046230.

corporate responsibility present significant ethical challenges. By learning from global perspectives and embracing innovative approaches, platforms can create safer, more equitable digital spaces while preserving the core values of free expression and user empowerment.

6.5 Navigating the Privacy Minefield

The Ethical Challenges of Urgency Versus Privacy

In moments of crisis—whether a pandemic, natural disaster, or terrorist attack—data collection often becomes a crucial tool for saving lives. Governments and organizations deploy technologies to track disease outbreaks, coordinate rescue operations, or monitor threats. However, these measures often place individual privacy in direct conflict with urgent societal needs, creating ethical dilemmas that are difficult to navigate.

During a crisis, the question of **urgency versus privacy** often arises: How much privacy should individuals sacrifice for the greater good? For example, in the early days of the COVID-19 pandemic, several countries used mobile location data to monitor the movement of infected individuals and enforce quarantines. While these measures helped control the spread of the virus, they also raised concerns about surveillance and the long-term implications of such data collection.

The ethical principles of **proportionality and necessity** are critical in these situations. Proportionality ensures that the scope of data collection is appropriate to the severity of the crisis, while necessity limits the use of data to what is strictly required to achieve specific goals. Without these safeguards, temporary measures risk becoming permanent, turning crisis-driven surveillance into a norm.

Case Study: Location Tracking During Crises

Location tracking is one of the most common tools used in emergencies, but its ethical implications vary depending on how it is implemented and governed. Two contrasting examples illustrate this complexity:

Hurricane Katrina (2005): During Hurricane Katrina, rescue teams used mobile location data to identify stranded individuals and coordinate evacuations. In this context, the data was used exclusively for humanitarian purposes, with no reports of misuse. This ethical use of technology highlighted how data could save lives without compromising individual rights.

COVID-19 in China (2020): In China, the government's Health Code app monitored citizens' movements and health status using GPS and QR codes. The app assigned color-coded statuses (green, yellow, or red) that determined individuals' access to public spaces.[18] While effective in controlling the virus, critics argued that the system lacked

18. James Gregory, "China Deactivates"; "As Chinese Authorities Expand Use of Health Tracking Apps."

transparency and could easily be repurposed for mass surveillance. This raised concerns about whether the benefits of the system outweighed its potential for abuse.

These cases underscore the need for **clear boundaries and oversight**. Data collection during emergencies should be limited in scope, time-bound, and subject to independent review to prevent misuse and ensure public trust.

Techniques for Protecting Privacy

To navigate the ethical minefield of data collection during crises, organizations can adopt privacy-preserving techniques that allow for data use without compromising individual rights. Two key approaches are **anonymization** and **pseudonymization**.

Anonymization removes all personally identifiable information (PII) from datasets, ensuring that individual users cannot be identified. This technique is commonly used in public health reporting, where aggregated data can reveal trends without exposing personal details. For example, Google's COVID-19 mobility reports anonymized location data to show changes in foot traffic to parks, grocery stores, and workplaces.[19]

However, anonymization has limitations. Researchers have demonstrated that even anonymized data can be de-anonymized by cross-referencing it with other publicly available datasets. For instance, a study published in Nature showed that 87 percent of Americans could be uniquely identified using just three data points: ZIP code, gender, and date of birth.[20] This highlights the need for stronger anonymization methods and the responsible use of anonymized data.

Pseudonymization replaces direct identifiers (e.g., names or Social Security numbers) with pseudonyms, such as random strings of characters. Unlike anonymization, pseudonymization allows for re-identification under controlled conditions, making it useful in contexts where follow-up analysis or verification is needed. For example, a hospital might use pseudonymized patient data to track treatment outcomes while maintaining the ability to reconnect the data to individual patients if necessary.

Balancing Public Benefit and Individual Rights

Navigating the privacy minefield requires a careful balance between maximizing public benefit and respecting individual rights. Achieving this balance involves three key principles:

Transparency: Organizations must clearly communicate the purpose, scope, and limitations of data collection. Users should understand how their data will be used, who will have access to it, and when it will be deleted. Transparency builds trust and reduces the likelihood of resistance.

19. Google, "Exposure-Notification-FAQ-v1.2."
20. Latanya Sweeney, "Simple Demographics Often Identify People Uniquely," Data Privacy Working Paper (Carnegie Mellon University, 2000).

For example, Iceland's COVID-19 contact-tracing app achieved high adoption rates by emphasizing transparency and voluntary participation.[21] The government provided detailed information about how the app worked and ensured that all data was stored locally on users' devices.

Time-Bound Measures: Data collection during emergencies should have a clear expiration date. Sunset clauses—policies that mandate the deletion of data after a specified period—are essential for preventing the long-term misuse of crisis-driven surveillance tools. Without such measures, temporary practices risk becoming permanent fixtures of daily life.

Independent Oversight: Independent oversight bodies can monitor data collection practices to ensure they adhere to ethical standards. These bodies should include diverse stakeholders, such as privacy advocates, ethicists, and legal experts, to provide a balanced perspective. Regular audits and public reports can further enhance accountability.

The Role of Privacy-Enhancing Technologies

Emerging privacy-enhancing technologies (PETs) offer new opportunities to navigate the privacy minefield. These tools enable data analysis without exposing individual information, making them ideal for high-stakes scenarios like public health crises or national security threats.

Federated Learning: This technique allows machine learning models to be trained across decentralized datasets without transferring raw data. For example, hospitals could use federated learning to develop predictive models for disease outbreaks without sharing patient records.

Homomorphic Encryption: Homomorphic encryption enables computations on encrypted data, allowing organizations to analyze sensitive information without decrypting it. This ensures that the data remains secure throughout the process.

Differential Privacy: Differential privacy adds statistical noise to datasets, ensuring that individual data points cannot be identified. This technique is widely used by companies like Apple and Google to collect aggregate insights without compromising user privacy.

By adopting these technologies, organizations can achieve the dual goals of utility and privacy, mitigating the ethical challenges of data collection during crises.

21. Yi Wu, Qianying Ye, Fei Shen, Zhian Zhang, and Crystal Li Jiang, "Country- and App-Level Factors Affecting the Adoption and Evaluation of COVID-19 Mobile Apps," *BMC Public Health* 22, no. 1 (2022): 2457, https://doi.org/10.1186/s12889-022-14918-8.

Lessons for the Future

The ethical challenges of navigating the privacy minefield are unlikely to disappear. As crises become more frequent and data-driven technologies become more sophisticated, organizations must develop robust frameworks for balancing urgency and privacy. Key lessons include the following:

- **Embedding Ethics in Design:** Privacy and ethical considerations should be incorporated into the design phase of data collection tools rather than treated as afterthoughts.
- **Building Public Trust:** Transparency, accountability, and voluntary participation are essential for fostering trust in data-driven initiatives.
- **Planning for the Long Term:** Temporary measures must have clear endpoints to prevent mission creep and safeguard individual rights.

By prioritizing these principles, we can ensure that technology serves the public good without compromising the fundamental values of privacy and autonomy. The path forward will require collaboration between governments, companies, and civil society, as well as a commitment to placing ethics at the center of decision-making.

6.6 Practical Applications of Digital Ethics

Developing Ethical Guidelines in Organizations

Organizations have a critical role to play in embedding digital ethics into their data governance and operational strategies. Ethical guidelines act as a compass, ensuring that decision-making aligns with both societal values and user expectations. While many companies prioritize legal compliance, those that adopt robust ethical frameworks often build stronger trust with their stakeholders and position themselves as industry leaders.

Creating an ethical culture requires more than drafting policies—it demands commitment at all levels of the organization. Leadership must set the tone by prioritizing ethical considerations alongside financial and operational goals. For example, appointing a Chief Ethics Officer or forming cross-functional ethics committees ensures that ethical concerns are integrated into decision-making processes.

Training programs are equally important. Employees at all levels, from engineers to marketing teams, should understand the principles of digital ethics and how they apply to their roles. For instance, engineers might receive training on **privacy-by-design principles**, while marketers could learn to identify and avoid manipulative practices like dark patterns.

Case Study: Mozilla's Ethical Approach

Mozilla, the organization behind the Firefox browser, provides a model for integrating ethics into corporate strategy. Mozilla has consistently championed user privacy, offering features like Enhanced Tracking Protection and a private browsing mode. Additionally, the company is transparent about its data collection practices, publishing annual reports on its ethical initiatives.[22]

Mozilla's commitment to ethics extends beyond its products. The organization actively participates in digital rights advocacy, supporting initiatives like net neutrality and open-source development. This dual focus on user empowerment and social impact highlights how companies can align profitability with ethical responsibility.

Ethical Training and Education

While organizational ethics are critical, individuals also play a significant role in shaping the digital ecosystem. As future professionals and active participants in online spaces, students must understand the ethical dimensions of their actions and decisions. Education is the key to fostering this awareness.

Universities and colleges should incorporate digital ethics into their curricula, particularly in fields like communications, business, and computer science. Courses on topics such as data privacy, algorithmic bias, and the societal impact of technology equip students with the knowledge to navigate ethical dilemmas in their careers.

For example, a communications student might learn how targeted advertising can influence public opinion, while a computer science student could explore the ethical challenges of designing AI systems. By integrating case studies, hands-on projects, and interdisciplinary discussions, these courses prepare students to think critically about the ethical implications of their work.

Beyond formal education, public awareness campaigns can help individuals make informed decisions about their digital lives. Initiatives like Google's **Be Internet Awesome** teach young users about online safety, privacy, and digital citizenship. Similarly, nonprofit organizations like the **Electronic Frontier Foundation (EFF)** provide resources on topics such as encryption and data security.

Empowering Consumers Through Tools and Resources

As individuals become more aware of digital ethics, they need practical tools to take control of their online privacy and security. Empowering consumers with the right resources ensures they can make informed decisions and protect their data in everyday interactions.

Privacy Tools

A wide range of tools are available to help users safeguard their information:

22. Ali Ateeq and Marwan Milhem, "Integrating Ethical Principles in Corporate Strategy: A Comprehensive Analysis of Business Ethics in Contemporary Enterprises," in *The AI Revolution: Driving Business Innovation and Research: Volume 1*, ed. Bahaa Awwad (Springer Nature Switzerland, 2024), 201–10, https://doi.org/10.1007/978-3-031-54379-1_17.

- **Ad Blockers:** Tools like uBlock Origin prevent tracking by blocking advertisements and third-party scripts.
- **Password Managers:** Applications like LastPass and Bitwarden generate and store strong, unique passwords for each account.
- **Privacy-Focused Browsers:** Browsers like Brave and Firefox offer features like tracker blocking and private browsing modes.
- **Virtual Private Networks:** VPNs encrypt internet traffic and hide users' IP addresses, enhancing anonymity.

Educating users about these tools is an essential step toward digital empowerment. For example, Mozilla's **Privacy Not Included** guide reviews popular apps and devices, highlighting their privacy features (or lack thereof).[23]

Understanding privacy policies can be daunting, but simplifying the process makes it more accessible. Tools like **Terms of Service; Didn't Read (ToS; DR**) summarize and rate privacy policies, providing users with a quick overview of potential risks.[24] Similarly, browser extensions like DuckDuckGo's Privacy Essentials analyze websites' tracking practices, helping users make informed choices.[25]

The Business Case for Ethics

Ethical practices are not just morally right—they also make good business sense. Companies that prioritize ethics often experience long-term benefits, including enhanced customer loyalty, reduced regulatory risks, and improved brand reputation.

Building Consumer Trust: Transparency and accountability are powerful drivers of trust. When users believe that a company values their privacy and acts responsibly, they are more likely to engage with its products and services. For instance, Apple's privacy-focused marketing campaigns have resonated with consumers, positioning the company as a leader in digital ethics.

Avoiding Scandals: Unethical practices can lead to reputational damage, legal penalties, and customer attrition. The Facebook-Cambridge Analytica scandal, for example, resulted in billions of dollars in fines and a significant loss of user trust. Companies that proactively address ethical concerns can avoid these pitfalls and create a more sustainable business model.

Attracting Ethical Investors: As environmental, social, and governance (ESG) investing gains traction, ethical practices are becoming a priority for investors. Companies with strong digital ethics are more likely to attract funding from investors who value account-

23. Mozilla Foundation, "*Privacy Not Included: A Buyer's Guide for Connected Products," accessed December 23, 2024, https://foundation.mozilla.org/en/privacynotincluded/.
24. Michiel de Jong, Jan-Christoph Borchardt, and Hugo Roy, "Terms of Service; Didn't Read," 2024, https://tosdr.org.
25. Salman Ravoof, "DuckDuckGo Review: The Privacy-Focused Search Engine," Kinsta, June 30, 2021, https://kinsta.com/blog/duckduckgo-privacy/.

ability and social impact. This trend underscores the growing recognition that ethical responsibility and financial performance are intertwined.

Emerging Technologies and Ethical Considerations

The rapid pace of technological innovation presents both opportunities and challenges for digital ethics. Emerging technologies like AI, blockchain, and the Internet of Things (IoT) require new frameworks for addressing ethical dilemmas.

Artificial Intelligence: AI systems are increasingly used for decision-making in areas such as hiring, lending, and law enforcement. However, algorithmic bias can perpetuate discrimination, and the lack of transparency in AI processes raises questions about accountability. Ethical AI development involves auditing algorithms for bias, ensuring explainability, and involving diverse stakeholders in the design process.

Blockchain and Decentralized Platforms: Blockchain technology offers transparency and user control but also raises concerns about environmental impact and misuse. For example, decentralized social media platforms could empower users to govern their communities but might also facilitate the spread of harmful content. Balancing these trade-offs requires careful consideration of governance structures and ethical safeguards.

The Internet of Things: IoT devices, from smart thermostats to wearable health monitors, collect vast amounts of data about users' daily lives. While these devices offer convenience, they also pose significant privacy risks. Ethical IoT development involves minimizing data collection, securing devices against hacking, and providing users with clear control over their information.

Moving from Awareness to Action

The practical applications of digital ethics are as diverse as the challenges they aim to address. From developing ethical guidelines in organizations to empowering consumers with tools and resources, these efforts require collaboration across sectors. As technology continues to evolve, the principles of transparency, accountability, and trust will remain essential for navigating the complexities of the digital age.

By embracing these practices, individuals and organizations can create a more ethical and equitable digital ecosystem. The path forward lies not only in recognizing the importance of digital ethics but also in translating that awareness into concrete actions that benefit both society and the individual.

6.7 Conclusion: Building an Ethical Digital Future

Revisiting the Ethical Landscape

The digital age presents extraordinary opportunities to enhance lives, connect people, and drive innovation. However, these advancements come with significant ethical responsibilities. From the foundational principles of digital ethics to the real-world challenges of privacy, security, and regulation, this chapter has explored the complexities of navigating a connected world with integrity and accountability. As technology becomes increasingly integral to every aspect of life, ensuring that its benefits outweigh its risks demands a multifaceted approach rooted in ethical awareness.

Ethical dilemmas in data privacy are not abstract—they manifest in decisions made by governments, corporations, and individuals every day. For instance, contact-tracing apps deployed during the COVID-19 pandemic demonstrated how data could save lives while simultaneously raising concerns about long-term surveillance. Social media platforms illustrated the tension between free speech and harm reduction, grappling with issues such as misinformation, hate speech, and extremist ideologies. These cases highlight the delicate balance required to address the trade-offs inherent in technology use.

Key Lessons and Takeaways

- **The Shift from Compliance to Ethics:** Legal frameworks like GDPR and CCPA are critical for establishing baseline protections, but true digital ethics extends beyond compliance. Organizations must consider not just what they can do with data but what they should do. Ethical decision-making prioritizes the well-being of users and society over short-term profit motives.
- **Balancing Privacy and Public Benefit:** Navigating the privacy minefield involves weighing individual rights against societal needs, particularly during crises. Techniques such as anonymization, pseudonymization, and privacy-enhancing technologies offer pathways to achieve this balance. However, these measures must be implemented transparently and with rigorous oversight.
- **The Role of Social Media Regulation:** Social media platforms wield significant influence over public discourse, making their ethical responsibilities paramount. Content moderation, algorithmic amplification, and transparency are key areas where ethical principles must guide action. Regulation must also adapt to global contexts, balancing cultural differences with universal values.
- **Empowering Consumers:** Ethical technology use is not solely the responsibility of corporations and governments—individuals also play a critical role. Education, awareness, and access to privacy tools empower users to make informed decisions about their data and online interactions.
- **The Promise and Perils of Emerging Technologies:** Technologies such as AI, blockchain, and IoT hold tremendous potential but also pose new ethical challenges. Addressing issues like algorithmic bias, data ownership, and security vulnerabilities requires proactive governance and multidisciplinary collaboration.

The Path Forward: Collaborative Solutions

Building an ethical digital future requires collective effort. Governments, corporations, civil society organizations, and individuals must work together to create a technology ecosystem that prioritizes trust, transparency, and accountability. Policymakers should develop regulations that protect user rights without stifling innovation. Companies must embed ethical principles into their operations, adopting privacy-by-design frameworks and engaging with diverse stakeholders. Educational institutions should equip students with the skills and knowledge to navigate ethical dilemmas, fostering a culture of critical thinking and responsible decision-making.

Global Collaboration: In a borderless digital world, addressing ethical challenges requires global cooperation. Initiatives like the **Christchurch Call**, which brings together governments and tech companies to combat online extremism, demonstrate the potential for collective action.[26] Similarly, international standards for privacy and data protection, such as the EU's **DSA**, offer models for harmonizing regulatory approaches across jurisdictions.[27]

Advancing Ethical Innovation: Ethical considerations should not be seen as barriers to progress but as catalysts for innovation. Companies that prioritize ethics often gain competitive advantages, attracting loyal customers, talented employees, and ethical investors. By integrating ethics into product development, organizations can create technologies that are not only effective but also equitable and trustworthy.

A Call to Action

As students, professionals, and global citizens, we all have a role to play in shaping the future of digital technology. The decisions we make today—whether in designing software, crafting policies, or simply choosing how we interact online—will determine whether technology serves as a tool for empowerment or exploitation.

The principles outlined in this chapter—autonomy, transparency, accountability, and fairness—provide a foundation for ethical decision-making in the digital age. By embracing these values, we can create a world where technology enhances human dignity, protects individual rights, and fosters collective progress.

The journey toward an ethical digital future is ongoing, and its success depends on our collective commitment to act with integrity, empathy, and foresight. Let this chapter serve as both a guide and an invitation to engage in this critical endeavor.

26. Rachel Wolbers, "The Future of the Christchurch Call to Action: How to Build Multistakeholder Initiatives to Address Content Moderation Challenges," *Journal of Law, Technology, & the Internet* 15, no. 1 (2024): 106.
27. Aina Turillazzi, Federico Casolari, Mariarosaria Taddeo, and Luciano Floridi, "The Digital Services Act: An Analysis of Its Ethical, Legal, and Social Implications," *SSRN Electronic Journal* (2022), https://doi.org/10.2139/ssrn.4007389.

Discussion Questions

1. **Defining Digital Ethics**

    - In your own words, explain the concept of digital ethics. Why is it important to go beyond legal compliance when addressing issues of data privacy and technology use?
    - Can you think of an example where a company acted legally but unethically? How could they have handled the situation differently?

2. **Balancing Privacy and Public Benefit**

    - Discuss the ethical challenges of data collection during emergencies, such as the COVID-19 pandemic. Do you believe public health needs should outweigh individual privacy rights in such cases? Why or why not?
    - How can governments and organizations ensure that temporary surveillance measures do not become permanent? What safeguards would you recommend?

3. **Social Media Regulation**

    - Social media platforms often face criticism for both over-moderating and under-moderating content. How should platforms balance the need for free speech with the obligation to reduce harm caused by misinformation or hate speech?
    - Do you agree with Twitter's decision to ban political advertisements? How might this policy impact smaller campaigns or grassroots movements?

4. **Privacy Tools and Consumer Empowerment**

    - How can individuals take control of their privacy in a digital world where data collection is pervasive? What tools or practices do you use, or would you recommend, to protect personal information?
    - Why do you think many people ignore or skim through privacy policies? How could organizations make these policies more accessible and meaningful?

5. **Emerging Technologies**

    - Discuss the ethical implications of AI in decision-making processes such as hiring or credit approval. What safeguards should organizations implement to reduce bias and ensure fairness?
    - The IoT provides convenience but also raises privacy concerns. How

should manufacturers balance data collection with user autonomy and security?

6. **Trust and Transparency**

    - Transparency is often cited as a cornerstone of ethical data practices. What does true transparency look like in practice, and how can organizations avoid overwhelming users with too much information?
    - Share your thoughts on whether companies like Apple, which market themselves as privacy-focused, are genuinely committed to digital ethics or if this is primarily a marketing strategy.

7. **Ethical Decision-Making Frameworks**

    - Apply the three-part ethical framework (purpose, proportionality, and accountability) to a real-world scenario, such as a health app collecting user data. What recommendations would you make to the organization involved?
    - Do you believe ethical decision-making should be a responsibility shared by all employees in an organization, or should it rest with leadership and specialized ethics teams? Why?

8. **Global Perspectives**

    - Compare the approaches to social media regulation in different countries (e.g., the EU, US, and China). Which approach do you believe is most effective, and why?
    - Should there be a universal standard for digital ethics and data privacy, or should cultural and political differences guide individual countries' regulations? Explain your reasoning.

Chapter 7

From Typewriters to Tweets

Media in the Age of Cybersecurity

Lamia Zia, PhD

Learning Outcomes

- Describe the evolution of journalism from pre-digital practices to today's cyber-driven media landscape.
- Explain the intersection between journalism and cybersecurity, identifying key risks journalists face in the digital age.
- Analyze the impact of digital platforms on journalistic practices, editorial independence, and source protection.
- Identify common cybersecurity threats to journalists and media organizations, including phishing, ransomware, surveillance, and data breaches.
- Evaluate tools and best practices for digital safety, such as encryption, VPNs, secure messaging apps, and newsroom cybersecurity protocols.
- Discuss ethical challenges in balancing speed, accuracy, and source confidentiality in modern journalism.
- Explore the implications of AI and emerging technologies on the future of journalism and media credibility.
- Develop critical awareness of digital media literacy, misinformation risks, and the importance of cyber hygiene in journalism.

Key Terms

- **Encryption**: A method of securing digital communication to prevent unauthorized access, widely used in protecting journalistic sources.
- **Phishing**: Fraudulent attempts to obtain sensitive information via deceptive digital communications.
- **End-to-End Encryption (E2EE)**: A secure communication protocol that prevents third parties from accessing data while it's transferred.
- **Misinformation**: False or inaccurate information that is spread regardless of

intent.

- **Disinformation**: Deliberately misleading or biased information spread to deceive.
- **Digital Literacy**: The ability to find, evaluate, and communicate information via digital platforms responsibly and securely.
- **Editorial Independence**: The freedom of journalists to make editorial decisions without influence from external pressures or corporate entities.
- **Panopticism**: A concept of constant surveillance that influences behavior, applied here to describe digital self-censorship.
- **Algorithmic Bias**: Systemic errors in AI and algorithms that result in unfair outcomes, often influencing news dissemination.
- **Deepfake**: AI-generated synthetic media used to impersonate individuals or falsify visual/audio content.
- **Citizen Journalism**: The collection, dissemination, and analysis of news by the general public using digital technology.
- **AI News Anchor**: Artificial intelligence-powered avatars used to present news content, a growing trend in media automation.
- **Signal**: A secure messaging app widely used by journalists for private communication.
- **Cyber Hygiene**: Habits and practices that ensure safe and secure use of digital devices and networks.

7.1 Before the Digital Deluge: A Journalist's Tale

Let me begin with a personal journey.

The year was 2003. I was a journalist in a bustling daily newsroom, one of those places where the air smelled of ink, urgency, and ambition. The good old days, as we now like to call them. But back then, they were simply the days we knew.

Journalism, at that time, was physical. It was about pounding the pavement, chasing leads, knocking on doors, and sitting face-to-face with sources. Truth was something you pursued with persistence, patience, and presence not with a search bar.

My mornings did not begin with a glowing digital screen. There were no notifications, no tweets, no endless stream of updates competing for attention. Instead, there was the sharp buzz of a traditional alarm clock, often followed by a call from the editor—brief, direct, and purposeful. That call set the tone for the day.

Armed with a worn-out pen, a trusty notebook, and an insatiable curiosity, I would step into the field. Reporting meant observation, conversation, and intuition. There were no digital distractions, no algorithmic pressures, and certainly no looming fear of cyber surveillance or invisible audiences watching every move. The story lived in the streets, in people's voices, and in the journalist's ability to listen and interpret.

Each day was an adventure. Covering events meant being on the scene, sharp as a tack, soaking up the details like a sponge. Meeting sources was a delicate dance of trust and persuasion, no encrypted apps, just a quiet corner in a café and a promise to keep their words safe. Information wasn't handed to you on a digital screen; you had to dig for it. And when I finally returned to the newsroom, head buzzing with stories, it felt like carrying a treasure chest of raw truth, ready to be shaped into something meaningful.

No Twitter, no Facebook, no rapid-fire WhatsApp messages that shrink communication to fractions of a second. And guess what? Life was simpler. Back then, communication moved at a human pace, meetings happened face-to-face, and stories took time to unfold. There were no doomscrolling or viral distractions pulling attention in a hundred different directions, just pure, undiluted focus. Jotting down notes by hand wasn't just a habit; it was second nature. Typing out stories on a clunky computer with no internet access felt almost meditative, allowing for deep reflection and deliberate storytelling.

Fast forward to today, and the landscape of journalism has transformed beyond recognition.

We no longer just report the news, we exist within it, in real time, across digital platforms. Journalism has moved from the newsroom to the network, from print columns to timelines, from deadlines to continuous updates. This shift has given rise to what we now call cyber journalism.

Cyber journalism is not merely journalism on the internet. It is a redefinition of how news is gathered, produced, distributed, and consumed in a digitally connected world. It is shaped by speed, interactivity, data, and global reach. A story can break, trend, evolve, and disappear within hours sometimes minutes.

But with this transformation comes a new set of challenges.

The journalist today is not only a storyteller but also a digital navigator. They must verify information in an age of misinformation, protect sources in a world of surveillance, and maintain credibility in an environment driven by clicks, shares, and algorithms. The tools have changed but so have the risks.

Where once the biggest challenge was accessing information, today the challenge is filtering it. Where once journalists feared missing a story, today they fear being misled by one.

This chapter explores that journey from the tactile, grounded practice of traditional journalism to the fast-paced, complex ecosystem of cyber journalism. It examines how technology has reshaped the profession, not just technically, but ethically, socially, and psychologically.

Because in the end, while the medium has evolved, the core question remains the same:

How do we find and tell the truth in a world where information is everywhere?

Anthony Giddens (1990) offers critical perspective on the transformation brought about by digital technology. He asserts that "the problem of order is here seen as one of time-space distanciation, the conditions under which time and space are organized so as to connect presence and absence. This issue has to be conceptually distinguished from that of the 'boundedness' of social systems" (p. 14). In the pre-digital era, the connection between presence and absence was more clearly defined; journalists had to be physically present to cover stories, relying on tangible interactions and firsthand experiences.

The absence of digital immediacy allowed for a more structured and less chaotic flow of information, offering a greater sense of control over narratives and timelines.

Today, those boundaries have all but dissolved. Digital media has fundamentally reorganized the way time and space intersect in journalism. Journalists can report in real-time from anywhere in the world, but this unprecedented connectivity comes at a cost. The pressure to be constantly available, to react instantly, and to produce content at an ever-accelerating pace has reshaped journalism into an unrelenting 24-7 cycle.

Cybersecurity? What cybersecurity? Back then, we didn't worry about our phones being hacked or our data being stolen. I used a phone, not a smartphone—no apps, no tracking, no breaches. It was a world where the biggest "hack" was someone peeking over your shoulder while you wrote.

In the early 2000s, journalism operated in a landscape markedly different from today's digitally driven environment. Before the widespread adoption of social media, the profession was deeply rooted in traditional methods of newsgathering and dissemination. Journalists like Christiane Amanpour and Robert Fisk (Fisk 2012) exemplified the era's commitment to on-the-ground reporting. During the 2003 Iraq War, Amanpour reported directly from conflict zones, relying on satellite communications and face-to-face interviews to convey the realities of war to the global audience. Similarly, Fisk's in-depth reports provided unique perspectives, shaped by firsthand experiences and direct interactions with sources, Public Broadcasting Service (PBS) reported (2023).

In local newsrooms, reporters pursued stories through personal interactions, attending community events, conducting in-person interviews, and sifting through physical records. The verification of information was a meticulous process, often involving cross-referencing multiple sources and consulting experts directly. The absence of digital tools meant that journalists had to rely heavily on their investigative skills and professional networks to uncover and confirm facts. The dissemination of news was also a more deliberate process. With print newspapers, television broadcasts, and radio as the primary channels, journalists worked within set publication schedules. This allowed for comprehensive editing and fact-checking before stories reached the public. The pace of news was measured, providing audiences with thoroughly vetted information at regular intervals.

However, this period was not without its challenges. The limitations in technology meant that real-time reporting was rare, and reaching a global audience required substantial resources. The lack of instant communication tools made coordinating coverage in rapidly developing situations more complex. Despite these hurdles, the foundational journalistic principles of accuracy, integrity, and firsthand reporting remained steadfast, guiding journalists in their mission to inform the public.

Fast-forward to today, and journalism has taken a digital nosedive or should I say, a quantum leap. The advent of the internet and social media changed the media landscape in ways we could never have imagined. What used to be a race to the story is now a race against algorithms and cyber threats. Information travels faster, but so do misinformation and data breaches. What changed the media? Everything. The tools, the risks, the pace, and even the storytelling. But at its core, journalism still carries the same torch: finding the truth and sharing it with the world. The journey just got a lot more complicated and a lot more digital.

In an increasingly interconnected digital age, the media faces both unprecedented opportunities and formidable challenges. Journalists now have access to vast pools of information and tools for instant communication, allowing them to deliver stories in real time. However, with these advantages come significant risks to data privacy, source protection, and information security. Cyber threats, surveillance, and data breaches are not just abstract concerns, they are tangible dangers that threaten journalistic integrity and freedom of the press.

This chapter offers a comprehensive analysis of cyber breaches that have impacted media organizations, exploring the challenges and vulnerabilities they face in the digital age. It includes a personal narrative from the author, who has firsthand experience working as an international journalist in the South Asian region, providing a valuable lens into the evolving landscape of journalism. The chapter also provides a comparative overview of traditional media practices before and after the advent of social media, examining how digital platforms have revolutionized the field of journalism and storytelling. With the rise of social media, traditional media has undergone a significant transformation, shifting the way news is gathered, disseminated, and consumed.

Furthermore, this chapter addresses the crucial aspect of how journalists safeguard their sensitive data and information in an increasingly digitalized world. As cyber threats continue to grow, the need for strong cybersecurity measures within media organizations has become more critical than ever. The discussion highlights what cybersecurity means to the media industry, emphasizing the importance of protecting journalistic integrity and source confidentiality in the face of evolving digital threats. By focusing on these key areas, this chapter aims to shed light on the complex relationship between cybersecurity and digital media, offering a comprehensive perspective on the ongoing challenges and opportunities that define modern journalism. By understanding these issues, we can better appreciate the importance of robust cybersecurity practices in ensuring that journalism remains a cornerstone of democratic society.

Key Questions to Explore in This Chapter

To deepen the understanding of the relationship between cybersecurity and digital media, this chapter explores several critical questions, including the following:

- Why is cybersecurity essential for modern journalism?
- What are the specific cyber threats that media organizations and journalists face today?
- How have these threats evolved over time, and what new risks are emerging?
- What are the most common cybersecurity challenges faced by journalists?
- How do journalists protect their sources from surveillance and digital attacks?

- What measures can journalists take to secure their communication and data storage?
- What happens when cybersecurity measures fail, and how do journalists recover from breaches?
- How effective are current cybersecurity measures, such as encrypted messaging and secure communication?

7.2 Life of Today's Journalist: A Digital Tightrope

The life of a journalist today is like walking a digital tightrope, fast, high-pressure, and full of surprises. Mornings often start not with coffee and a quiet read of the paper but with a cascade of notifications. Breaking news, trending hashtags, press releases, and emails flood in before the day even begins. The pace is relentless, and the journalist's phone is practically an extension of their hand. Today's journalists experience a world where information flows like water from a firehose. Leads come not just from sources but from social media platforms, forums, and even algorithmic suggestions. A story might break on Twitter, spread across Instagram, and spiral into a full-blown media frenzy on TikTok before noon. Fact-checking is no longer just about knocking on doors; it's about sifting through digital trails and verifying viral claims, all while the clock is ticking.

The Multitasking Maestro

Gone are the days of focusing solely on writing. Today's journalist wears many hats, researcher, writer, photographer, videographer, and sometimes even social media manager. They're expected to record interviews, edit videos, and post updates in real-time, all while juggling deadlines. The newsroom has extended into coffee shops, home offices, and anywhere with a strong Wi-Fi signal.

In the age of data breaches and cyber hackers, today's journalist lives with the constant shadow of cyber threats. Sensitive stories require encrypted communication, secure storage, and often anonymity for sources. Journalists must master digital tools to protect their work and identities while also staying alert to phishing attempts and hacking risks. It's a digital battlefield, and the stakes couldn't be higher.

Social media is both a blessing and a curse in all means. It's a goldmine for stories, feedback, and reach, but it's also a minefield of trolls, misinformation, and cancel culture. Growing up in this era, one must tread carefully, knowing that one misstep could spark a digital backlash. However, as college students preparing to enter the professional world, it's equally important to focus on building a strong personal brand, engaging effectively with audiences, and staying ahead of constantly evolving trends.

Case Study: Online Harassment of Journalists in Hong Kong – A Global Warning

In September 2024, Reuters (2024) reported a concerning escalation in the harassment of journalists in Hong Kong. According to the Hong Kong Journalists Association (HKJA), at least 15 journalists, along with their families and professional associates, were subjected to targeted intimidation campaigns. Anonymous complaints were sent by self-proclaimed "patriots" via email and letter, while others were doxed and attacked within private Facebook groups. Some even received threats against their lives or found their names smeared with defamatory edits on Wikipedia pages.

This pattern of coordinated digital harassment is not an isolated incident, it reflects a broader, global trend in which journalists are increasingly vulnerable to online abuse, surveillance, and psychological intimidation. In Hong Kong, these attacks are occurring within the broader context of a crackdown on dissent following the 2019 pro-democracy protests. But similar tactics are being used in other regions as well, often as a strategy to silence critical voices and erode press freedom without overt censorship.

The case illustrates how cyber harassment can now transcend individual journalists, threatening their families, employers, and even their personal data privacy. What once may have occurred behind closed doors is now being played out across social media platforms, coordinated chat groups, and anonymous communication channels, often leaving little trace of accountability.

The Reward Amid the Chaos

Despite the challenges, today's journalist is still driven by the same core values: uncovering the truth, holding power accountable, and telling stories that matter. The tools may have changed, and the stakes may be higher, but the heart of journalism remains. It's a life of constant motion, where every day brings new stories, new challenges, and the chance to make a difference. The intersection of media and cybersecurity has become a critical area of study in the digital age. Journalists, as frontline information gatherers, face increasing threats to their data security and privacy due to the proliferation of cyberattacks and digital interference.

7.3 Tools and Techniques for Data Protection

In today's digital landscape, data protection is a critical concern for journalists, who often work with sensitive information and vulnerable sources, as explained in detail in other chapters of this book. Encryption has become a fundamental tool for safeguarding communications and end-to-end encryption (E2EE) services are widely recommended for secure interactions. According to Pearlman (2020), encryption is essential for journalists operating in hostile environments, ensuring that their conversations remain confidential and protected from surveillance or interception. The Freedom of the Press Foundation emphasizes that "encryption should be part of every journalist's toolkit," highlighting its role in protecting data such as computer files or messages from unauthorized access (Abrams 2024). This has been discussed in detail in other chapters of the book.

According to the Electronic Frontier Foundation (EFF), a digital and free-speech activist group, "Signal is widely used by human rights activists and journalists." Signal provides strong E2EE that secures both text messages and voice calls. EFF states that while other applications, such as WhatsApp, use similar cryptographic techniques, Signal is considered superior because it implements the best practices for secure messaging (Trilling 2017). Additionally, due to Signal's privacy-centric architecture, even under legal pressure, the only user data that can be provided to authorities includes minimal metadata, such as the date and time of registration and last connectivity to the service.

For example, in 2016, Open Whisper Systems, the developers of Signal, received a subpoena from the US government seeking user data as part of an ongoing criminal investigation. Due to Signal's stringent data retention policies, the company was unable to provide any meaningful user information beyond the bare minimum—specifically, the date and time of account registration and the last recorded connection to the service. This incident highlights Signal's unwavering commitment to user privacy and its effectiveness in protecting communication from external scrutiny, reinforcing its reputation as a trusted tool for secure messaging (Farivar 2016).

Is Cybersecurity Training in Newsrooms Adequate Enough?

As cyber threats continue to evolve and target the media industry, a critical question arises: Are journalists adequately equipped to protect their work and sources from digital risks? The increasing reliance on digital tools for communication and reporting has exposed journalists to cyber threats such as hacking, surveillance, and data breaches. However, despite the growing awareness of these risks, many newsrooms still lack sufficient cybersecurity training, leaving journalists vulnerable to attacks that can compromise their professional integrity and the safety of their sources.

According to a UNESCO report (2018), a significant number of journalists, particularly those in developing countries, lack the technical skills and resources needed to implement advanced cybersecurity measures. This gap in knowledge not only jeopardizes sensitive information but also poses a significant threat to press freedom and journalistic independence. Without adequate training, journalists are at a higher risk of exposing confidential data and compromising their investigative work.

Recognizing the pressing need to bridge the cybersecurity gap, major media organizations have proactively initiated measures to safeguard their operations and personnel such as PBS (n.d.), which has developed the "PBS Cyber Champions" program. This initiative offers comprehensive courses covering topics such as phishing, social engineering, malware defense, and mobile security, equipping individuals with essential skills to protect their data and networks.

In addition to internal programs, collaborative efforts have emerged to bolster journalists' cybersecurity competencies. The Global Cyber Alliance (GCA n.d.), for instance, has introduced the "Cybersecurity Toolkit for Journalists." This resource provides independent journalists and small newsrooms with tools and information to protect their sources and maintain the integrity of their reporting. The toolkit includes best practice recommendations from the Center for Internet Security (CIS), ensuring that journalists can stay updated on current threats and defenses.

An article in Forbes highlights that while specific cases of journalists successfully thwarting phishing attacks due to cybersecurity training are not widely documented in public sources, the overall effectiveness of such training programs is well-supported. For example, a report by USecure, citing the Ponemon Institute, indicates that cybersecurity risk can be reduced from 60 percent to as low as 10 percent with a good training program (Forbes Technology Council 2023). A study by Beu et al. (2023) conducted in a naturalistic phishing simulation to investigate individual differences that influence susceptibility to such attacks. Their findings suggest that factors such as personality traits, digital literacy, and prior cybersecurity awareness significantly impact one's likelihood of falling victim to phishing.

As phishing tactics evolve in sophistication, relying solely on technological defenses would not be sufficient. Individuals must be equipped with the critical thinking skills necessary to identify deceptive tactics commonly used in phishing attempts. The study demonstrates that while some users may possess technical knowledge, their behavioral tendencies such as overtrusting online sources or failing to verify authenticity, render them vulnerable. To contest these threats effectively, academic institutions, organizations and policymakers must prioritize cybersecurity trainings, workshops, or programs that address cyber issues and teach a culture of vigilance. Strengthening awareness through real-world simulations, such as those conducted in the study, can bridge the gap between knowledge and practice, ensuring that users are prepared to handle evolving cyber threats

Digital Vulnerabilities and Editorial Independence: A Panoptic Dilemma in the Cyber Era

According to Reporters Without Borders (2022), cyber threats pose a growing danger to press freedom and the safety of journalists worldwide. Among the numerous challenges faced by journalists in the cyber era, the overreliance on digital platforms controlled by corporate entities presents a significant threat to editorial independence. The increasing dependence on platforms such as social media, cloud storage, and digital communication tools, many of which are owned by technology conglomerates, introduces vulnerabilities that can undermine journalistic autonomy and ethical reporting. This concern is closely aligned with Jeremy Bentham's concept of panopticism, which Michel Foucault later expanded upon, highlighting the ways in which surveillance leads individuals to regulate their behavior under the assumption that they are constantly being watched (Foucault 1977). In the digital context, journalists are subjected to a modern form of panopticism, wherein the pervasive surveillance capabilities of digital platforms create an environment of self-censorship and restrained editorial decision-making.

According to Lyon (2018), this constant state of digital observation can lead to "anticipatory compliance," where individuals adjust their behavior preemptively to avoid perceived risks. In the journalistic field, such compliance may manifest as self-censorship, avoidance of controversial topics, or hesitance in pursuing investigative leads that could attract unwanted scrutiny from powerful entities.

While journalists and media organizations have sought to implement robust cybersecurity measures, such as encrypted communication channels and decentralized data storage, these efforts are often insufficient in the face of systemic surveillance mechanisms that are deeply embedded in the digital ecosystem. The challenge, therefore, is not only technological but also structural, necessitating broader discussions on media governance, digital sovereignty, and ethical use of technology in journalism. Furthermore, the findings contribute to broader discussions on media literacy, highlighting the need for continuous education on cybersecurity risks within the digital media landscape. Media consumers must not only be aware of misleading information and fake news but also of deceptive cyber tactics that can compromise their personal data and security.

7.4 How Cyber Technologies Have Transformed Media and Journalism

McLuhan's famous dictum, "the medium is the message," from *Understanding Media: The Extensions of Man*, is an essential lens for analyzing how technology shapes journalism and communication. McLuhan's idea about how media technologies transform human perception applies to digital tools and cybersecurity. For example, smartphones, encrypted communication, and social media not only enable journalism but also shape how stories are reported and consumed. Social media itself has become a message for the audience, and the cyber technologies have transformed the media industry, influencing how journalists work, how stories are presented, and how audiences engage with information. This digital revolution presents both opportunities and challenges, reshaping journalism in significant ways:

- Cyber technology enables instant communication and real-time reporting, allowing journalists to gather, verify, and publish news faster than ever. Digital platforms have expanded global reach, removing geographical barriers to media access.
- The pressure to report quickly often compromises accuracy, leading to rushed or incomplete verification processes. The fast-paced nature of digital news amplifies misinformation and the spread of "fake news."
- Journalists are prime targets for cyberattacks, including hacking, phishing, and surveillance, due to their access to sensitive information.
- Leaks of sensitive data, such as source identities and unpublished stories, can endanger lives and careers.

- Freelancers and underfunded organizations struggle to invest in cybersecurity training and tools.
- Platforms like Twitter, Facebook, and Instagram have become vital for information gathering, story dissemination, and audience engagement. Citizen journalism, enabled by smartphones and social media, has democratized reporting, allowing nonprofessionals to break news.
- The rise of unverified and sensationalized content from nonprofessional sources undermines public trust in credible media. Algorithm-driven platforms prioritize engagement over accuracy, amplifying misinformation and sensationalism.
- The shift to digital has disrupted traditional revenue models, with advertising revenue shifting to tech giants like Google and Meta.
- Many journalists now work in freelance or precarious roles, lacking the resources to protect themselves from cyber threats. Reduced funding for investigative journalism limits the ability to invest in cybersecurity and innovation. Journalists are expected to take on multiple roles, including social media management and video production, increasing workloads and job complexity.
- The spread of "deepfakes" and artificial intelligence (AI)–generated content complicates fact-checking and makes it harder to distinguish between truth and fiction. Journalists must dedicate more time and resources to verifying content and debunking falsehoods.
- Online harassment and trolling, often coordinated, have become a significant occupational hazard for journalists. Female and minority journalists face higher levels of online abuse, which can escalate into physical threats.
- Constant exposure to cyber harassment leads to mental health challenges such as anxiety, depression, and burnout. Media organizations need to invest in mental health support and policies to combat online abuse, though many fail to provide adequate support.
- Multimedia storytelling, integrating text, video, audio, and interactive graphics has become more accessible and engaging for audiences. Smaller outlets and independent journalists face challenges in adopting new technologies due to high investment costs.
- Overreliance on digital tools may detract from traditional journalistic values, such as in-depth reporting and human connection.

Hypothetical Scenario: The Case of the Leaked Source

It's 10:00 p.m. on a rainy Thursday night in a metropolitan city. Sophia, an investigative journalist at the digital news outlet, sits in her dimly lit apartment with a mug of cold coffee. She's working on what could be the biggest story of her career: exposing corruption in a powerful multinational corporation. Her source, an anonymous whistleblower known only as "Phoenix," has provided exclusive documents detailing years of fraud and environmental violations. Maya is determined to uncover the truth. What she doesn't realize is that someone is already watching her.

As Sophia reads through the leaked files on her laptop, her phone pings. It's a strange message from an unknown number: "Be careful, Sophia. You're being watched." Her heart skips a beat. She brushes it off as a prank, but an hour later, her laptop freezes. A red warning screen flashes:

"Your files have been encrypted. Pay $50,000 in Bitcoin to recover them."

Sophia feels the weight of the world on her shoulders. Her work, months of investigation, hours of interviews, and sensitive files from Phoenix, might be gone. Worse, if the attackers get access to her source's identity, Phoenix could be in grave danger. She calls her editor, who reminds her of the cybersecurity protocols the newsroom implemented after a similar attack last year. But Sophia didn't follow all the steps. She'd skipped setting up two-factor authentication on her accounts, thinking it would slow her down. She also stored some of Phoenix's documents on her personal cloud drive for quick access something she now regrets deeply.

Determined not to give up, Sophia contacts the newsroom's cybersecurity team. They help her isolate her infected laptop and retrieve some backup files from the organization's secure server. Meanwhile, the editor reminds her to use encrypted communication tools to contact Phoenix and let them know about the potential breach. But time is running out. The ransomware attackers email her again, threatening to leak her files if she doesn't pay. The newsroom refuses to negotiate with criminals, leaving Sophia feeling both relieved and terrified.

As Sophia continues to fight to secure her files, she faces a moral dilemma. Should she rush to publish the story with the limited files she has recovered, risking inaccuracy and legal challenges? Or should she delay, giving the newsroom's tech team more time to retrieve the data, even though it might alert the corporation to her investigation? Her editor warns her of another layer of risk: the possibility that Phoenix's identity might be revealed. If that happens, not only will her source's safety be jeopardized, but future whistleblowers may fear coming forward.

The Outcome

The next morning, Sophia stands in the newsroom, exhausted but reflective. The cybersecurity team managed to recover most of her files and safeguard Phoenix's identity, but she knows the outcome could have been disastrous. Speaking to her colleagues, she shares her experience.

"Journalism today isn't just about chasing stories, it's about protecting them. We're not just fighting against lies and cover-ups anymore; we're fighting against cyberattacks, surveillance, and data breaches. If we don't secure our work, we risk losing more than just a story. We risk lives, careers, and trust."

Takeaway: This scenario highlights the tightrope journalists walk in the digital age. It highlights the importance of using secure communication tools and implementing strong cybersecurity practices (e.g., two-factor authentication, secure backups).

7.5 From Typewriters to Tweets: A Journalist's Tale Across Time

It's 1995. The newsroom hums with the rhythmic clack of typewriters, punctuated by the occasional ring of a rotary phone. The air smells faintly of coffee and ink-stained paper. Journalists like Sam are the boots-on-the-ground truth seekers, armed with a notepad, a pen, and a stubborn determination to uncover the facts. Sam's day begins with a handshake and a knowing nod to his editor. There are no smartphones to ping with breaking news updates; Sam gets his assignments face-to-face. By mid-morning, he's off to city hall, interviewing officials and flipping through dusty archives to piece together the story of a brewing scandal.

No email, no Google. Just Sam, his instincts, and a trusty landline to check in with sources. The day ends back at the newsroom, where he types his findings on a battered typewriter. When the final draft is handed in, the story is out of his hands until it's inked onto paper and delivered to the public with the morning coffee. It's slow, deliberate, and tangible. The only "data breach" Sam worries about is losing his notebook or misplacing a critical source's phone number.

The Present: Digital Chaos

Fast-forward to 2025. The newsroom looks and sounds entirely different. Journalists like Sam's granddaughter, Alina, no longer carry notebooks; they carry smartphones, laptops, and external hard drives. The once noisy typewriters have been replaced by the silent hum of sleek computers. And the quiet anticipation of tomorrow's headline is drowned out by the constant clamor of the 24-7 news cycle. Alina wakes up to a flood of notifications. Breaking news. Viral tweets. Comments from readers halfway across the globe. Her day starts not at the city hall archives, but on social media. She scours Twitter hashtags, Reddit threads, and live videos for leads. Instead of meeting her editor in person, they communicate via Slack or Zoom.

When she chases a story, Alina doesn't just face the challenge of finding the truth, she faces the digital minefield of misinformation, phishing attempts, and cyberattacks. Her notes are stored in encrypted cloud drives, her communications happen over digital devices, and she's acutely aware that one mistake in cybersecurity could cost her source their anonymity or their life.

Unlike her grandfather, Alina doesn't have the luxury of a nightly deadline. Her stories are published online the moment they're written, often updated in real time. Comments pour in instantly, some constructive, others trolling or abusive. And while Sam only worried about how his story would land with readers, Alina worries about how algorithms will rank her story and whether it will cut through the noise of millions of competing narratives.

Sam and Alina may live worlds apart, but they share a core purpose: to tell the truth. Yet their tools, challenges, and environments couldn't be more different. Sam worked with limited resources, relying on in-person interviews and paper archives. Alina, by contrast, has the internet at her fingertips but must investigate a flood of unverified and misleading information. For Sam, deadlines came once a day, giving him time to dig deep. Alina lives in a world of constant deadlines, racing to keep up with the pace of breaking news online.

Sam never worried about his work being stolen or hacked. Alina, however, encrypts every file and triple-checks her digital defenses, knowing her work and her sources could be exposed at any moment. Despite the vast technological and cultural shifts, one thing hasn't changed: journalism's mission to inform and empower the public. Both Sam and Alina are bound by the same ethical responsibilities to protect their sources, verify their facts, and hold power accountable. The medium has evolved, but the message remains the same.

The Future: A Shared Legacy

As a former media practitioner and a current media educator, I have had the unique opportunity to witness and experience both the pre-digital and post-digital landscapes of journalism. Having experienced the practices and challenges of both eras, I can attest to the profound transformations brought about by the digital revolution. Contemporary journalists face an increasingly complex array of challenges, ranging from the data privacy in the face of cyber threats to adapting their workflows and strategies to meet the expectations of a digitally savvy and hyperconnected audience. This dual perspective allows for a comprehensive understanding of the evolving dynamics of media production, dissemination, and consumption in the digital age.

Traditional journalists operating within traditional newsrooms now face the formidable challenge of keeping pace with social media influencers, vloggers, and content creators who wield significant power in shaping public discourse. The power of agenda-setting, once predominantly held by established media institutions, has increasingly shifted to these digital creators. Social media platforms empower influencers to reach vast audiences directly, bypassing traditional gatekeeping mechanisms. This democratization of content creation has disrupted the conventional hierarchy of media, allowing individuals without institutional affiliations to set trends, drive narratives, and influence public opinion. Consequently, traditional journalists must navigate a media landscape where their authority to define and prioritize issues is no longer uncontested, adapting their practices to remain relevant in this rapidly evolving digital ecosystem.

Journalists today find themselves in an increasingly complex and multifaceted professional landscape, grappling with challenges that span both technological and cultural domains. On one front, they must protect their stories, sources, and data from cyber threats, including hackers, phishing attempts, and surveillance. The rise of digital tools has introduced vulnerabilities that make sensitive journalistic work a prime target for malicious actors, putting not only their work but also their sources' safety at risk.

On another front, journalists are contending with the rapid evolution of social media and the rise of influencers and digital content creators. These new players have reshaped the media ecosystem, often setting public agendas with speed and reach that traditional journalism struggles to match. This competition for audience attention, coupled with the pressure to adapt to algorithms, trends, and the nonstop news cycle, adds to the already heavy burden journalists carry. As a result, today's journalists must master both cybersecurity practices and digital storytelling strategies to protect their credibility and relevance in a media environment that is more dynamic and demanding than ever before.

7.6 What Journalists Think About Cybersecurity?

There was a time when cybersecurity felt like something that belonged in the IT department, something journalists didn't have to worry about. They were more concerned with tracking down sources, verifying facts, and chasing deadlines than with encrypting our emails or worrying about hackers lurking in the shadows. During my journalism days, "security" meant locking up our notes in a drawer or meeting a source in a café, not setting up complex passwords or navigating encrypted communication platforms.

But the world has changed. Cybersecurity is no longer just a technical field or issue; it's for everyone! Whether you're a journalist, a communications student, or simply someone exploring the digital age, the reality is that every piece of information you share, store, or consume carries inherent risks and responsibilities. The same platforms that empower us to connect, report, and share ideas are also vulnerable. For instance, social media platforms like Twitter (now X), Facebook, and Instagram, which serve as essential tools for journalists and communicators to disseminate news and engage with audiences, have been exploited for misinformation campaigns, account takeovers, and data breaches. In 2020, Twitter experienced a major security breach, where high-profile accounts, including those of journalists and political figures, were hacked to promote cryptocurrency scams (BBC News, 2020). Similarly, Facebook's Cambridge Analytica scandal exposed how the personal data of millions of users was harvested without consent, raising concerns about privacy and manipulation of public opinion (Confessore 2018).

These incidents highlight the double-edged nature of digital platforms: While they provide unprecedented opportunities for communication and storytelling, they also present significant vulnerabilities that can jeopardize privacy, security, and credibility. The fight for truth has always been tough, but today, it's not just fought with words and reporting, it's fought in cyberspace, in encrypted files, and behind firewalls.

Best Practices for Secure Communication

Whether you're interviewing a whistleblower, discussing sensitive leads with your editor, or just trying to keep your sources safe, secure communication is no longer a luxury, it's a necessity. So, how do journalists stay ahead of cyber threats without losing their minds? They rely on a mix of savvy tech tools, smart habits, and a bit of good old-fashioned caution. Let's say you're a top investigative journalist, think James Bond, but with a laptop instead of a martini. You wouldn't just text a source using your regular phone, right? That's why many journalists use tools like Signal, an encrypted messaging app that ensures your conversations remain private. Signal's latest feature allows users to chat without sharing phone numbers, ideal for journalists who don't want their personal digits floating around in the digital ether.

Second, major traditional media organizations now have dedicated cybersecurity teams, advising reporters on how to avoid pitfalls like phishing scams and spyware attacks. Some outlets even provide journalists with dedicated devices or access to "sandboxed" environments, where they can work on sensitive stories without leaving digital breadcrumbs behind. Think of it like a secret bunker anything happening inside stays protected, making it harder for snoopers to track or intercept critical information. Whether covering cybercrime or political scandals, journalists know that the safer their workspace, the more secure their story.

Third, A journalist's inbox can be a battlefield loaded with dodgy links, too-good-to-be-true tips, and fake PR requests. The golden rule? If something looks suspicious, it probably is. Reporters are trained to spot red flags and think twice before opening unexpected attachments or clicking links from unknown senders. Cyber hygiene might not be glamorous, but it's the difference between securing a groundbreaking story and becoming the story yourself. And let's not forget password managers and VPNs are the unsung heroes of secure digital habits.

Thus, media organizations operate in a high-risk digital environment, where journalists routinely handle sensitive information and interact with vulnerable sources. With cyber threats such as phishing, data breaches, and surveillance becoming more sophisticated, the need for proactive cybersecurity measures is no longer optional, it's essential. According to the Forbes Technology Council (2023), cybersecurity risk can be reduced from 60% to as low as 10% with effective training programs. This statistic underscores a crucial reality: well-informed, well-trained employees are the first line of defense against cyberattacks.

Given their role as guardians of public information and accountability, newsrooms have a particular responsibility to protect their operations and personnel from digital threats. Training programs should cover practical skills such as identifying phishing attempts, using encrypted communication, managing passwords securely, and understanding the ethical implications of digital reporting. As journalists increasingly work across digital platforms and store data online, these competencies are critical not just for individual safety, but for upholding journalistic integrity and protecting the confidentiality of sources.

Breaking News: We've Been Hacked!

It was a regular Tuesday night in the newsroom. The buzz of keyboard clacks and muted phone calls filled the air as reporters chased deadlines. Stories about politics, climate change, and the economy were all lined up, ready to go live by midnight. But then, without warning, the screens started going black. At first, people thought it was a power surge. "Check the main server," the IT tech muttered, already rushing to the back room. Within minutes, the realization sank in this wasn't a glitch. This was a full-blown cyberattack.

This wasn't the first time a media organization had been hit. Back in 2021, Sinclair Broadcast Group, one of the largest television operators in the United States, suffered a crippling ransomware attack (GJIN 2022). Hackers had infiltrated their systems, locking out employees from their files and encrypting crucial data. Entire broadcasts were halted, leaving local stations unable to deliver the nightly news. Ads stopped running, revenue bled out, and the company lost millions. But this attack wasn't just about money. It was about control. Sinclair's ability to communicate with its audience had been silenced, a chilling reminder of how vulnerable the media is in the digital age.

Back in the newsroom, the head of security was piecing together how the attack might have started. "It's always an email," he sighed, holding up the evidence. The phishing email had been crafted perfectly disguised as a message from a trusted executive, complete with the company's logo. Someone in accounting had clicked the link, and that was all it took. The hackers were in.

Media organizations are prime targets for cyberattacks. They hold vast amounts of sensitive information confidential sources, unpublished stories, internal communications—all of which can be exploited. These attacks can have various motivations. For example, in April 2015, the French television network TV5Monde experienced a politically motivated cyberattack where hackers claiming allegiance to the Islamic State (ISIS) disrupted broadcasts and defaced social media accounts with pro-ISIS messages, Associated Press (2015) reported. The media's role as a watchdog makes it a natural target for those seeking to suppress the truth or manipulate public perception. A compromised newsroom isn't just a financial problem; it's a direct threat to democracy.

For the reporters and editors, the attack was deeply personal. Journalists pride themselves on their ability to uncover stories and hold power accountable. Losing control of their platforms felt like a betrayal not just to them, but to the public they served. At Sinclair, broadcasts eventually resumed, but the damage had been done. The company spent months recovering, upgrading security protocols, and rebuilding trust with viewers. Meanwhile, the hackers got away with the data, leaving no trace of their identities. In today's media landscape, cyberattacks aren't an "if" but a "when." Newsrooms worldwide have started to adapt. Organizations are investing in cybersecurity training, teaching employees how to spot phishing attempts, and implementing encrypted communication tools to protect their sources. But the threats keep evolving, and staying one step ahead is a constant battle.

That Tuesday night, as the newsroom's lights flickered back on and reporters returned to their desks, there was a lingering tension in the air. The attack was a stark reminder that in the fight for truth, the battlefield isn't just on the streets or in interviews, it's also in cyberspace. As mentioned earlier in the chapter, for journalists, the job has always been about uncovering the truth. Now, it's also about protecting it.

7.7 The Biggest Dilemma of a Journalist

In today's fast-paced and interconnected world, journalists face a profound and multifaceted dilemma: how to balance the core principles of truth and integrity with the demands and challenges of the digital age. This dilemma is not a single issue but a complex intersection of ethical, technological, and societal pressures that shape the modern journalist's role.

One of the most significant challenges for journalists today is combating the flood of misinformation and disinformation. Social media platforms have democratized the spread of information, allowing anyone with internet access to shape narratives and influence opinions. While this openness has empowered marginalized voices, it has also created a fertile ground for falsehoods to thrive. Journalists now not only compete with these unverified sources but are also tasked with debunking misinformation, often in real time. This adds an immense burden to their work, as the speed of news dissemination often leaves little room for the rigorous verification that journalism traditionally requires.

Balancing Speed and Accuracy

The relentless 24-7 news cycle demands constant updates and breaking news, pressuring journalists to publish quickly. The rise of digital platforms and social media means that being the first to report a story often matters as much as or more than getting it right. This tension between speed and accuracy creates a dangerous environment where the risk of error increases, potentially damaging credibility and public trust. Journalists must tread carefully, ensuring that the race to break news does not compromise the integrity of their reporting.

Protecting Sources in the Age of Cyber Threats

Another pressing concern is the protection of sources in a world increasingly vulnerable to cyber threats and surveillance. Whistleblowers and confidential sources often place their lives and careers in jeopardy to share information with journalists. However, the digital age has made anonymity more challenging to maintain. From email hacks to advanced tracking technologies, the risks to source confidentiality have multiplied. Journalists now have to be not just storytellers but also cybersecurity experts, adopting encrypted communication tools and secure data storage practices to protect their sources and themselves. Despite these challenges, media professionals remain critical to the health of democratic societies. Their work informs the public, exposes injustice, and amplifies voices that might otherwise go unheard. To navigate the dilemmas they face, journalists must adapt and evolve embracing new technologies, prioritizing ethical standards, and fostering deeper connections with their audiences. As emphasized by the International Federation of Journalists (IFJ, 2021), cybersecurity tools and practices are essential for protecting journalists and the integrity of their sources in today's high-risk digital landscape.

7.8 Back to the Future: A Vision for 2050

A new media vision is emerging one shaped by unprecedented integration of technology into human experience, offering both powerful opportunities and profound challenges. The strengths of future media lie in its ability to engage audiences in immersive, personalized, and real-time ways, blurring the lines between content creator and consumer. From holographic journalism to AI-generated investigative reports, the tools of storytelling will become more dynamic, intuitive, and data-rich than ever before.

However, this vision is not without its weaknesses. Increasing reliance on AI and algorithmic curation raises critical concerns about bias, misinformation, and loss of editorial independence. As media systems become more automated and predictive, the risk of eroding human judgment, ethical reasoning, and critical inquiry becomes all the more urgent. There is also the danger of surveillance and data exploitation in the name of personalization, challenging fundamental rights to privacy and autonomy.

Yet, within these tensions lie opportunities: to design more inclusive, secure, and equitable media ecosystems; to train journalists who are not just content creators but ethical technologists; and to reimagine storytelling as a collaborative, global dialogue. Already, the lines between man and machine are beginning to blur. According to The Hindu (2023), India introduced its first AI news anchor, raising questions about whether this innovation represents a groundbreaking milestone or a potential menace to traditional journalism. This development signals the beginning of a new era one where artificial intelligence may not just assist journalism but also perform it.

Fifty years ago, Marshall McLuhan predicted that media would not just shape society but become an extension of human consciousness itself. Today, as we look toward 2050, his vision takes on new dimensions media is no longer confined to screens or printed pages; it has become a living, breathing entity seamlessly interwoven into the fabric of our daily existence. In the world of tomorrow, media will not simply inform us; it will surround us, anticipate us, influence us, and engage us in ways we can scarcely imagine today.

As Dr. Safiya Umoja Noble's Algorithms of Oppression (2018) reveals how algorithmic systems, particularly search engines, can perpetuate harmful racial and gender biases under the guise of neutrality. Her work exposes the reality that without transparency and accountability, AI systems may not correct biases, they may entrench them further. Thus, as journalism increasingly depends on AI-driven tools for data analysis, content delivery, and audience engagement, Noble's study serves as a cautionary lens. It urges media professionals to critically assess whether these tools are truly advancing truth or subtly distorting it based on hidden biases and commercial incentives.

In this context, the promise of AI as a guardian of integrity must be tempered with vigilance, ethical oversight, and an ongoing commitment to exposing and addressing systemic algorithmic discrimination. Noble's work is a reminder that in a digital age, defending journalism requires not only protecting sources and stories, but also interrogating the very tools used to tell them.

The newsroom of 2050 will be no longer a physical space filled with the sound of hurried typing and ringing phones. Instead, it exists in an interconnected, fluid ecosystem powered by AI, quantum computing, and augmented reality. Media and journalists of the future will work side by side with AI co-reporters sentient, data-driven assistants capable of conducting interviews, analyzing vast troves of data in milliseconds, and even predicting events before they unfold. The questions rises here whether these highly sophisticated AI companions will act as protectors of journalistic integrity, constantly scanning the digital landscape for cyber threats, disinformation campaigns, and algorithmic biases, ensuring that the truth remains untarnished.

In this future, the barrier between the physical and digital worlds will dissolve. Satellites and Drones equipped with real-time translation, facial recognition, and deepfake detection will capture breaking news with unprecedented accuracy, broadcasting events to global audiences instantaneously no more language barriers, no more misinformation. Every detail will be verified before the public even hears about it.

And what about experiencing the news? Holo-journalism will transport people to the heart of the story—whether it's walking through a melting glacier to understand climate change, standing amid a protest in a foreign land, or witnessing the aftermath of natural disasters firsthand. Virtual journalists will guide them through these experiences, providing real-time analysis and context. The public will not just consume the news; they will live it.

To combat the inevitable flood of misinformation, personalized AI news companions will serve as trusted curators, filtering out noise and delivering only the most relevant and credible content. These AI agents will learn user preferences, biases, and intellectual curiosities, offering multiple perspectives on complex issues and even challenging cognitive biases. Just like in 2023, India witnessed the emergence of AI news anchors, marking a significant shift in the media landscape. According to Business Standard (2023) Odisha Television Ltd (OTV) introduced "Lisa," India's first regional AI news anchor, capable of delivering news in multiple languages, including Odia and English. Similarly, the India Today Group unveiled "Sana," an AI anchor designed to present news updates in various languages, aiming to enhance audience engagement. These AI developments and rapid integration of AI into journalism are setting the stage for a future where AI-driven news presentation becomes commonplace.

But with great power comes great responsibility. As media becomes more immersive, so do the potential threats. Cybersecurity in 2050 will no longer be about secure passwords and robust firewalls; it will be an arms race of AI against AI. As we advance race in AI, we should also remember what Albert Einstein advised, “It has become appallingly obvious that our technology has exceeded our humanity.”

Just as self-driving cars have revolutionized transportation, self-generating media will redefine journalism. AI-driven programs will monitor global events, cross-reference information from millions of sources, and autonomously produce unbiased reports faster than any human team ever could. However, the human element—curiosity, empathy, and ethical judgment will remain irreplaceable. While AI can analyze patterns and anticipate events, it is the journalist’s heart and intuition that will continue to breathe life into storytelling.

In this future, journalism will not merely be about reporting the facts; it will be about shaping the collective human experience. It will be deeply personal yet globally interconnected, blending technology with humanity in ways we can only begin to fathom. Marshall McLuhan once said, “The medium is the message.” In 2050, the medium will no longer be separate from us, it will be us. Media will no longer just inform our reality; it will create it, challenge it, and ultimately redefine what it means to know the truth.

Conclusion

Cyber threats ranging from hacking and surveillance to misinformation and online harassment—have become a persistent reality, forcing journalists to find a delicate balance between fast speed, accuracy, and security. One of the most pressing issues in this digital landscape is the vulnerability of journalists to cyberattacks. With media organizations becoming prime targets for corporate espionage, and malicious actors, the need for robust cybersecurity measures has never been greater. The protection of sensitive data, source confidentiality, and the prevention of misinformation require constant vigilance and adaptation to evolving threats. However, many journalists, especially freelancers and those working in resource-strapped organizations, face significant barriers in accessing the necessary tools and training to secure their work.

Social media has emerged as both a boon and a bane for journalism. While it has democratized access to information and enabled real-time reporting, it has also contributed to the spread of misinformation, erosion of trust in traditional media, and increased competition with nonprofessional content creators. The rapid dissemination of unverified news, fueled by algorithm-driven engagement models, challenges journalists to uphold credibility and fact-checking standards in an era of click-driven media consumption.

Looking ahead, the future of media in the age of cybersecurity will be shaped by the evolving interplay of technology, regulation, and audience expectations. To thrive, journalists must adopt a proactive approach to cybersecurity, embrace innovation, and continue to serve as vigilant watchdogs of society in an era where the stakes are higher than ever before. As veteran journalist Bob Woodward once said, "The central dilemma in journalism is that you don't know what you don't know" (Smith 2019). In the digital age, staying ahead requires not only uncovering the truth but also protecting it at all costs.

References

Abrams, M. 2024. "Encryption Should Be Part of Every Journalist's Toolkit." Freedom of the Press Foundation, November 4. https://freedom.press/issues/encryption-should-be-part-of-every-journalists-toolkit.

Beu, N., Jayatilaka, A., Zahedi, M., Babar, A., Hartley, L., Lewinsmith, W., & Baetu, I. 2023. "Falling for Phishing Attempts: An Investigation of Individual Differences That Are Associated with Behavior in a Naturalistic Phishing Simulation." *Computers & Security* 131, 103313. https://doi.org/10.1016/j.cose.2023.103313.

BBC News. 2020. "Major US Twitter Accounts Hacked in Bitcoin Scam." July 16. https://www.bbc.com/news/technology-53425822.

BS Web Team. 2023. "Odisha Television Introduces Lisa, India's First AI News Presenter." Business Standard, July 10. https://www.business-standard.com/technology/tech-news/odisha-television-introduces-lisa-india-s-first-ai-news-presenter-123071000767_1.html.

Associated Press. 2015. "ISIS-Allied Hackers Claim Worrying New Attack." CBS News, April 9. https://www.cbsnews.com/news/french-tv-network-tv5-monde-hacked-by-cybercaliphate-in-name-of-isis/.

Confessore, N. 2018. "Cambridge Analytica and Facebook: The Scandal so Far." *The New York Times*, April 4. https://www.nytimes.com/2018/04/04/us/politics/cambridge-analytica-scandal-fallout.html.

Committee to Protect Journalists. 2023. "Press Freedom and Digital Surveillance." cpj.org

Fisk, R. 2012. "The Heroic Myth and the Uncomfortable Truth of War Reporting." *The Independent*, March 2. https://www.independent.co.uk/voices/commentators/fisk/robert-fisk-the-heroic-myth-and-the-uncomfortable-truth-of-war-reporting-7499735.html.

Foucault, M. 1977. *Discipline and Punish: The Birth of the Prison.* Pantheon Books.

Giddens, A. 1990. *The Consequences of Modernity.* Polity Press.

Global Cyber Alliance (GCA). n.d. "GCA Cybersecurity Toolkit for Journalists." https://globalcyberalliance.org/gca-cybersecurity-toolkit-for-journalists.

Farivar, Cyrus. 2016. "Feds Demand Signal's Private Data, but There's None to Hand Over." https://arstechnica.com/tech-policy/2016/10/fbi-demands-signal-user-data-but-theres-not-much-to-hand-over/.

Forbes Technology Council. 2023. "How Cybersecurity Training Lowers Risk Among Employees." *Forbes*, October 24. https://www.forbes.com/councils/forbestechcouncil/2023/10/24/how-cybersecurity-training-lowers-risk-among-employees/.

GJIN. 2022. "Sinclair Broadcast Group Hit by Ransomware Attack." *The Hill*, May 17. https://thehill.com/policy/cybersecurity/577203-sinclair-broadcast-group-hit-by-ransomware-attack/

International Federation of Journalists (IFJ). 2021. "Cybersecurity Toolkit for Journalists." https://www.ifj.org/media-centre/reports/detail/ifj-cybersecurity-toolkit-for-journalists.

Lyon, D. 2018. *The Culture of Surveillance: Watching as a Way of Life.* Polity Press.

Noble, S. U. 2018. *Algorithms of Oppression: How Search Engines Reinforce Racism.* New York University Press.

Public Broadcasting Service (PBS). n.d. "PBS Cyber Champions. Public Media Learns." https://catalog.publicmedialearns.org/browse/pbs/programs/pbs-cyber-champions.

Public Broadcasting Service (PBS). 2003. "Christiane Amanpour: The Pool System. Reporting America at War." https://www.pbs.org/weta/reportingamericaatwar/reporters/amanpour/poolsystem.html.

Pearlman, S. J. 2020. *America's Critical Thinking Crisis: The Failure and Promise of Education.* Rowman & Littlefield.

Reuters. 2024. "Hong Kong Journalist Group Says Dozens of Journalists Harassed." https://www.reuters.com/world/asia-pacific/hong-kong-journalist-group-says-dozens-journalists-harassed-2024-09-13.

Reporters Without Borders. 2022. "Cyber Threats to Press Freedom." rsf.org

Smith, C. 2019. "A Collection of Bob Woodward Quotes on Watergate, Reporting." Deseret News, January 10. https://www.deseret.com/2019/1/10/20663057/a-collection-of-bob-woodward-quotes-on-watergate-reporting.

The Hindu. 2023. "India Gets Its First AI News Anchor: Milestone or Menace?" https://frontline.thehindu.com/news/india-gets-its-first-ai-news-anchor-milestone-or-menace/article66766751.ece.

Trilling, D. 2017. "Digital Security Tips for Journalists: Protecting Sources and Yourself." The Journalist's Resource, March 9. https://journalistsresource.org/economics/digital-security-tips-protecting-sources-journalist/?utm_source=chatgpt.com.

UNESCO. 2018. "World Trends in Freedom of Expression and Media Development." https://unesdoc.unesco.org.

Chapter 8

Privacy in a Digital Networking World

Lamia Zia, PhD

Chapter Learning Objectives

- Understand the evolution of social media platforms from early communication tools to data-driven ecosystems.
- Understand the concept of the "Fish Tank Digital World" as a metaphor for constant digital surveillance and loss of autonomy.
- Evaluate the ethical implications of TikTok's platform design, including features that contribute to compulsive use and their psychological impact on youth.
- Analyze how social media platforms collect, track, and monetize user data through algorithms, cookies, third-party apps, and behavioral profiling.
- Identify the types of data collected by social media platforms, including how it is gathered and used.
- Analyze privacy policies and user agreements, including their implications for data ownership and third-party sharing.
- Examine real-world examples of data breaches and privacy violations and their impact on users and public trust.
- Explore key privacy theories, including surveillance capitalism, the privacy paradox, and the digital panopticon.
- Apply practical strategies to protect personal information online, such as managing privacy settings, avoiding phishing, and limiting third-party access.

Key Terms

- **Privacy Paradox** – The conflict between users' concerns about privacy and their actual online behaviors.
- **Surveillance Capitalism** – A term coined by Shoshana Zuboff describing the monetization of personal data by tech companies.
- **Panopticon** – A concept introduced by Michel Foucault to describe a form of surveillance where individuals regulate their own behavior due to the perception of being constantly watched.

- **Data Mining** – The process of analyzing large datasets to discover patterns, often used by social media platforms to profile users.
- **Biometric Data** – Personal data derived from biological characteristics, such as facial recognition and voice prints.
- **Third-Party Sharing** – The act of social media platforms sharing user data with outside entities, such as advertisers or analytics firms.
- **User Agreement** – A contract users accept when joining a platform, often outlining data collection and sharing practices.
- **Cookies and Tracking Pixels** – Tools used to track user behavior across websites and platforms.
- **Informed Consent** – The process of clearly informing users about data collection practices and obtaining their voluntary agreement.
- **Digital Footprint** – The trail of data users leave behind when engaging online.
- **Data Breach** – A security incident where sensitive, protected, or confidential data is accessed or disclosed without authorization.
- **Algorithmic Personalization** – The use of algorithms to tailor content and ads based on user behavior and preferences.
- **Two-Factor Authentication (2FA)** – An extra layer of security requiring users to verify their identity using two forms of identification.
- **Social Engineering** – The manipulation of people into sharing confidential information, often used in phishing and scam attacks.

Introduction

What does privacy mean to you? Is it the ability to walk freely in public without being watched? To exist without being recorded, analyzed, or exposed? Or has privacy quietly shifted into something we only expect behind locked doors and password-protected screens?

In today's digital world, the boundaries of privacy are no longer clear. The line between public and private has blurred often without our consent. A recent investigation by BBC forces us to confront this uncomfortable reality. The report revealed that men are covertly filming women during nights out and uploading the footage online for profit. Disguised as "walking tours" or "nightlife content," these videos circulate widely across platforms such as YouTube, TikTok, Facebook, and Instagram. They often focus on women in dresses or skirts, filmed from behind or at low angles, sometimes exposing intimate parts of their bodies without their knowledge (BBC, 2026).

The scale of the issue is staggering. The BBC identified more than 65 channels producing such content, collectively amassing over three billion views in just three years. The recordings span major cities across the world from London and Oslo to Miami and Bangkok highlighting how this is not an isolated problem, but a global phenomenon. But beyond the numbers lies a more disturbing truth: many of the women filmed had no idea it had happened.

When tracked down, nearly 50 women expressed feelings of fear, humiliation, and violation. One 21-year-old woman, who discovered footage of herself filmed from a low angle and uploaded online, described how the experience left her feeling paranoid every time she stepped outside. What was once an ordinary night out had been transformed into a lasting psychological burden without her consent, and without her control (BBC, 2026). This example forces us to rethink a fundamental assumption: that being in a public space means giving up privacy.

But privacy in the digital age is not only a personal or social issue, it is also deeply political.

Consider what happened in India in June 2020. The government abruptly banned TikTok, owned by the Chinese company ByteDancenalong with dozens of other Chinese apps following a deadly border clash between India and China. Citing concerns over data privacy, national security, and sovereignty, Indian authorities argued that these apps posed a threat to the country's digital integrity (PBS, 2024). What followed was a sudden disappearance of a platform used by millions, demonstrating how personal data flows can become entangled with geopolitical conflict. This incident reveals a critical dimension of privacy: it is not just about individuals being watched, it is also about nations being vulnerable.

Privacy, therefore, operates at multiple levels. At the personal level, it protects dignity and autonomy. At the societal level, it shapes trust and behavior. And at the political level, it influences power, control, and security.

This chapter explores what privacy means in such a world. It examines how digital technologies have redefined personal boundaries, how surveillance has become normalized, and how individuals often without realizing it, are constantly exposed to new forms of vulnerability. Because the question is no longer whether we are being watched.

The question is: who is watching, why and what happens to us when they are?

Growing up in the digital age, these questions are more urgent than ever. As we all know, social media has become a cornerstone of our lives, enabling us to connect with loved ones, share milestones, and perform everyday tasks. Yet, this connectivity comes with a hidden cost: the gradual erosion of privacy. As we embrace the benefits of these platforms, we also enter a trade-off, often unknowingly surrendering control over our personal information.

According to Roy et al. (2020), "Eavesdropping on private conversations is one of the most common yet detrimental threats to privacy." This argument captures the essence of a growing concern in the digital age: the pervasive surveillance of our interactions, often without our explicit knowledge or consent. Social media platforms, designed to build connection and convenience, have also become ecosystems where personal data is constantly collected.

This reality becomes even more complex with the rise of facial recognition technologies. Facial recognition systems, powered by artificial intelligence and vast datasets, can identify, track, and profile individuals in real time. What was once the domain of high-security environments has now expanded into everyday life, airports, shopping malls, public streets, and even social media platforms. A photograph uploaded online is no longer just an image; it becomes a data point that can be analyzed, matched, and stored indefinitely.

These technologies raise profound questions about consent and control. Unlike passwords or personal identifiers that can be changed, a face is permanent. When facial data is collected without knowledge or permission, individuals lose agency over one of their most fundamental identifiers their identity itself.

The implications are both personal and societal: At the personal level, facial recognition can lead to unauthorized tracking, profiling, and exposure. At the societal level, it introduces the possibility of mass surveillance, where movements, associations, and behaviors are continuously monitored. In such an environment, anonymity in public spaces, once considered a basic aspect of freedom begins to disappear.

This connects directly to earlier examples of covert filming and digital exposure. Whether through hidden cameras capturing unsuspecting individuals or algorithms scanning faces in crowds, the underlying issue remains the same: the transformation of human presence into data.

Social media platforms further amplify this transformation. Designed to build connection, they have evolved into data-driven ecosystems where every click, like, share, and image contributes to a larger surveillance infrastructure. Facial recognition tools embedded in these platforms can automatically tag individuals, map social networks, and infer behavioral patterns often without users fully understanding the extent of this data collection.

These platforms blur the line between public and private spheres, where even seemingly intimate conversations or actions contribute to a vast network of surveillance. As we explore this digital landscape, we confront fundamental questions about what we are willing to trade for connectivity and whether the erosion of privacy is an inevitable cost of participating in the modern world or a challenge we can collectively address to protect the boundaries of personal freedom.

Let's run a quick hypothetical scenario: Imagine a new social media platform called Locus Café, designed to simulate the feeling of sitting in a bustling coffee shop. When you join, you're handed a personalized digital table where you can chat, share updates, and interact with others around you.

At first, it feels cozy. You share a picture of your latte (ten likes instantly!), chat with friends at neighboring tables, and even join a virtual book club meeting at the café. But as you sip your coffee, you notice something odd: the café staff is taking detailed notes on every move you make. They jot down what you ordered, how long you spent at each table, who you interacted with, and even the title of the book you mentioned. Occasionally, they whisper to advertisers standing by the counter, who begin offering you ads for new coffee mugs or bean subscriptions.

Curious, you explore the café's policies. A cheerful sign at the door reads,

"By entering the Café, you agree to let us use your actions to improve your experience! Don't worry, we're committed to keeping things fun!" However, buried in the café's fine print is a long document that reveals what you really agreed to:

- Your conversations may be used to develop targeted ad campaigns.
- Every "cheers" you send to a friend (the platform's equivalent of a "like") helps train algorithms to better predict your behavior.
- Your profile information can be shared with "trusted partners" (a term the café doesn't clearly define).

This scenario mirrors the real-world dynamics of social media platforms like Instagram or Facebook. The café's appeal (connection and engagement) is challenged by this realization that users' actions and behaviors are being observed, analyzed, and monetized. Just as Marlon Brando stated, "Privacy is not something that I'm merely entitled to, it's an absolute prerequisite," privacy is not a perk but a foundational need. Without it, users begin to feel exposed, manipulated, and ultimately disconnected from the authentic experience they sought in the first place. This sentiment is echoed by Arias-Cabarcos et al. (2022), whose study on Facebook highlights the critical importance of institutional transparency. Their study revealed that users were "surprised, shocked, [and] worried" upon discovering the extent of Facebook's data collection from third parties. They emphasize that for users to feel informed and capable of making privacy decisions, platforms must provide clarity and enable informed consent regarding the processing of personal data.

Yet, many social media platforms operate within a framework of ambiguity, where users unknowingly trade privacy for convenience. While these platforms promise connection and engagement, the underlying practices of observation, analysis, and monetization of user behavior often leave individuals feeling exposed and manipulated. In this context, the erosion of privacy is not just a by-product of modern technology, it's a direct challenge to autonomy and trust in the digital age.

A study by Arias-Cabarcos et al. (2022) supports this, revealing that users were "surprised, shocked, [and] worried" upon discovering the extent of Facebook's data collection from third parties.

This indicates that when users become aware of how their data is utilized, it can significantly impact their comfort levels and trust in the platform. Furthermore, the documentary *The Social Dilemma* highlights how social media companies design algorithms to maximize user engagement, often leading to feelings of manipulation and addiction. This aligns with Marlon Brando's timeless words: "Privacy is not something that I'm merely entitled to, it's an absolute prerequisite."

The abovementioned quote asserts that privacy isn't a luxury or an optional feature; it's the foundation upon which our autonomy and individuality are built. In the context of social media, this principle becomes more critical. Platforms encourage us to share intimate details of our lives our interests, relationships, and even our real-time locations all while operating systems that analyze, monetize, and sometimes exploit this information.

Fish Tank Digital World

This chapter introduces the term "Fish Tank Digital World" to articulate the unsettling nature of life in the age of surveillance capitalism. The metaphor powerfully captures how the digital environment, though presented as a private and personalized space, is in fact a transparent enclosure where users' every movement is tracked, analyzed, and monetized by unseen observers such as corporations, algorithms, and governments. In this metaphorical tank, individuals swim freely but are under constant observation, stripped of meaningful privacy and control. What appears to be a space for self-expression and connection is, in truth, a meticulously surveilled ecosystem where data extraction is the currency of participation.

The "fish tank" analogy critically exposes the illusion of digital autonomy. Social media platforms promise intimacy and community yet embed their services with mechanisms of surveillance designed to manipulate behavior and maximize profit. The user, believing they are the subject, is in fact the object monitored and modeled to serve commercial interests. This form of visibility is not benign; it erodes psychological safety, fosters self-censorship, and undermines individual agency. The constant cataloging of behaviors reduces the user to a predictable profile, transforming rich, human experiences into commodified data points.

Moreover, the normalization of this surveillance disguised as personalization renders users complicit in their own exposure. As platforms blur the lines between public and private, individuals gradually accept visibility as the default condition of existence. The "Fish Tank Digital World" thus serves not merely as a metaphor, but as a call to action. It challenges us to confront the ethical implications of our digital lives and to advocate for a reimagined internet one where privacy is a right, not a relic, and where users can reclaim agency over their digital identities.

Living in a digital world does not require surrendering privacy. Instead, it demands an intentional stance rooted in awareness, critical literacy, and resistance to exploitative systems. We must question who benefits from our visibility, whose interests are being served, and how we might rebuild digital ecosystems that prioritize dignity over data.

"It is because of the internet and associated social media tools of human communication that we are witnessing a new era of global memory themes, which are not static, but continue to be reshaped on digital media platforms. This phenomenon is resulting in the rise of global social movements where the idea of a Collective We is no more about the experiences of people located in a region or a country, but about the experiences of digitally connected global citizens" (Arif 2020, 193).

Social media's allure lies in its unprecedented ability to bring people together, amplifying voices and fostering global conversations. As Arif (2020) notes, these digital platforms have reshaped collective memory, transforming it into a dynamic, evolving entity.

Today, global social movements no longer hinge on physical proximity or cultural ties. Instead, they emerge from the shared experiences of digitally connected citizens, bound by common values and causes. Climate change advocacy, human rights campaigns, and other movements demonstrate the immense potential of social media to unite people and drive meaningful change. Yet, this interconnectedness comes with a price: the erosion of privacy. In the digital realm, our personal lives are cataloged and commodified, reducing us to data points in an algorithmic marketplace.

This chapter explores the delicate balance between the opportunities social media offers and the risks it poses to personal freedom and autonomy. It invites readers to think critically about how privacy serves as the bedrock of selfhood and the foundation for authentic participation in a globalized digital society. For example, the Black Lives Matter (BLM) movement demonstrates how social media reshapes global memory and creates a shared sense of purpose among people worldwide. Originating in the United States, BLM gained global traction through platforms like Twitter, Instagram, and TikTok. Hashtags such as #BlackLivesMatter allowed individuals from different countries to share their own experiences of systemic racism and police brutality, creating a global narrative about racial injustice. The movement's messages were not confined to American experiences but resonated with diverse audiences, highlighting the universal need for equality and justice.

Here is another example, the #MeToo movement is another example of how social media has redefined collective memory and solidarity. What started as a hashtag on Twitter quickly became a global campaign against sexual harassment and assault. Survivors from various countries and cultural contexts shared their stories, creating a universal narrative about gender-based violence. The movement united individuals across geographical and cultural divides, amplifying voices and shaping a global conversation about accountability and empowerment.

As we explore this complex digital landscape, we are faced with a choice: to relinquish control over our digital identities or to reclaim the power to set boundaries and protect our most personal spaces. This chapter will examine the evolving role of privacy in social media, offering strategies into how individuals, platforms, and policymakers can work together to build a more equitable and respectful digital environment. Because in the end, preserving privacy isn't just about protecting our data, it's about ensuring we remain human in a world that never stops watching.

In this chapter, readers will gain a comprehensive understanding of the evolving role of privacy in the digital landscape, particularly within the context of social media. Specifically, they will achieve the following:

- Learn how social media has transformed from basic communication tools to sophisticated ecosystems driven by data collection and algorithmic personalization.
- Understand why privacy is a fundamental requirement in the digital age and how it influences freedom, individuality, and autonomy.

- Explore how social media platforms have transformed from networking tools to data-centric ecosystems that shape our digital interactions.
- Explore the nature of data collected, including personal information, browsing habits, and location data, and the mechanisms used to gather it.
- Learn how to critically analyze social media privacy policies, identify key clauses, and comprehend what users are consenting to when they join these platforms.
- Examine real-world examples of data breaches, privacy violations, and their consequences, along with their impact on public trust in social media platforms.
- Learn practical strategies to safeguard personal data, understand privacy settings, and make informed choices about sharing information online.
- Understand key theories like surveillance capitalism, the privacy paradox, and the digital panopticon.

8.1 The Evolution of Social Media Platforms

Social media, as we know it today, has undergone a remarkable evolution, transforming from simple tools for communication into complex ecosystems of data-driven interaction, community building, and global influence. To understand this evolution, it is essential to explore its historical milestones, grounded in academic research and industry observations.

Early Roots of Social Media: The Precursors (1960s–1990s)

The origins of social media can be traced back to the development of early networking technologies. The first computer-based communication systems, such as ARPANET in the late 1960s, laid the groundwork for digital connectivity (Leiner et al. 1997). These early systems were primarily designed for research and academic purposes, facilitating the exchange of information among limited users.

By the 1980s, technologies like Bulletin Board Systems (BBS) and Internet Relay Chat (IRC) emerged, allowing users to post messages, share files, and engage in real-time discussions. These platforms provided the first glimpses of digital communities, where users could connect based on shared interests, despite geographic barriers (Rheingold 1993). Howard Rheingold, often referred to as the "first citizen of the internet," provides a compelling exploration of these early digital spaces in his seminal work, *The Virtual Community* (1993). In his book, Rheingold describes these online networks as real and multifaceted communities, comparable to physical ones. He observes that people in these virtual spaces talk, argue, seek information, organize politically, fall in love, and even deceive one another.

Rheingold (2000) recounts moving stories of individuals who received emotional support from online communities during devastating illnesses, demonstrating the profound positive potential of these connections. However, he also acknowledges a darker side, noting that people's behavior online often mirrors their actions in physical communities, including conflict and manipulation. His reflections underline that while these early platforms offered unprecedented opportunities for connection, they also introduced challenges in managing relationships, trust, and ethical behavior in a digital environment.

The Rise of Web-Based Social Networks (1990s–2000s)

The late 1990s marked a turning point with the advent of web-based platforms that began to resemble modern social media. Sites like Six Degrees, launched in 1997, allowed users to create profiles, connect with friends, and engage in early forms of online networking (Boyd and Ellison 2007). Named after the idea of "six degrees of separation," Six Degrees was built on the premise that any two people in the world are connected through a chain of six or fewer intermediaries. The platform enabled users to do the following:

- Create Personal Profiles: Users could build profiles showcasing their interests and personal information, a feature that would later become a staple of social media.
- Form Connections: It allowed users to invite friends to join the network and establish direct links with them.
- Engage in Early Online Networking: The platform featured a rudimentary form of networking where users could see and interact with friends of friends, creating a sense of community and interconnectedness.

While Six Degrees was innovative, it struggled with challenges like limited internet adoption in the late 1990s and a lack of sustained engagement from users. These factors eventually led to its decline by 2001. However, its foundational features—profiles, connections, and networking laid the groundwork for future social media platforms. Following Six Degrees, the early 2000s saw the emergence of several platforms that refined and expanded the concept of online social networking such as LinkedIn. Unlike its predecessors, LinkedIn targeted professionals, offering features focused on career networking, job searches, and industry connections. It demonstrated the versatility of social networking, showing that it could serve niche audiences.

The Social Media Boom: Facebook, Twitter, and Beyond (2004–2010s)

On February 4, 2004, Mark Zuckerberg and his cofounders launched thefacebook.com, a web service initially available exclusively to Harvard University students in Cambridge, Massachusetts. The platform enabled students to create profile pages, share personal information, and maintain contact with each other. Access to thefacebook.com required an email address ending in harvard.edu, ensuring exclusivity, and users had to be at least 18 years old. This focus on a closed, real-name network helped building trust and authenticity among users (Brugger 2015).

Thefacebook.com quickly gained traction, expanding to other Ivy League universities and later opening to the general public in 2006 as Facebook. Its simple, intuitive design and focus on real-world connections set it apart from earlier platforms like Friendster and Myspace. By allowing users to share updates, post photos, and interact with friends in real time, Facebook transformed social networking into an integral part of daily life.

Twitter, founded in 2006, introduced the concept of microblogging, enabling users to share thoughts in real time within a 140-character limit. It became a critical tool for breaking news, celebrity engagement, and grassroots activism (Murthy 2013). The platform's simplicity and immediacy redefined how people consumed and disseminated information.

Modern Social Media Ecosystem (2010s–Present)

The 2010s saw the diversification of social media platforms, each catering to specific user needs and interests. Instagram, launched in 2010, focused on visual storytelling through images and videos, while Snapchat introduced ephemeral content that prioritized privacy and spontaneity (Piwek and Joinson 2016). Meanwhile, platforms like LinkedIn emerged as professional networking tools, and TikTok (launched internationally in 2018) captured the attention of younger audiences with its short-form video content and algorithm-driven personalization (Kaye et al. 2021).

Social media has since become deeply integrated into daily life, influencing politics, culture, commerce, and even mental health. Platforms now rely heavily on algorithms, data collection, and targeted advertising to enhance user engagement and drive revenue (Zuboff 2019). This era also marked a significant shift in how users interact with content, particularly with features like the "like" button. Platforms such as Instagram capitalized on this simple yet powerful tool to foster engagement and strengthen social connections. As Arif et al. (2024) highlight, the motivations behind "liking" a post on Instagram go far beyond a mere acknowledgment of content. Their study reveals that users are driven by reciprocity, relationship-building, and even the desire to deepen offline connections. The act of liking is not just a personal gesture but a form of metacommunication, subtly shaping and maintaining relationships within digital and social contexts.

However, this seemingly innocuous feature also has far-reaching implications. Platforms leverage liking behavior as a data point, feeding algorithms that curate personalized content, target advertisements, and drive user engagement (Zuboff 2019). While users may view their likes as personal expressions or social currency, these interactions are analyzed to create detailed behavioral profiles, often without their explicit awareness.

The dual nature of social media platforms becomes evident: They serve as spaces for authentic connection and expression while simultaneously operating as systems for data collection and monetization. As platforms like Instagram evolve, the social and emotional motivations behind features like likes remain central to user engagement, but the corporate use of this data raises critical questions about privacy, consent, and the ethics of algorithmic design.

In this modern ecosystem, social media is no longer just a tool for communication, it is a mirror of societal behavior, a marketplace for data, and a stage for cultural evolution.

The findings of Arif et al. (2024) emphasize the complex role of user behavior in shaping these platforms and highlight the need for greater transparency and accountability in how data from these interactions is used.

TikTok and the Crisis of Digital Privacy, Sovereignty, and Mental Health

"Social media and smartphones are designed to hack our brains and press our emotional buttons. We are constantly flooded with information and it is vital we find the time to disconnect in order to protect our mental well-being," renowned scholar Yuval Noah Harari stated in a social media post.

He aptly captures the social media concerns while emphasizing the importance of disconnecting to preserve mental well-being. In the context of TikTok, these dynamics are especially pronounced among younger users, where constant exposure to curated content not only shortens attention spans but also fuels unrealistic social comparisons and compulsive use patterns. Harari's warning calls for a broader ethical dilemma: platforms like TikTok are not merely passive entertainment spaces rather they are sophisticated systems built to influence thought and behavior at a neurological level.

TikTok, a leading force in the global social media ecosystem, has emerged as a focal point in debates surrounding digital privacy, national sovereignty, and mental health. The platform's meteoric rise is matched by the complexity of its controversies most notably the concerns regarding its data practices and psychological impact on youth. TikTok's parent company, ByteDance, is based in China, prompting U.S. lawmakers to question the security of American user data in light of China's cybersecurity laws. These concerns culminated in legislative action demanding ByteDance divest its ownership or face a nationwide ban. While enforcement timelines have fluctuated due to political transitions and executive orders, the underlying issue remains potent: in a digitally interconnected world, data governance has become a geopolitical flashpoint.

Yet, the scrutiny of TikTok extends beyond the borders of statecraft into the intimate realms of behavior and psychology. Critics argue that TikTok's design architecture short-form, personalized videos propelled by a powerful algorithm intentionally maximizes user engagement by fostering compulsive, even addictive, behaviors. Multiple lawsuits filed by U.S. states and international families allege that the platform contributes to rising levels of anxiety, depression, and exposure to harmful trends among adolescents. These lawsuits claim that TikTok's algorithm prioritizes emotionally triggering or risky content to increase screen time and advertising revenue, often at the expense of users' mental well-being.

In response, TikTok has introduced features like screen time management and parental controls, but these measures are often regarded as superficial or easily circumvented. The platform's case reveals a broader dilemma in platform governance: whether corporate social responsibility can meaningfully mitigate the harms of algorithmic manipulation in attention-based economies.

TikTok's algorithm is central to its user engagement strategy. It curates content based on user interactions, leading to a personalized "For You" feed that encourages prolonged usage. This design leverages the principles of the stimulus–organism–response (S–O–R) model and flow theory, where users experience deep immersion, often losing track of time while engaging with content (Qin et al.). At the center of each lawsuit is TikTok's algorithm that plaintiffs argue are intentionally addictive. These include infinite scrolling, attention-triggering push notifications, and augmented face filters that promote unrealistic beauty standards among young users (Associated Press).

The case of TikTok illustrates a central tension of the modern digital experience between innovation and intrusion, engagement and exploitation. It exemplifies the "Fish Tank Digital World," where individuals exist in environments that feel personal and empowering but are, in reality, subject to constant observation, behavioral manipulation, and opaque data extraction. As TikTok continues to evolve and face regulatory scrutiny, its trajectory will likely remain emblematic of the larger questions confronting all digital platforms: How should societies balance the promise of global connectivity with the imperative to protect individual autonomy, democratic accountability, and mental health?

This enduring relevance makes TikTok more than a case study, it is a barometer for how the digital future will be shaped and contested.

8.2 The Nature of Data on Social Media

Let's explore the nature of the data through this hypothetical scenario: Imagine walking into a marketplace where every step you take, every item you glance at, and every word you speak is meticulously recorded. At first, it seems harmless, your preferences are noted, and vendors use this information to make recommendations tailored just for you. But as you walk further, you realize that this isn't just about what you choose to share. It's about the invisible eyes watching you, drawing conclusions from every move you make.

Welcome to the world of social media, where the currency isn't money, it's your data.

Platforms like Facebook and Instagram analyze your likes, shares, and comments to build detailed profiles of your behavior, interests, and even emotional states. For example, Facebook's algorithms track how long you pause on a post, while Instagram predicts your preferences based on the photos and videos you linger on. These platforms don't just collect data you actively provide; they infer your habits and tendencies through advanced machine learning models.

Consider TikTok, where every swipe contributes to an extraordinarily precise algorithm. If you spend a fraction longer on a video about fitness, the platform deduces that you might enjoy similar content, even without your explicit input. Over time, this leads to a hyperpersonalized feed designed to maximize engagement often at the cost of user well-being, as studies link excessive use of these tailored feeds to anxiety and reduced attention spans (Kaye et al. 2021).

The Many Faces of Data

When you create a profile on a social media platform, you're not just signing up to share photos and connect with friends. You're opening a door to a system that thrives on collecting as much information about you as possible. Social media platforms gather personal information, your name, age, email, and even the way you describe yourself in your bio. But they don't stop there. They want to know about your behavior: the posts you like, the accounts you follow, the time you spend scrolling through certain content. Even your location, yes, where you are at any given moment becomes part of the treasure trove of data these platforms collect.

Take Snapchat, for example. Its Snap Map feature allows users to see their friends' real-time locations. On the surface, it feels like a fun way to connect. But think about the implications, your location is being shared constantly, potentially without you even realizing it. In fact, many users were surprised to discover this feature was active by default, leaving them exposed without their consent. This raises critical questions about data privacy:

- How can platforms ensure that users fully understand and actively consent to data-sharing features, especially those enabled by default?
- What measures are in place to protect sensitive information, such as real-time location data, from unauthorized access or misuse? And where should the line be drawn between enhancing user experience and exploiting personal data for profit or engagement, particularly when users may not fully grasp the implications of these features?

These are essential considerations as social media platforms continue to innovate while grappling with the ethical responsibility of protecting user privacy.

How Platforms Collect Your Data

The mechanisms for collecting data are as complex as the platforms themselves.

Cookies and Tracking Pixels

Imagine you're browsing for a new pair of shoes online. Later, you log into Facebook, and suddenly, your feed is filled with ads for shoes. That's not a coincidence. Cookies, tiny pieces of data stored on your browser, track your activity and report it back to social media platforms. Facebook Pixel, a tool used by businesses, goes a step further by connecting your browsing habits to your Facebook profile.

User Input

Every post you make, every photo you upload, every search you perform; this is data you willingly provide. But did you know platforms like Instagram analyze your hashtags, captions, and even the objects in your photos? That cute picture of your dog? It's helping Instagram refine its advertising algorithms.

Third-Party Apps

Here's where things get tricky. In 2018, the world was rocked by the Cambridge Analytica scandal. A seemingly innocent personality quiz app collected data not only from users who took the quiz but also from their entire friend lists without their consent. This data, amounting to over 87 million profiles, was then used to influence political campaigns, including the 2016 US presidential election.

Device Data

Even the device you use tells a story. TikTok, for instance, tracks not just what videos you watch but how you interact with them, your screen taps, pauses, and replays. This allows its algorithm to serve you eerily accurate recommendations, creating an addictive feedback loop. The power of this data collection lies in its ability to predict and influence behavior. Social media platforms don't merely reflect your interests; they shape them. As harmless as it may seem to accept cookies or consent to data collection, the depth of insight these platforms gain into your life raises serious ethical concerns about privacy, autonomy, and the commodification of personal information.

The Stories Behind the Data

Every case of data collection reveals a deeper story about how these platforms operate.

Consider Facebook. In 2018, they quietly updated Instagram's terms of service to allow data sharing between the two platforms. Many users clicked "Agree" without reading the fine print, inadvertently allowing their personal data to flow freely between the two giants. It wasn't until privacy advocates raised alarms that people realized the extent of their exposure.

Or look at TikTok, the rising star of social media. Its algorithm is a master of personalization, showing users content so perfectly aligned with their interests that it feels magical. But behind the magic lies a complex system analyzing everything from your viewing habits to subtle facial expressions captured by your device's camera. Even Snapchat's Snap Map sparked controversy when users discovered just how detailed its location tracking could be. For some, it was a fun way to see where friends were hanging out. For others, it became a chilling reminder of how much privacy they had unknowingly surrendered.

According to CNN (2025), with uncertainty surrounding TikTok's future in the United States, many American users have shifted to Xiaohongshu, a Chinese app often referred to as RedNote in the United States, which topped the Apple App Store recently. CNN reported, "Users are finding creative ways to transcend language barriers, navigate cultural differences, and co-exist in fascinating ways. This community building happening in real time could have lasting impact, and I'm cautiously optimistic" (CNN 2025). While this shift builds global community and cultural bridges, it also raises significant concerns about data privacy. Chinese platforms, like RedNote, operate under the Cybersecurity Law of China, which mandates that data be stored locally and may allow government access to it. For US users, this means that the personal data they share on the platform could be managed in a jurisdiction with different and potentially less stringent privacy protections, raising questions about the trade-offs between cultural connectivity and individual data security.

How Much Do Users Really Know?

Here's the startling truth: most people have no idea how much data they're sharing. A 2019 study by Pew Research Center found that nearly three-quarters of Americans didn't know Facebook tracks their interests and demographics through its ad preferences page. Why? Because the process is designed to be invisible. Terms of service agreements are notoriously long and full of legal jargon, discouraging users from reading them. Features like Snap Map are often enabled by default, catching users off guard. And the convenience of personalized recommendations makes it easy to ignore the trade-offs.

What This Means for You

Social media promises connection, creativity, and the thrill of belonging. But beneath the filters and trending hashtags lies a hidden truth: these platforms aren't just spaces for you to share your life—they're engines designed to collect it. Every swipe, every click, and every second of your attention feeds a system that's learning more about you than you might know about yourself.

As Tristan Harris, Google's former design ethicist and cofounder of the Center for Humane Technology, aptly puts it, "If you're not paying for the product, then you are the product" (McCormick 2021). The truth is, you're not just sharing posts or pictures, you're sharing yourself. Your habits, preferences, and even your vulnerabilities are packaged as data, turning you into the most valuable commodity on the platform.

The real question isn't whether your data is being collected, it's how much, and whether you're okay with what's happening behind the scenes. In this marketplace of information, understanding what's being gathered, how it's being used, and the hidden story behind these platforms is no longer optional. It's the key to reclaiming your digital identity. Awareness is power, and it's time to use it because in a world where data is currency, protecting your privacy is an act of self-preservation.

8.3 Privacy Policies and User Agreements

What Do Privacy Policies Actually Say?

At first glance, privacy policies seem to promise safety and transparency. They often begin with phrases like, "Your privacy matters to us," or, "We are committed to protecting your data." But beneath these assurances lies a complex web of permissions, conditions, and loopholes. For instance, Facebook's privacy policy outlines its ability to collect personal data, track browsing habits, and share this information with third parties. While this is stated explicitly, the language used is often technical and buried in lengthy documents. In 2021, TikTok updated its privacy policy to include the collection of biometric data, such as facial and voice prints, raising significant concerns about user consent and awareness.

The User Agreements We Don't Read

Let's face it: most of us don't read user agreements. A study by Deloitte (2017) revealed that 91 percent of consumers accept terms and conditions without reading them. And who can blame them? These agreements are notoriously long, filled with legal jargon, and designed to be skimmed or ignored. But what are we actually agreeing to?

Data Ownership and Usage

Many agreements state that while users "own" their content, platforms have a license to use, modify, and distribute it. This means that the photos, videos, and posts you share could be used in ways you didn't anticipate. Instagram's terms, for example, allow them to use your content for advertising without explicit notification.

Third-Party Sharing

A key clause in many agreements involves sharing data with third parties. This often includes advertisers, data analytics firms, and even governments. Facebook's infamous Cambridge Analytica scandal highlighted how user data shared with third parties could be exploited for political purposes without direct user consent.

Tracking Across Platforms

Many policies permit cross-platform tracking. For instance, if you're logged into Google, your activity on YouTube, Gmail, and even non-Google sites can be linked to create a detailed profile of your behavior.

The Devil in the Details: Key Clauses and Implications

The fine print in privacy policies is where the real story unfolds. These clauses often appear innocuous but have far-reaching implications:

"We may update this policy at any time."

Most platforms reserve the right to change their privacy policies without notifying users. For example, WhatsApp faced backlash in 2021 when it updated its terms to mandate data sharing with its parent company, Facebook, sparking concerns about user privacy.

"Your data may be shared with trusted partners."

The term "trusted partners" is intentionally vague, leaving users unsure of who has access to their information. In some cases, this includes advertisers, political organizations, or even law enforcement agencies.

"Data collected may include biometrics or geolocation."

Platforms like Snapchat and TikTok explicitly state their ability to collect sensitive data, including precise location tracking and even voice or facial recognition data. The implications for misuse, from surveillance to identity theft, are significant.

A Case Study: Instagram's Terms of Service

In 2020, Instagram updated its terms to clarify that it could use user content in advertisements. While this wasn't a new policy, the backlash was immediate. Users felt betrayed, believing their photos and videos could be used without their explicit consent. This case highlighted a recurring issue: the gap between what platforms legally disclose and what users understand. Many users threatened to delete their accounts, but Instagram's defense was simple: the policy had always been there. The outrage stemmed from users' lack of awareness, not from Instagram's lack of disclosure.

Why It Matters

Privacy policies and user agreements may seem like mundane formalities, but they define the boundaries of our digital lives. These documents determine what platforms can do with our data, how they track us, and who else gets to see our information. The implications are far-reaching, from targeted advertising to potential data breaches. Yet, the sheer length and complexity of these agreements create a dynamic where users feel powerless. By clicking "Agree," they unknowingly relinquish control over their digital identities, trusting platforms to act responsibly, an expectation that history has shown to be misplaced.

The Path Forward

Understanding privacy policies doesn't mean reading every word of every document. It means recognizing patterns, questioning vague clauses, and pushing for greater transparency. It's about demanding clarity in a system designed to obscure so that when we sign on the dotted line, we know exactly what we're giving up and what we're getting in return. Because at the end of the day, privacy policies are more than just a formality. They are the rules of engagement in a digital world, and it's up to us to ensure we're playing on terms that protect our rights and freedoms.

So, the next time you're faced with a user agreement, take a moment to pause. Beneath the legalese lies a story, one that deserves your attention, because it's about you, your data, and your digital future.

8.4 Major Data Privacy Concerns in Social Media

The allure of connection and convenience offered by social media comes at a hidden cost: the exposure of personal data. Social media platforms, designed to bring people closer together, often collect immense amounts of user information, turning them into lucrative targets for data breaches and exploitation. The repercussions of mishandling this data are far-reaching, eroding individual privacy and public trust in these platforms. Real-world incidents, like the Cambridge Analytica scandal, underscore how data misuse can shake the foundations of user confidence and highlight the need for stronger data protection measures (Isaak and Hanna 2018).

Case Studies of Data Breaches and Privacy Violations

The Facebook–Cambridge Analytica scandal is widely recognized as one of the most significant examples of data misuse in social media history. The scandal unfolded in 2018, when it was revealed that Cambridge Analytica, a British political consulting firm, had harvested data from more than 87 million Facebook users through a seemingly innocuous personality quiz app. The app not only collected data from users who participated but also from their friends, often without their knowledge or consent (Isaak and Hanna 2018).

This data was then utilized to create detailed psychological profiles, which were strategically employed to influence voter behavior during critical events like the 2016 US presidential election and the Brexit referendum. The revelation of such extensive data exploitation led to global outrage, significant scrutiny of Facebook's data practices, and a historic $5 billion fine imposed on Facebook by the Federal Trade Commission (FTC) for violating user privacy (FTC 2019). The incident also resulted in multiple lawsuits and prompted widespread calls for stricter data protection regulations.

The scandal's impact on public trust was profound. A 2018 Pew Research Center study found that 44 percent of Facebook users aged 18–29 reported deleting the app from their phones following the incident, highlighting a significant erosion of confidence in the platform (Pew Research Center 2018).

Twitter's Data Breach (2020)

In July 2020, a daring group of hackers executed one of the most notorious breaches in Twitter's history. They infiltrated the accounts of high-profile individuals such as Barack Obama, Elon Musk, and Bill Gates, turning these influential platforms into unwitting promoters of a Bitcoin scam. The attackers pulled off this audacious scheme by exploiting Twitter's internal tools and manipulating employees to gain access. While their primary motive was financial, the hack underscored deeper issues, spotlighting vulnerabilities in Twitter's security framework and the troubling potential for such breaches to disrupt critical events, like elections or crise (The Guardian 2020).

Snapchat's "Snappening" (2014)

In 2014, Snapchat faced backlash after approximately 200,000 private images sent via the app were leaked online. The breach, dubbed "The Snappening," occurred when third-party apps that users had integrated with Snapchat were hacked. Although Snapchat wasn't directly at fault, the incident highlighted how third-party apps can jeopardize user data on social media platforms.

Consequences of Data Mishandling for Users

Identity Theft and Financial Fraud

Data breaches often expose sensitive information, such as email addresses, phone numbers, and even credit card details. For example, the LinkedIn data breach in 2021 exposed the personal information of over 700 million users, making them vulnerable to phishing scams and identity theft (Mathews 2021).

Emotional and Psychological Impact

The misuse of private photos, as seen in Snapchat's 2014 breach, can cause severe emotional distress. Victims may experience anxiety, shame, or harassment, particularly when private images are distributed without their consent (BBC News 2014).

Erosion of Digital Autonomy

When users discover their data has been used without their knowledge, they experience a profound loss of control over their digital presence. This was evident in the Cambridge Analytica scandal, where many Facebook users were unaware that their personal data had been harvested and weaponized for political purposes (Isaak and Hanna 2018). The incident highlighted the risks associated with opaque data practices and underscored the need for greater transparency in how personal information is collected and used.

Public Perception and Trust in Social Media Platforms

Declining Trust in Facebook

After the Cambridge Analytica scandal, surveys revealed a sharp decline in trust toward Facebook. A 2018 Pew Research Center study found that 44 percent of users aged 18–29 had deleted the app from their phones (Pew Research Center 2018). Although Facebook remains a dominant player, its reputation has been significantly tarnished, particularly among younger users.

Misinformation and Transparency Issues

Platforms like Twitter and YouTube have faced criticism for their role in spreading misinformation, exacerbating the trust deficit. For example, during the COVID-19 pandemic, false information about vaccines proliferated on social media, leading to public health challenges and calls for stricter moderation policies (Cinelli et al. 2020). This highlighted the urgent need for improved transparency and accountability in how platforms handle false or misleading content.

8.5 The User's Role in Data Privacy

Let's imagine you receive a notification from your favorite social media app: "We've updated our privacy policy." You skim past it, assuming nothing significant has changed, and click "Agree." But what if that update included permissions to access your microphone, track your location, or share your browsing history with advertisers? Would your decision have been different if you had known the details?

This scenario features a critical issue: how often do we, as users, take the time to thoroughly understand the privacy settings and policies of the platforms we use daily? Research shows that a vast majority of users—particularly younger audiences—routinely ignore these updates, either due to a lack of awareness or because they assume they have no other choice (Obar and Oeldorf-Hirsch 2018). The interplay of psychological and theoretical frameworks can help explain this phenomenon. For example, the "privacy paradox" refers to the discrepancy between users' expressed concerns about data privacy and their actual behaviors. While many users claim to value privacy, they often act in ways that suggest otherwise like accepting terms of service without reading them or oversharing on social media. This paradox is influenced by convenience, trust in platforms, and a lack of understanding about the implications of data sharing (Barnes 2006).

Foucault's Theory of Surveillance Michel Foucault's concept of the panopticon in his work Discipline and Punish is particularly relevant in the context of social media. Foucault described a system of power where individuals behave as if they are always being watched. On social media, this translates into self-censorship and compliance with norms established by platforms. Users may not fully understand the extent of data collection, but they accept surveillance as a trade-off for access to digital spaces (Foucault 1977).

The “Nothing to Hide” Fallacy

When asked about their data privacy habits, many young people often express indifference, echoing sentiments like, “I have nothing to hide, so why should I care?” Many users, particularly younger ones, subscribe to the “nothing to hide” argument, believing that privacy concerns are irrelevant if they have done nothing wrong. However, this fallacy, addressed by legal scholar Daniel Solove (2007), overlooks the broader implications of data collection. Privacy is not merely about concealing wrongdoing; it is about maintaining control over personal information, preventing misuse, and safeguarding against broader societal consequences, such as surveillance or discrimination.

For instance, data thieves and malicious actors can exploit even seemingly innocuous information. Your browsing habits, location history, or purchase preferences can be weaponized for identity theft, targeted scams, or manipulative advertising. Furthermore, extensive profiling by social media platforms can lead to algorithmic biases, such as unfair credit decisions or employment discrimination based on inferred characteristics. While social media platforms bear significant responsibility for safeguarding user data, individuals also have the power to protect themselves. Here are some actionable steps:

Best Practices for Safeguarding Your Digital World

Protecting your data on social media isn’t just about avoiding scams, it’s about being proactive in managing your online presence. Here’s how to fortify your digital defenses:

- Got a text from an unknown number? Don’t trust it. Verify by contacting the person through a known and secure method.
- Received a friend request from someone already in your list? It’s likely a fake. Double-check with your friend and report impersonators immediately.
- Think of your social media posts as a public bulletin board. Before posting, ask, Would I want a stranger to see this?
- Real-life tip: Sharing vacation photos in real time might seem fun, but it also signals to bad actors that your home is unattended. Save those snapshots for after you return, it’s a small delay that protects you while you’re away.
- A strong password is your first line of defense. Avoid predictable choices like “password123” or your pet’s name. Instead, create a mix of letters, numbers, and symbols.
- Enable two-factor Authentication (2FA) for an extra layer of security. Platforms like Instagram and Facebook offer 2FA in their settings, requiring a second verification step like a code sent to your phone. Even if someone guesses your password, 2FA can stop them cold.
- Remember the Cambridge Analytica scandal? It all started with a seemingly harmless quiz app. Many third-party apps request access to your social media accounts, but not all are trustworthy.

- Actionable tip: Regularly review the apps connected to your accounts and remove those you no longer use. Only grant access to apps you trust and truly need.
- If someone impersonates you or a friend, inform the affected person immediately.
- Report the fraudulent account to the platform without delay. A quick response can prevent further harm.
- A suspicious profile? Report it.
- An unknown message? Verify before clicking.
- By staying mindful, cautious, and proactive, you can turn your social media experience into a safer, smarter space. Remember: your data is valuable—guard it like treasure.

Understanding Privacy Settings and Tools

Privacy settings on social media are like the locks and shutters of your digital home, they give you control over who gets to see your world. But many people don't take the time to use them properly. Here's how to make these tools work for you, explained in simple terms:

Control Who Sees Your Content

- Most social media platforms (like Facebook, Instagram, and Twitter) let you choose who can see what you post. You can share with everyone, just your friends, or even specific people.
- Think of it this way: If you were hosting a party, would you invite everyone in your neighborhood or just a few close friends? Your posts deserve the same kind of care. Use privacy settings to keep your personal content shared only with those you trust.

Be Cautious with Location Sharing

- Did you know many apps track your location automatically? This can be handy for tagging your favorite café or checking in at a concert, but it's not always safe.
- Quick Fix: Turn off location sharing unless it's absolutely necessary. Apps like Snapchat even have a "Ghost Mode," so you can use location features without broadcasting your whereabouts to everyone.

Manage Ad Preferences

- Social media platforms use your data to show you targeted ads. While it might seem harmless, this tracking can feel intrusive. Thankfully, platforms like Facebook allow you to control what data advertisers can use.
- Pro Tip: Take a moment to explore the "Ad Preferences" section on your favorite platform. You can reduce unnecessary tracking and get a bit more privacy.

Think Before You Click

- Ever seen a link that promises free gifts or exclusive content? It's tempting, but these are often phishing scams designed to steal your information.
- Story Example: Imagine a stranger knocking on your door with a free prize. You'd probably ask for ID before accepting, right? Treat online links the same way. If it seems suspicious, verify it first.

Stay Educated

- Social media platforms frequently update their privacy settings and policies. Staying informed is like keeping your digital house locks updated—essential for security.
- Tip: Spend five minutes exploring the privacy section of your social media account. You might find helpful tools you didn't know existed, like extra account protections or content filters.

Advocate for Yourself

- If you feel like a platform isn't respecting your privacy, don't stay silent. Most platforms have reporting tools or customer support for privacy concerns.
- Example: If an app starts sharing your data in ways you're uncomfortable with, you can usually report it or reach out for help to address the issue.

Conclusion

To conclude, privacy in the age of social media is more than a personal concern; it is a cornerstone of autonomy, trust, and the broader ethical digital society, and the power to protect privacy is a shared responsibility among individuals, social media platforms, and policymakers. As the chapter discussed, the cases such as the Cambridge Analytica scandal and the repeated failures of platforms to adequately inform users about their data rights highlight the urgent need for greater transparency and accountability.

At the heart of this digital ecosystem lies the individual user. The ability to make informed choices, utilize privacy tools, and critically evaluate the platforms we engage with is paramount. However, the responsibility cannot rest solely on individuals. Social media companies must take proactive steps to simplify privacy policies, implement robust security measures, and prioritize user trust over profit. Similarly, policymakers must enforce regulations that protect data rights and promote equitable access to digital platforms.

In essence, this chapter calls for a collective reevaluation of privacy in the digital world. The choices we make today both as users and as a society will shape the future of social media and its role in our lives. Privacy is not just about shielding information; it is about preserving the dignity, freedom, and individuality that define us as human beings. To protect digital privacy is to protect the foundation of a connected yet ethical digital future. As Tim Cook once said, "Privacy is one of the top issues of the 21st century." In light of this, the question remains: What path will you choose to protect your privacy and contribute to a more ethical digital future?

References

Arias-Cabarcos, P., S. Khalili, and T. Strufe. 2022. "'Surprised, Shocked, Worried': User Reactions to Facebook Data Collection from Third Parties." https://arxiv.org/abs/2209.08048.

Arif, R. 2020. *Movements for Change: How Individuals, Social Media and Al Jazeera Are Changing Pakistan, Egypt and Tunisia.* Peter Lang Publishing.

Arif, R., L. Ragsdale, and M. Ittefaq. 2024. "What Does a 'Like' on Social Media Mean? Understanding the Motivations and Interpretations of Likes on Instagram." *Journal of Social Media Studies* 13 (2). https://www.thejsms.org/index.php/JSMS/article/view/1411.

Associated Press. 2024. "TikTok Is Designed to Be Addictive to Kids and Causes Them Harm, US States' Lawsuits Say." AP News, October 8. https://apnews.com/article/tiktok-lawsuit-youth-mental-health-2993f8e70d2e3d4eab9988df168fb948.

Barnes, S. B. 2006. "A Privacy Paradox: Social Networking in the United States." *First Monday* 11 (9). https://firstmonday.org/ojs/index.php/fm/article/view/1394.

BBC News. 2014. "Hackers Threaten to Post More Snapchat Photos Online." BBC News, October 11. https://www.bbc.com/news/newsbeat-29581386.

BBC. (2026). Men covertly filming women on nights out for online content. https://www.bbc.com/news/articles/c9wxx97jlveo

Boyd, D. M., and N. B. Ellison. 2007. "Social Network Sites: Definition, History, and Scholarship." *Journal of Computer-Mediated Communication* 13 (1): 210–30. https://academic.oup.com/jcmc/article/13/1/210/4583062?login=false.

Brugger, N. 2015. "A Brief History of Facebook as a Media Text: The Development of an Empty Structure." *First Monday* 20 (5). https://doi.org/10.5210/fm.v20i5.5423.

Cinelli, M., W. Quattrociocchi, A. Galeazzi, C. M. Valensise, E. Brugnoli, A. L. Schmidt, P. Zola, F. Zollo, and A. Scala. 2020. "The COVID-19 Social Media Infodemic." *Scientific Reports* 10 (1): 16598. https://doi.org/10.1038/s41598-020-73510-5.

CNN. 2025. "The Great Social Media Migration: Sudden Influx of US Users to RedNote Connects Chinese and Americans Like Never Before." CNN, January 14. https://www.cnn.com/2025/01/14/tech/rednote-china-popularity-us-tiktok-ban-intl-hnk/index.html.

Federal Trade Commission (FTC). 2019. "FTC Imposes $5 Billion Penalty and Sweeping New Privacy Restrictions on Facebook." https://www.ftc.gov/news-events/news/press-releases/2019/07/ftc-imposes-5-billion-penalty-sweeping-new-privacy-restrictions-facebook.

Foucault, M. 1977. *Discipline and Punish: The Birth of the Prison.* Translated by A. Sheridan. Pantheon Books. (Original work published 1975).

Isaak, J., and M. J. Hanna. 2018. "User Data Privacy: Facebook, Cambridge Analytica, and Privacy Protection." *Computer* 51 (8): 56–59. https://ieeexplore.ieee.org/document/8436400.

Kaye, D. B. V., X. Chen, and J. Zeng. 2021. "The Co-Evolution of Two Chinese Mobile Short Video Apps: Parallel Platformization of Douyin and TikTok." *Mobile Media & Communication* 9 (2): 229–53. https://doi.org/10.1177/2050157920952120.

Leiner, B. M., Vint Cerf, David Clark, Robert Kahn, L. Kleinrock, Daniel C. Lynch, Jon Postel, Lawerence Roberts, and Stephen Wolff. 1997. "The Past and Future History of the Internet." *Communications of the ACM* 40 (2): 102–08.

Mathews, L. 2021. "Details on 700 million LinkedIn Users for Sale on Notorious Hacking Forum." *Forbes*, June 29. https://www.forbes.com/sites/leemathews/2021/06/29/details-on-700-million-linkedin-users-for-sale-on-notorious-hacking-forum/.

McCormick, A. 2021. "If You're Not Paying for the Product, Then You Are the Product." Saucon Panther, August 8. https://sauconpanther.org/2535/arts-and-entertainment/if-youre-not-paying-for-the-product-then-you-are-the-product/.

Murthy, D. 2013. *Twitter: Social Communication in the Twitter Age.* Polity Press. https://www.dhirajmurthy.com/wp-content/uploads/2012/04/vol32BookReview.pdf.

Obar, J. A., and A. Oeldorf-Hirsch. 2018. "The Clickwrap: A Political Economic Mechanism for Manufacturing Consent on Social Media." *Social Media + Society* 4 (3). https://doi.org/10.1177/2056305118784770.

PBS. (2024). Here's what happened when India banned TikTok. https://www.pbs.org/newshour/world/heres-what-happened-when-india-banned-tiktok

Pew Research Center. 2018. "Americans Are Changing Their Relationship with Facebook." September 5. https://www.pewresearch.org/short-reads/2018/09/05/americans-are-changing-their-relationship-with-facebook/.

Piwek, L., and A. N. Joinson. 2016. "'What Do They Snapchat About?' Patterns of Use in Time-Limited Instant Messaging Service." *Computers in Human Behavior* 54: 358–367.

Qin, Yao et al. "The addiction behavior of short-form video app TikTok: The information quality and system quality perspective." Frontiers in psychology vol. 13 932805. 6 Sep. 2022, doi:10.3389/fpsyg.2022.932805

Reuters. 2025. "TikTok Ban: Why Does the US Want to Shut Down This App?" January 16. https://www.reuters.com/technology/factbox-why-does-us-want-ban-tiktok-allegations-against-it-2025-01-16/

Rheingold, H. 1993. *The Virtual Community: Homesteading on the Electronic Frontier.* MIT Press.

Rheingold, H. 2000. *The Virtual Community: Homesteading on the Electronic Frontier* (rev. ed.). The MIT Press. https://doi.org/10.7551/mitpress/7105.001.0001.

Roy, N., M. Srivastava, P. Mishra, and R. Chandra. 2020. "LidarPhone: Acoustic Sensing Using LIDAR to Enable Speech Recognition and Voice Interfaces." Association for Computing Machinery. https://www.cs.umd.edu/~nirupam/images/2_publication/papers/LidarPhone_SenSys20_nirupam.pdf.

Solove, D. J. 2007. "'I've Got Nothing to Hide' and Other Misunderstandings of Privacy." *San Diego Law Review* 44 (4): 745–72. https://papers.ssrn.com/sol3/papers.cfm?abstract_id=998565.

The Guardian. 2020. "Twitter Hack: Accounts of Prominent Figures, Including Biden, Musk, Obama, Gates, and Kanye Compromised. *The Guardian*, July 16. https://www.theguardian.com/technology/2020/jul/15/twitter-elon-musk-joe-biden-hacked-bitcoin.

Zuboff, S. 2019. "The Age of Surveillance Capitalism: The Fight for a Human Future at the New Frontier of Power." PublicAffairs.

Chapter 9

Safe Screens, Safe Minds

The New Cyber Strategy

Lamia Zia, PhD

Learning Objectives

- Learn how digital algorithms and echo chambers contribute to misinformation and the illusion of knowledge in online environments.
- Analyze philosophical frameworks, such as Plato's Allegory of the Cave and Aristotle's knowledge categories, to understand the challenges of modern digital perception.
- Define and evaluate the role of digital literacy and cyber literacy in protecting youth from misinformation, cyberbullying, and online threats.
- Assess global and institutional responses to digital safety, including cyber literacy initiatives in schools and policy strategies in countries like Finland, Singapore, and Canada.
- Identify the risks associated with unregulated digital environments, including identity theft, misinformation, screen addiction, and cyber harassment.
- Propose actionable strategies for educational institutions, parents, governments, and tech companies to build a cyber-safe generation.
- Evaluate the ethical and societal implications of algorithm-driven media, surveillance capitalism, and the erosion of data privacy.
- Design a framework for cyber literacy education, incorporating critical thinking, digital ethics, and online safety into curriculum development.

Key Terms

- **Cyber Literacy**: The ability to understand and responsibly engage with digital technologies, including identifying cyber threats and practicing safe online behavior.
- **Digital Illusion**: The false sense of knowledge or control fostered by algorithmic curation and filtered information online.

- **Echo Chamber**: An environment where a person only encounters information or opinions that reflect and reinforce their own, often due to algorithms.
- **Algorithmic Bias**: Systematic and unfair discrimination embedded in the automated decision-making processes of digital platforms.
- **Cyberbullying**: The use of digital platforms to harass, threaten, or humiliate others, especially prevalent among youth.
- **Misinformation**: False or misleading information spread without malicious intent.
- **Digital Citizenship**: Responsible and ethical behavior in digital environments, involving privacy, respect, and critical engagement.
- **Privacy Turbulence**: Disruption in perceived control over one's personal information in digital contexts, especially on platforms like Snapchat.
- **Digital Literacy Programs**: Educational initiatives aimed at equipping individuals with the skills to analyze, evaluate, and create digital content responsibly.
- **Parental Digital Involvement:** Active participation of parents in monitoring and guiding children's digital behavior and cybersecurity awareness.
- **Filter Bubble**: A state of intellectual isolation caused by personalized search results and algorithmic sorting that limits exposure to diverse perspectives.
- **Surveillance Capitalism**: A system where personal data is commodified and used to influence behavior and decision-making.

Introduction

The biggest enemy of knowledge is not ignorance; it's the illusion of knowledge.

Stephen Hawking

Does humanity still live in Plato's Allegory of the Cave, where illusion is mistaken for reality? In an era dominated by digital media, misinformation, and algorithm-driven echo chambers, the illusion of knowledge has become one of the greatest intellectual challenges of our time. Hawking's assertion that illusion, not ignorance, is the enemy of knowledge aligns with Plato's philosophical argument that people often mistake perceived reality for absolute truth.

In Plato's *Republic*, the "Allegory of the Cave" presents a scenario where prisoners are confined from birth in a cave, seeing only shadows cast on a wall. These shadows represent their reality, yet they are mere distortions of the actual world outside the cave. When one prisoner escapes and discovers the true world, he realizes that what he and his fellow captives believed reality was, is, in fact, an illusion (Plato c. 380 BCE., trans. Grube and Reeve 1992). Hawking's argument reflects this concept in the modern digital landscape: Social media algorithms create self-reinforcing bubbles, where individuals only see information that aligns with their existing beliefs, preventing intellectual growth (Pariser 2011).

But do you ever ask yourself the following?

- Why do you keep seeing the same type of content on your social media feed?
- Why do certain ads, reels, or videos always seem to "match" your thoughts, interests, or even conversations?
- Is this really your choice, or are you being guided toward an illusion of choice?

Every click, every like, every share is not just an action; it's data. Tech companies use this data to shape what you see, think, and even believe. The result? A digital echo chamber that reinforces your biases rather than challenging them. Just like Plato's prisoners in the cave, many of us unknowingly accept the shadows on the wall our personalized social media feeds as reality. The question is, Are you willing to step outside the digital cave and seek the truth and not a version of truth?

Scholars argued that advancements in AI and digital media allow for the creation of hyperrealistic fabrications, blurring the line between reality and illusion (Citron and Chesney 2019). People favor information that reinforces their preconceived notions, rejecting opposing viewpoints regardless of factual accuracy (Nickerson 1998). The modern world is increasingly dominated by simulations of knowledge rather than knowledge itself, a phenomenon closely resembling Plato's cave where the shadows on the wall have evolved into social media narratives, fake news, and AI-generated content, creating a world of manipulated perception. While Plato's cave is a metaphor for enlightenment, Aristotle distinguished between different kinds of knowledge episteme (theoretical knowledge), techne (practical knowledge), and doxa (opinion or belief) (Aristotle 350 BCE). Many individuals mistake opinion (doxa) for fact, influenced by online discourse and algorithmic curation rather than empirical evidence (Carr 2010).

Let's look at these emerging issues from Greek scholars: Aristotle argued that true knowledge requires rational inquiry and direct experience. The digital world, however, trivializes critical thinking offering information so effortlessly that users rarely question its validity (Postman 1985). Aristotle emphasized habitual learning and logic as the foundation of knowledge (340 BCE). Without structured digital literacy education, the modern world remains trapped in a cave of misinformation and cognitive shortcuts.

The only way to escape the cave of digital illusion is through critical thinking, cyber literacy, and intellectual humility: Teaching individuals to differentiate fact from manipulation can help break the cycle of algorithmic misinformation (Wineburg and McGrew 2017). Encouraging self-examination and skepticism leads to intellectual autonomy, preventing blind acceptance of digital "shadows" (Paul and Elder 2006). Aristotle's holistic approach to knowledge emphasizes integrating science, ethics, and philosophy to cultivate well-rounded, critical thinkers (Nussbaum 1997). If Plato's cave still exists in digital form, then education, not blind acceptance of information, is the only path toward digital enlightenment. Breaking free from illusion requires embracing uncertainty, questioning narratives, and seeking truth beyond the walls of algorithmic perception.

In today's world, younger generations are digital natives, they've grown up with technology in their hands, swiping before they could write, clicking before they could talk. Because of this, many believe they fully understand the digital world.

But do they?

- They know how to post, but do they know how to protect themselves online?
- They know how to share, but do they know how to fact-check misinformation?
- They know how to comment, but do they understand the lasting impact of cyberbullying?

The truth is most teens don't realize the risks of the digital world until it's too late. They have the illusion of knowledge believing they are in control of their online lives, when they are unprotected, uninformed, and unprepared for the consequences. This is where cyber literacy and digital safety policies in the society must step in. Children and teenagers are growing up with gadgets in their hands, seamlessly trying to navigate online spaces for learning, social interaction, and entertainment. However, with these learning opportunities come significant challenges cyberbullying, misinformation, privacy breaches, and online exploitation—that pose serious risks to young users. If we don't teach students how to use the online world responsibly, we are leaving them vulnerable in this fast-growing digital planet.

In a recent class discussion with my students on cyber related issues, the urgency for action became clear. They weren't just aware of the problems they wanted to fix them. From cyberbullying to online privacy, from digital responsibility to misinformation, they recognized that schools, colleges, and universities must implement a comprehensive cyber strategy one that ensures students begin learning about digital privacy, responsible social media usage, digital ethics, and online etiquette from an early age. In an era where technology permeates every aspect of life, digital literacy should no longer be an option but a fundamental part of modern education. Equipping students with these skills early on is essential to creating a generation that is not only technologically proficient but also ethically responsible and critically aware of the digital landscape.

This chapter calls for robust cyber strategy, outlining the critical role of educational institutions in creating cyber literacy programs and courses that teach digital responsibility. By implementing structured policies and proactive measures, they can take immediate action to ensure that students are equipped with the necessary skills to navigate the digital world safely, critically evaluate online information, and protect themselves from cyber threats. The challenge is not technology itself; rather, it is the illusion that individuals already possess sufficient digital knowledge. Thus, it is imperative to shift from assumption to education ensuring that cyber literacy is not an afterthought but a fundamental component of modern education. Now is the time to lay out the foundation for a "Cyber-Safe Generation" one that is informed, resilient, and prepared for the complexities of the digital era.

This chapter also examines key strategies, framework, and recommendations to build "cyber-safe educational institutions." where social media corporations, academic institutions, and policymakers collaborate to create a safer digital environment. Ultimately, the goal is not just to implement protective measures but to empower young individuals to become responsible digital citizens in an era where knowledge, security, and ethical engagement online are more crucial than ever.

9.1 Policies and Regulations for Cybersecurity in Schools

Educational institutions are increasingly targeted by cyber threats, including phishing attacks, data breaches, and ransomware. The integration of technology into classrooms, while enhancing learning experiences, has expanded the attack surface for cybercriminals. The US Department of Education highlights that school districts nationwide face an average of five cyber incidents per week, emphasizing the critical need for robust security measures in educational environments. The Cybersecurity and Infrastructure Security Agency (CISA n.d.) notes that, on average, there is more than one cyber incident per school day in K–12 schools.

Governments worldwide have introduced policies to strengthen cybersecurity in educational institutions. The Children's Internet Protection Act (CIPA) in the US mandates schools to use internet filters and implement cybersecurity awareness programs (US Department of Education 2022). Similarly, the European Union's General Data Protection Regulation (GDPR) imposes strict guidelines on schools to protect student data (Gogolin 2021).

The Role of Digital Literacy in Cyber Safety

Digital literacy extends beyond basic computer skills to include critical thinking, responsible online behavior, and cybersecurity awareness. One successful initiative aimed at enhancing digital and media literacy is the PBS NewsHour Student Reporting Labs Program (Hobbs 2016). This project-based learning model connects middle and high school students with professional journalists, equipping them with the tools to critically assess news content, synthesize information, and develop responsible reporting skills. The program's impact is evident: Students who participated demonstrated significant improvements in collaboration, intellectual curiosity, self-expression, and the ability to evaluate news credibility (Hobbs 2016).

Buckingham (2006) has extensively discussed the necessity of integrating digital literacy into educational curricula. He argues that digital literacy enables students to learn the internet safely and critically evaluate online content, which is essential in the digital age. In his 2006 article, "Defining Digital Literacy—What Do Young People Need to Know About Digital Media?" Buckingham outlines a framework for digital literacy based on key concepts from media education. He emphasizes that developing critical approaches to digital media is a necessary prerequisite for using them as resources for learning.

Research supports the idea that teaching digital citizenship reduces online risks for students (Ribble 2021). Digital citizenship programs promote ethical online behavior, data privacy awareness, and responsible social media use (Livingstone and Helsper 2013). Studies also show that students who receive formal digital literacy training are less likely to fall victim to cyber threats and misinformation (Shao et al. 2018). Educators play a vital role in creating cyber awareness and digital ethics. However, research indicates that many teachers lack sufficient training in cybersecurity (Manca et al. 2021).

In today's hyperconnected world, cyber threats lurk behind every click, message, and data exchange. Yet, research shows that many educators and professionals lack the training needed to navigate the ever-evolving digital landscape. Addressing this critical gap, the University of Maryland's Department of Communication has stepped up in 2024 with a groundbreaking course: "Cybersecurity and Digital Communication." This forward-thinking program is designed to empower students with the knowledge and hands-on expertise required to tackle cybersecurity challenges in digital communication. The curriculum goes beyond theory, it immerses students in real-world scenarios where they learn to detect, prevent, and respond to cyber threats effectively. In launching this course, the Department of Communication at University of Maryland is taking a proactive stance in closing the cybersecurity knowledge gap and ensuring that future communicators are equipped to protect themselves and others in an increasingly digital world. These cutting-edge educational programs aren't just about learning the dos and don'ts of cybersecurity, they're about shaping a generation of savvy digital citizens. By blending media literacy, digital security, and ethical awareness, these initiatives equip students with the superpowers they need to perform in the ever-evolving digital world with confidence.

Emerging Cyber Issues

Cyberbullying has become a significant concern in educational settings, with studies indicating that nearly one in three students experience some form of online harassment (Patchin and Hinduja 2020). According to a study by Kowalski et al. (2021), cyberbullying is linked to increased anxiety, depression, and academic difficulties among victims. This growing issue has led scholars and policymakers to advocate for stronger anti-cyberbullying policies in schools, emphasizing preventative education, digital accountability, and stricter enforcement measures.

Research indicates that nearly 37 percent of teenagers have experienced cyberbullying (Patchin and Hinduja 2020), leading to anxiety, depression, and even suicide in extreme cases. According to the FBI, one in five children who use the internet have been approached by an online predator (Wolak et al. 2021). A study by Stanford University found that 82 percent of middle school students could not distinguish between real news and fake news (Wineburg and McGrew 2017). Young users often overshare personal information online, making them easy targets for identity theft and online scams (Livingstone and Helsper 2022).

However, cyberbullying is not the only digital threat affecting young internet users. Misinformation and fake news present another significant challenge, particularly for children and teenagers who lack the media literacy skills necessary to distinguish between credible and misleading content (Guess et al. 2020). A study by Metzger and Flanagin (2013) explored the complexities of credibility and trust in the digital age, emphasizing the necessity for users to develop critical evaluation skills to navigate online information effectively. They highlighted that the proliferation of user-generated content requires individuals to be more discerning about the sources and accuracy of the information they encounter.

Building on this foundation, a study Jones-Jang et al. (2021) examined the impact of media literacy education on the ability to identify fake news. The research found that information literacy significantly enhances individuals' capacity to discern false information, whereas other forms of literacy did not show the same effect. This underscores the importance of targeted educational interventions in fostering critical thinking and evaluative skills. These findings collectively suggest that as misinformation becomes increasingly sophisticated, there is a pressing need to prioritize digital information literacy in educational curricula. Equipping individuals with the tools to critically assess online content is essential in combating the spread of fake news and ensuring an informed public. To counter misinformation, researchers emphasize the need for media literacy programs in schools (Wineburg and McGrew 2022). These programs teach students how to fact-check information, analyze sources, and identify biases.

These two issues: cyberbullying and misinformation are interconnected, as both thrive in digital spaces where young users engage without sufficient digital literacy training. The rise of social media platforms as primary sources of news and peer interaction has created an environment where false information spreads rapidly and online harassment becomes more accessible and anonymous. Without strong educational interventions and institutional policies, students remain at risk of both emotional harm from cyberbullying and intellectual harm from misinformation.

One notable initiative is Finland's "digital leap" project, launched by the Ministry of Education and Culture in 2015. This project aimed to modernize the information and communication technology (ICT) infrastructure and pedagogy in Finnish schools. Research indicates that teachers' professional development plays a crucial role in the successful digitalization of education. However, challenges such as limited time and resources have been identified as barriers to effective ICT integration (Kupiainen 2022).

Building digital security and cyber literacy requires cooperation between schools, social media companies, governments, and tech organizations. According to West (2023), collaborative efforts can lead to

- better digital safety regulations,
- enhanced cybersecurity infrastructure in schools,

- more effective digital literacy programs, and
- stronger content moderation policies by tech companies.

By making cyber literacy a mandatory subject in middle and high schools, students will be equipped with the knowledge to protect themselves from the digital and cyber threats. For example, countries like Finland and Estonia have successfully integrated cyber literacy into their national curricula, resulting in lower incidents of cybercrime and misinformation exposure among students (Rintala and Kankaanranta 2022). The United States and other nations must follow such innovative strategies. Many students, especially from underserved communities, lack basic digital skills (Kim et al. 2023). A mandatory cyber literacy course ensures that every student, regardless of socioeconomic background, receives essential knowledge to safely navigate the internet, use digital tools effectively, and protect their personal and academic data. Cyber threats do not discriminate by profession as students in business, healthcare, engineering, journalism, communication, and the arts all interact with digital platforms, making cyber literacy essential across academic disciplines.

In the digital age, these cyber vulnerabilities are no longer confined to institutions—they affect each and every individual in society. While businesses, government agencies, and schools face significant cybersecurity risks, ordinary citizens are just as vulnerable to data breaches, identity theft, financial fraud, and manipulation through false information. Cyberattacks are often perceived as problems for large organizations, but individuals bear the brunt of these threats daily. The impact of cyber threats on individuals is profound and far-reaching: Because every individual is at risk, tackling cyber threats and misinformation requires collective action. Solutions must go beyond protecting institutions and focus on empowering individuals with digital literacy and cybersecurity awareness.

Global Cyber Literacy

Globally, several countries have integrated cyber literacy programs into their educational systems to equip students with essential digital skills and promote safe online behaviors. For example, Finland has implemented a comprehensive media literacy curriculum nationwide, aiming to enhance students' critical thinking and resilience against misinformation. This initiative has contributed to Finland consistently ranking high in media literacy indices, reflecting its commitment to comprehensive digital education (Cord 2022).

Educational institutions in Canada are integrating digital literacy into their curricula. East Hill Elementary School in Montreal, for example, offers a Digital Literacy/Online Safety Program as part of its Media and Technology academic curriculum. This program educates students about online safety, screen time management, and responsible digital behavior, addressing issues like screen addiction and cyberbullying (Gentile 2025).

This initiative is designed to address critical digital challenges faced by young students, including the following:

- The program teaches students how to identify online risks, including cyber threats such as phishing scams, identity theft, and online predators.
- It emphasizes safe browsing habits, guiding students on recognizing trusted websites and avoiding harmful digital interactions.
- With children increasingly exposed to screens at an early age, the program educates students on healthy digital habits and encourages balanced technology use.
- Students learn about the impact of excessive screen time on mental health, physical well-being, and academic performance.
- The curriculum promotes positive online engagement, teaching students about digital footprints, online etiquette, and the consequences of inappropriate content sharing.
- It reinforces the importance of respectful communication in online spaces, combating issues such as trolling, hate speech, and cyber harassment.

Singapore has also taken a structured and forward-thinking approach to digital literacy through its National Digital Literacy Programme (NDLP), launched by the Ministry of Education in March 2020. The program is designed to equip students with essential digital skills, ensuring they become confident, responsible, and effective users of technology in an increasingly digitized world. At the core of NDLP is the "Find, Think, Apply, Create" framework, which fosters critical thinking, responsible digital engagement, and innovative problem-solving skills (Ministry of Education, Singapore n.d.).

Key Components of the NDLP Initiative:

- The NDLP ensures that every secondary school student receives a Personal Learning Device (PLD)—such as a tablet or laptop—enhancing their ability to learn beyond traditional classroom settings.
- Students are trained to manage their digital devices responsibly, with schools integrating cyber wellness education into the curriculum to promote safe and ethical online behavior.
- Students are taught how to search for reliable information, verify sources, and detect misinformation—an essential skill in the era of fake news and digital propaganda.
- The program incorporates fact-checking exercises and media literacy workshops to help students critically analyze online content.

These examples demonstrate a global recognition of the importance of cyber literacy in education, with various countries adopting programs to prepare students for the challenges of the digital age.

9.2 The Cyber Strategy Recommendations

According to the Ministry of Education Singapore, digital literacy and technological skills are central to preparing students for a rapidly evolving digital world. Considering the accelerating pace of technological advancement and the corresponding rise in cyber threats, it is imperative that educators, policymakers, and technology stakeholders recognize the shared responsibility for a secure digital environment. Ensuring cyber safety for future generations necessitates a multistakeholder approach, wherein schools, families, social media platforms, and government agencies collaboratively engage in the ongoing development of comprehensive digital safety education.

The creation of a resilient and secure digital ecosystem cannot rest solely on the shoulders of any single institution. Rather, it demands a coordinated, proactive, and systemic response that integrates efforts across sectors. To ensure the efficacy of cyber literacy education, educational institutions must implement robust curricular frameworks; policymakers must enact supportive legislation and allocate resources; and technology companies must enhance content moderation tools, privacy protections, and user education initiatives. Through these collaborative strategies, stakeholders can collectively build a digitally literate, ethically responsible, and cyber-aware generation. This chapter recommends the following strategies:

In today's digital age, cyber literacy is not a luxury, it is a necessity. With the increasing prevalence of cyber threats, misinformation, online harassment, and privacy breaches, it is imperative that middle and high schools make cyber literacy a mandatory course requirement. Furthermore, universities across disciplines should integrate cyber literacy into their curricula, ensuring that all students, regardless of their field of study, graduate with a fundamental understanding of digital security, privacy, and responsible online behavior.

- All institutions, including schools, colleges, and universities must implement end-to-end encryption, secure cloud storage, and multifactor authentication (MFA) to protect sensitive personal data.
- Schools need to implement cybersecurity awareness programs from elementary to high school levels and incorporate digital citizenship education into the curriculum, teaching students about responsible online behavior, privacy, and security.
- Encourage peer-led digital safety initiatives where older students' mentor younger ones on safe internet practices in schools.

Public libraries must host weekly or monthly cyber safety discussion sessions where children engage in guided conversations about online risks, cyberbullying, misinformation, privacy, and digital ethics. Example: The British Library's "Digital Skills for Life" initiative runs interactive workshops teaching children how to recognize online threats, protect personal data, and respond to digital harassment.

Libraries should host age-appropriate, interactive workshops where children learn through games, storytelling, and role-playing scenarios about online scams, safe social media habits, and recognizing misinformation. Example: Singapore's National Library Board runs the "S.U.R.E. Campaign," teaching children how to evaluate online information critically and avoid digital manipulation.

- Work collaboratively with educators to design educational campaigns on cybersecurity and responsible social media use. Promote cyber ethics and digital literacy policies in national education frameworks.
- Schools should develop comprehensive cybersecurity policies that outline rules for internet usage, digital communication, and online behavior.
- Regular cyber hygiene training should be conducted to teach students how to recognize phishing attempts, protect passwords, and handle cyber threats.
- Implement strict anti-cyberbullying policies with clear reporting mechanisms for victims.
- Train teachers and school counselors on how to identify, address, and prevent cyberbullying incidents.

Introduce cyber literacy programs that teach students how to identify reliable sources and fact-check information and partner with tech companies to develop fact-checking tools accessible to students and educators.

Schools must integrate mandatory critical thinking exercises into cyber literacy curricula, where students analyze real-life examples of fake news, misinformation, and digital manipulation. Classroom activities should include fact-checking exercises where students evaluate news articles, social media posts, and viral content. Example: Finland's media literacy program teaches students to systematically fact-check online content as part of their standard curriculum, ensuring they develop strong analytical skills to identify misinformation.

Schools, universities, and educational ministries must host annual international cyber literacy conferences to share research findings, cybersecurity trends, and educational innovations. For example, Finland's global partnerships in media literacy education provide collaborative opportunities for educators worldwide to share best practices in combating misinformation and digital manipulation.

Cyber literacy is not just about security; it is about responsible digital behavior. Teaching students about ethical online engagement, media literacy, and cybersecurity awareness will encourage respectful communication and reduce online harassment. Cyber literacy should be a mandatory subject alongside math, science, and history. Cyber literacy should be a core course requirement for all undergraduate students, regardless of major.

According to the US Department of Education (2024) strengthening K–12 cybersecurity is essential to maintaining safe and secure learning environments. Schools should adopt hands-on cybersecurity training, misinformation detection exercises, and privacy awareness programs. Federal and State Governments should allocate funding for teacher training in cybersecurity and data privacy.

Academic institutions should partner with cybersecurity experts, tech companies, and government agencies to provide real-world training. Universities should integrate cyber literacy education into general education courses.

Governments should enact policies mandating cyber literacy education nationwide to create a digitally secure and informed society.

Schools must implement mandatory digital literacy programs to teach students how to detect misinformation, protect their privacy, and use the internet responsibly.

Social media corporations must improve content moderation algorithms to reduce the spread of fake news and cyber threats, and government should enforce stronger data privacy laws to protect users from exploitation by tech giants.

Tech companies must enforce strict anti-bullying policies, allowing users to report and remove harmful content efficiently.

Social media companies must disclose how their algorithms recommend content to prevent manipulation and misinformation.

Schools must actively track and document incidents of cyberbullying, digital harassment, and online exploitation to assess program effectiveness. Annual reporting on digital well-being metrics will be required to ensure that intervention strategies are working.

Students learn how to verify sources, fact-check news, and avoid spreading false information. Create class activities on these topics and involve students in practical scenarios finding solutions.

Integrate cyber literacy as a mandatory subject in middle and high schools. Include topics such as online privacy, misinformation detection, cyber hygiene, and ethical digital behavior.

Educators must receive training in cybersecurity and digital media literacy to effectively teach students.

Schools should partner with cybersecurity experts, universities, and tech companies to provide up-to-date resources.

Tech companies must enhance child protection policies, enforce stronger content moderation, and provide cybersecurity resources for schools.

With the rise of social media platforms such as Snapchat, digital self-disclosure and privacy boundaries have become increasingly blurred. Many users are unaware of the long-term consequences of sharing personal content in disappearing-message apps, making it critical for educational institutions to teach privacy management strategies within cyber literacy programs (Velten et al. 2017). Schools should introduce interactive workshops focused on the three key privacy concepts identified in the study—privacy ownership, privacy control, and privacy turbulence—to help students navigate digital disclosure responsibly.

9.3 Parental Intervention Strategies

Parental involvement is crucial in creating a safe digital environment at home. Research indicates that when parents actively monitor their children's online activities and engage in open discussions about internet safety, adolescents are less likely to engage in risky behaviors. According to the Centers for Disease Control and Prevention (2024) effective parental monitoring is associated with reductions in various adolescent risk behaviors, including substance use, sexual activity, and experiences of violence such as bullying and cyberbullying. However, Blum-Ross and Livingstone (2022) highlights that many parents lack the necessary digital skills to guide their children effectively. To create a safer digital environment for students, educational institutions must proactively engage parents in addressing cyberbullying, online harassment, and digital threats. Parental intervention plays a critical role in reinforcing responsible digital behavior and ensuring that students receive support both at school and at home. Cyber literacy education must extend beyond schools to involve parents, guardians, and the wider community.

Governments must establish nationwide digital literacy programs in partnership with schools, cybersecurity agencies, and child protection organizations to educate parents on cyber threats, privacy risks, and digital safety strategies. Example: Finland's media literacy program actively includes parents in training sessions, ensuring they can guide their children in identifying misinformation and practicing safe online interactions.

Schools must host quarterly digital literacy workshops where parents receive hands-on training on parental control tools, social media settings, and cyber threat detection. Example: Singapore's NDLP incorporates parental workshops to educate families on cybersecurity, data privacy, and responsible online communication.

State-sponsored initiatives must run nationwide public awareness campaigns through media, social media, and community events to emphasize the importance of parental involvement in online safety.

Example: Australia's eSafety Commissioner runs targeted campaigns for parents, providing guidelines on safe technology use, detecting cyberbullying, and reporting digital crimes.

Parents must complete a certified digital literacy course as part of school engagement programs, ensuring active participation in their child's online safety education.

Schools that successfully integrate parental digital literacy workshops into their curriculum will receive state grants and funding to expand cybersecurity resources. Example: Canada's Digital Literacy Exchange Program (DLEP) provides funding for community and school-based training programs that promote cyber literacy and online safety awareness among families

9.4 The Subtle Spread of Fake News Requires Strategic Digital Literacy Education

While much of the discourse around fake news paints a picture of rampant disinformation overwhelming social media platforms, the study by Guess, Nagler, and Tucker (2020) complicates this narrative. Their research, published in Science Advances, found that the actual prevalence of fake news dissemination on Facebook is lower than popularly assumed, yet the phenomenon remains highly concentrated among a small subset of users, particularly older adults and individuals with lower levels of digital media literacy.

This nuanced finding has significant implications for how we address fake news. It suggests that the danger is not necessarily in the quantity of fake news, but in its targeted impact and the mechanisms of its spreadincluding algorithmic amplification, confirmation bias, and a lack of critical engagement with online content. This supports the argument that blanket censorship or platform-wide panic is not the solution. Instead, what is needed is strategic, targeted digital literacy education one that focuses on teaching indlviduals how to verify sources, question narratives, and resist emotionally manipulative content.

In the context of this chapter, ff we acknowledge that the spread of disinformation is less about volume and more about vulnerability, then educational systems must prioritize fact-checking skills, source evaluation, and psychological resilience as essential components of cyber literacy curricula. Particularly in schools and universities, these skills must be cultivated early and consistently, so that students not only recognize misinformation but also understand the cognitive biases that make them susceptible to it.

Moreover, Guess et al. remind us that the solution is not just technological, it is deeply human. The ability to discern truth from falsehood depends on critical thinking, not just machine learning. Their findings reinforce the chapter's broader thesis: without digital literacy education grounded in ethics and critical inquiry, students are not empowered citizens but passive recipients of algorithmically filtered content. In this sense, building cyber-safe and intellectually resilient communities depends not just on software updates or fact-checking tools, but on the deliberate cultivation of informed, skeptical, and responsible media users.

Conclusion

Cyberbullying remains a persistent threat to student well-being in the digital age. According to the Cyberbullying Research Center (2023), cyberbullying is defined as "when someone repeatedly and intentionally harasses, mistreats, or makes fun of another person online or while using cell phones or other electronic devices." Their findings indicate that approximately 34% of students surveyed reported experiencing cyberbullying at some point in their lives. In the 30 days prior to the survey, 26% of students reported being cyberbullied two or more times across one or more of eleven specific types. The most commonly reported behaviors included mean or hurtful comments (22.5%) and the spreading of online rumors (20.1%), reflecting the emotional harm that digital harassment can inflict. These statistics highlight the urgent need for schools, parents, and policymakers to implement stronger cyber safety education and intervention programs.

The cyber strategy is essential to protect young users from online risks such as cyberbullying, misinformation, and privacy threats. Schools, parents, policymakers, and tech companies must work collaboratively to ensure a safe and responsible digital environment for future generations. While progress has been made in digital literacy education and cybersecurity awareness, challenges remain, particularly in enforcing policies and ensuring cross-sector cooperation. The lack of mandatory cyber literacy education poses a major risk to young users and future professionals. Cyber threats are no longer hypothetical—they are real, constant, and evolving. Failing to address these risks in the education system leaves students vulnerable to identity theft, cyberbullying, misinformation, and digital exploitation.

The academic institutions must integrate cyber literacy as a mandatory course, ensuring that students grow up with the knowledge to protect themselves and others online. Universities must make cyber literacy a cross-disciplinary requirement, preparing students for an increasingly digital workforce. By investing in cyber literacy education today, we can build a digitally responsible, secure, and empowered generation that is ready to face the challenges of tomorrow's cyber landscape. Data privacy isn't just a policy decision—it's a fundamental human right, as crucial as freedom of speech or personal security. In a world where digital footprints are tracked, stored, and sold, the right to control one's own data must be protected with unwavering urgency. It cannot be an afterthought, a secondary concern, or a compromise; it must be a nonnegotiable cornerstone of the digital age. The chapter concludes with the haunting words of T. S. Eliot's "The Hollow Men" that serves as a reminder of what happens when a society loses its pursuit of true knowledge when it becomes filled with illusion, yet devoid of depth and understanding. When illusion replaces truth, when we trade depth for distraction, privacy for convenience, and awareness for apathy, we risk becoming just as Eliot describes a world filled with voices that whisper but mean nothing, faces that exist but hold no soul, and actions that move but lead nowhere. Eliot says,

"We are the hollow men
We are the stuffed men
Leaning together
Headpiece filled with straw.
Our dried voices, when
We whisper together
Are quiet and meaningless
As wind in dry grass
Or rats' feet over broken glass
In our dry cellar
Shape without form, shade without colour.

Paralysed force, gesture without motion;
Those who have crossed
With direct eyes, to death's other Kingdom
Remember us—if at all—not as lost
Violent souls, but only
As the hollow men."[1]

Eliot critiques a world where voices are meaningless, gestures are empty, and knowledge is hollow—a sentiment that echoes Hawking's warning about the illusion of knowledge. Today, in an era where misinformation spreads faster than truth, where clickbait headlines replace critical inquiry, and where social media algorithms dictate our perception of reality, we are in danger of becoming "hollow men"—passive consumers of content, unable or unwilling to think critically about the information we absorb. This chapter has explored how cyber literacy education, digital responsibility, and institutional accountability can serve as safeguards against intellectual emptiness, providing individuals with the tools to distinguish fact from fiction, recognize digital manipulation, and protect themselves online.

If Eliot were to observe our present world, he might see a society where people, despite having access to limitless information, are more disconnected from true knowledge than ever before. But unlike the hollow men in his poem, we are not yet doomed to silence. Through education, awareness, and a commitment to intellectual honesty, we can ensure that the next generation is not merely stuffed with fragmented information but truly empowered by knowledge. It is time to step out of the cave, break free from illusion, and reclaim our pursuit of truth.

References

Aristotle. 340 BCE. *Nicomachean Ethics*. Translated by J. A. K. Thomson.

Aristotle. 350 BCE. *Metaphysics*. Translated by W. D. Ross.

Buckingham, D. 2006. "Defining Digital Literacy – What Do Young People Need to Know about Digital Media? *Nordic Journal of Digital Literacy* 1 (4): 263–77. https://doi.org/10.18261/ISSN1891-943X-2006-04-03.

Carr, N. 2010. *The Shallows: What the Internet Is Doing to Our Brains.* W.W. Norton & Company.

Centers for Disease Control and Prevention. "Parental Monitoring." Centers for Disease Control and Prevention, https://www.cdc.gov/healthy-youth-parent-resources/positive-parental-practices/parental-monitoring.html

Citron, Danielle K., and Robert Chesney. 2019. "Deepfakes and the New Disinformation War." Foreign Affairs. https://scholarship.law.bu.edu/shorter_works/76.

Cord, D. J. 2022. "Educated Decisions: Finnish Media Literacy Deters Disinformation." Finland.fi, June. https://finland.fi/life-society/educated-decisions-finnish-media-literacy-deters-disinformation/.

Cyberbullying Research Center. 2023. "Cyberbullying Data & Trends 2023." https://cyberbullying.org/.

Cybersecurity and Infrastructure Security Agency. n.d. "K–12 Cybersecurity: Protecting Our Future." U.S. Department of Homeland Security. https://www.cisa.gov/K12Cybersecurity.

Eliot, T. S. 1925. *The Hollow Men.* Faber & Faber.

1. T. S. Eliot, "The Hollow Men," Collected Prose of T.S. Eliot Volume 1, Faber & Faber, Inc., 1925.

Gentile, A. 2025. "Screen Addiction and Cyberbullying: Montreal Students Learn Online Safety in Much-Loved Digital Literacy Class." CityNews Montreal, January 20. https://montreal.citynews.ca/2025/01/20/east-hill-media-literacy-online-safety/.

Gogolin, G. 2021. *Digital Forensics and Cyber Crime.* Elsevier.

Guess, A. M., J. Nagler, and J. Tucker. 2020. "Less Than You Think: Prevalence and Predictors of Fake News Dissemination on Facebook. *Science Advances* 6 (14).

Hobbs, R. 2016. "When Teens Create the News: Examining the Impact of PBS News Hour Student Reporting Labs." *Journalism Education* 5 (1): 61–73.

Jones-Jang, S. M., T. Mortensen, and J. Liu. 2021. "Does Media Literacy Help Identification of Fake News? Information Literacy Helps, but Other Literacies Don't." *American Behavioral Scientist* 65 (2): 371–88. https://doi.org/10.1177/0002764219869406.

Kowalski, R. M., G. W. Giumetti, A. N. Schroeder, and M. R. Lattanner. 2021. "Bullying in the Digital Age: A Critical Review and Meta-Analysis of Cyberbullying Research Among Youth. *Psychological Bulletin* 147 (3), 118–45.

Kupiainen, R. 2022. "Making the 'Digital Leap' in Finnish Schools. Nordisk tidsskrift for pedagogikk og kritikk, Special Issue." *Digitalisering av utdannings- og oppvekstspraksiser* 8, 287–297. https://doi.org/10.23865/ntpk.v8.4068.

Livingstone, S., and E. J. Helsper. 2013. "Children, Internet and Risk in Comparative Perspective. *Journal of Children and Media* 7 (1): 1–8. https://eprints.lse.ac.uk/48952/1/Children_internet.pdf.

Manca, S., V. Grion, and L. Caviglione. 2021. "Teaching Digital Literacy: Strategies for K–12 Education." *Educational Technology & Society* 24 (2): 88–102.

Metzger, M. J., and A. J. Flanagin. 2013. "Credibility and Trust of Information in Online Environments: The Use of Cognitive Heuristics." *Journal of Pragmatics* 59: 210–20. https://doi.org/10.1016/j.pragma.2013.07.012.

Ministry of Education Singapore. n.d. "Digital Literacy and Technological Skills." https://www.moe.gov.sg/education-in-sg/educational-technology-journey/edtech-masterplan/digital-literacy-and-technological-skills

Nickerson, R. S. 1998. "Confirmation Bias: A Ubiquitous Phenomenon in Many Guises." *Review of General Psychology* 2 (2): 175–220.

Nussbaum, M. C. 1997. *Cultivating Humanity: A Classical Defense of Reform in Liberal Education.* Harvard University Press.

Pariser, E. 2011. *The Filter Bubble: How the New Personalized Web Is Changing What We Read and How We Think.* Penguin Press.

Patchin, J. W., and S. Hinduja. 2020. *Cyberbullying Prevention and Response: Expert Perspectives.* Routledge.

Paul, R., and L. Elder. 2006. *Critical Thinking: Tools for Taking Charge of Your Learning and Your Life.* Prentice Hall.

Plato. c. 380 BCE. *The Republic.* Translated by G. M.A. Grube and C. D. C. Reeve, 1992. Hackett Publishing.

Postman, N. 1985. *Amusing Ourselves to Death: Public Discourse in the Age of Show Business.* Penguin Books.

Ribble, M. 2021. *Digital Citizenship in Schools: Nine Elements All Students Should Know.* ISTE.

Shao, C., G. L. Ciampaglia, O. Varol, A. Flammini, and F. Menczer. 2018. "The Spread of Low-Credibility Content by Social Bots. *Nature*. https://www.nature.com/articles/s41467-018-06930-7.

US Department of Education. n.d. K–12 Cybersecurity: Keeping Schools Safe Online. Last updated December 1, 2024. https://www.ed.gov/teaching-and-administration/safe-learning-environments/school-safety-and-security/k-12-cybersecurity.

US Department of Education. 2022. "Children's Internet Protection Act (CIPA) Compliance Guidelines." https://www.ed.gov/.

Velten, J. C., R. Arif, and D. Moehring. 2017. "Managing Disclosure Through Social Media: How Snapchat Is Shaking Boundaries of Privacy Perceptions." *The Journal of Social Media in Society* 6 (1): 220–50.

Wineburg, S., and S. McGrew. 2017. "Lateral Reading: Reading Less and Learning More When Evaluating Digital Information." *Teachers College Record* 121: 1–40. https://ssrn.com/abstract=3048994.

Wolak, J., D. Finkelhor, and K. J. Mitchell. 2021. "Online Predators and Their Victims: Understanding the Threat." *Journal of Child Exploitation and Cybercrime* 15 (1): 89–103.

Chapter 10

Building a Layered Data Privacy Plan

Shane McNeil

Privacy is not an option, and it shouldn't be the price we accept for just getting on the Internet.

Gary Kovacs

Learning Outcomes

- **Understand the concept of a layered data privacy plan:** Students will be able to explain the concept of a layered data privacy plan and its importance in safeguarding sensitive information.
- **Identify the principles of a layered data privacy plan:** Students will be able to identify the principles of a layered data privacy plan, including defense in depth and least privilege.
- **Analyze the components of a layered data privacy plan**: Students will be able to analyze the components of a layered data privacy plan, including internet protocol (IP) address protection, Media Access Control (MAC) address security, Domain Name System (DNS) privacy, and implementation of end-to-end encryption (E2EE) communications such as commercial encrypted messaging apps, encrypted payment apps, encrypted web browsers, Virtual Private Networks (VPNs), and encrypted file storage.
- **Evaluate the effectiveness of a layered data privacy plan:** Students will be able to evaluate the effectiveness of a layered data privacy plan by examining real-world case studies and examples.

Key Terms

- **IP address:** A unique identifier assigned to every device that connects to the internet, such as a computer, a smartphone, or a router. It consists of four numbers, separated by dots, such as 192.168.0.1. An IP address is used to communicate with other devices on the internet and to access websites and services.

- **MAC address:** A unique identifier assigned to every network device, such as a computer, a smartphone, a router, or a printer. It consists of 12 hexadecimal digits, usually separated by colons or dashes, such as 00:1A:C2:7B:00:47. A MAC address is used to communicate with other devices on the same network, such as a local area network (LAN) or a wireless network.
- **DNS:** The Domain Name System, a service that translates human-readable domain names, such as www.example.com, into machine-readable IP addresses, such as 192.0.2.1. The DNS is essential for the functioning of the internet, as it allows users to access websites and services by using easy-to-remember names rather than complex numbers.
- **E2EE:** End-to-end encryption, a method that encrypts your data on your device before sending it over the internet and decrypts it on the recipient's device after receiving it. E2EE ensures that no one, not the app or platform provider, can see or modify your data in transit or at rest.
- **Encryption:** The process of transforming data into an unreadable form using a secret key or a password to prevent unauthorized access or disclosure. Encryption can be symmetric, where the same key is used to encrypt and decrypt the data, or asymmetric, where different keys are used to encrypt and decrypt the data.
- **Decryption:** The process of transforming encrypted data back into its original form, using the same or a different key or password, to allow authorized access or disclosure. Decryption is the reverse of encryption.
- **Authentication:** The process of verifying the identity or the legitimacy of a person or a device using a password, a code, a fingerprint, a face, or a key to allow or deny access or communication. Authentication can be one-way, where only one party is verified, or two-way, where both parties are verified.
- **Verification:** The process of confirming the integrity or the origin of the data using a checksum, a signature, a certificate, or a code to ensure that the data has not been tampered with or altered. Verification is a part of authentication.

Introduction

In previous chapters, we learned about common security threats, fundamental concepts, encryption techniques, various communication technologies, and ethical considerations for safeguarding sensitive information in our interconnected world. However, knowing these concepts is not enough to ensure data privacy. Using a layered data privacy plan, we must also apply them systematically and effectively.

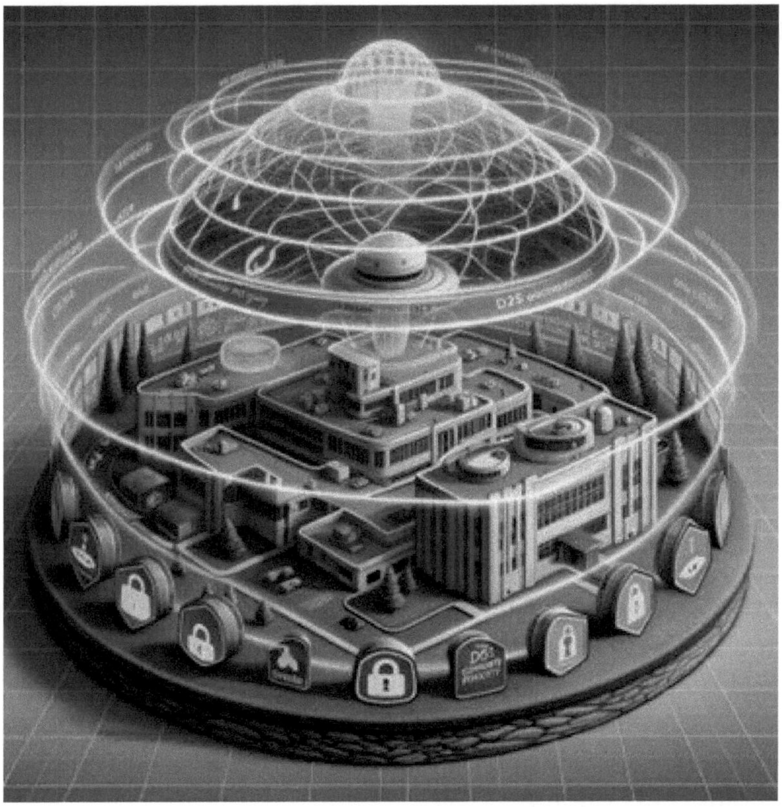

Figure 10.1 Multilayered Data Privacy and Security System: An Illustration of Defense in Depth Strategy

A layered data privacy plan is a strategy that combines multiple methods and tools to protect data from unauthorized access, modification, or disclosure. A layered data privacy plan is based on the principle of defense in depth, which means that if one layer of protection fails, there are other layers to prevent or mitigate the damage. A layered data privacy plan also follows the principle of least privilege, which means that only the minimum amount of data and access is granted to the users or systems that need it.

This chapter will explore building a layered data privacy plan for personal and professional contexts. We will cover four main aspects of data privacy: (1) internet protocol (IP) address protection, (2) Media Access Control (MAC) address security, (3) Domain Name System (DNS) privacy, and (4) implementation of end-two-end encryption (E2EE) communications such as commercial encrypted messaging apps, encrypted payment apps, encrypted web browsers, Virtual Private Networks (VPNs), and encrypted file storage. We will explain these aspects, why they are essential, and how to use them effectively. We will also provide real-world case studies and examples to illustrate the benefits and challenges of implementing a layered data privacy plan.

10.1 IP Address Protection

An IP address is a unique identifier assigned to every device connecting to the internet. It allows data to be sent and received between different devices over the IP, which is the foundation of the internet. Your IP address can reveal your device, location, and online activities. For example, your IP address can be used to track your browsing history, your online purchases, your streaming preferences, and your social media interactions. It can also target you with personalized ads, censor or restrict your access to certain content, or launch cyberattacks against you.

Therefore, concealing your IP address is crucial to prevent tracking and maintain privacy. You can use several techniques to hide or mask your IP address, such as VPNs, proxy servers, or Tor. In this section, we will explain these techniques, how they work, and their advantages and disadvantages.

VPNs

A VPN is a service that creates an encrypted tunnel between your device and a remote server. When you use a VPN, your internet traffic is routed through this tunnel, and the IP address of the VPN server replaces your IP address. This means that anyone who tries to see your IP address will only see the IP address of the VPN server, not your real one. This also means you can access content blocked or restricted in your region by connecting to a VPN server in a different country.[1]

VPNs are one of the most popular and effective methods to hide your IP address. They offer several benefits, such as providing high security and encryption, protecting your data from hackers, ISPs, and government surveillance, bypassing geo-restrictions and censorship, and accessing any content you want online, and being easy to use and compatible with most devices and platforms.

However, VPNs also have some drawbacks, such as slowing down your internet speed, depending on the quality and location of the VPN server, being blocked or detected by some websites and services, which may prevent you from accessing them or require you to solve captchas, and being expensive, depending on the VPN provider and the features you need.

Therefore, when choosing a VPN service, you should consider the following factors: the reputation and reliability of the VPN provider, whether they have a no-logs policy and a kill switch feature, the number, and location of the VPN servers, and whether they offer fast and stable connections, the compatibility and functionality of the VPN software, and whether it supports multiple devices and protocols, and the price and value of the VPN service, and whether it offers a free trial or a money-back guarantee.

1. Zhiwei Xu and Jie Ni, "Research on Network Security of VPN Technology," in *2020 International Conference on Information Science and Education (ICISE-IE)* (IEEE, 2020), 539–42, https://doi.org/10.1109/ICISE51755.2020.00121.

Proxy Servers

Proxy servers act as intermediaries between a user's device and the internet, allowing the user to access web content without revealing their actual IP address. An IP address is a unique identifier that can reveal information about the user's location, device, and online activity. By hiding the user's IP address, proxy servers can provide some level of privacy and security and enable the user to access content that is blocked or restricted in their region.

However, proxy servers are not the same as VPNs, which are more advanced and secure tools that encrypt the user's internet traffic and route it through a remote server. Proxy servers only encrypt the user's web requests and responses and do not affect other types of internet traffic, such as email or file transfers. Moreover, proxy servers do not guarantee the user's anonymity, as they may keep logs of the user's activity or leak the user's IP address through various methods, such as DNS queries or WebRTC leaks.[2]

Therefore, proxy servers should be used cautiously and aware of their limitations and risks. Users should also be aware of the different types of proxy servers and choose the one that best suits their needs and preferences. Some of the common types of proxy servers are as follows:

Forward proxy: This is the most basic type of proxy server, which passes the user's requests from an internal network to the internet through a firewall. Forward proxies can help users bypass network restrictions and access any web content. However, forward proxies can also expose the user's identity and activity to the proxy server operator or anyone accessing the proxy server's logs or cache.[3]

Reverse proxy: This is the opposite of a forward proxy, which passes the requests from the internet to an internal network through a firewall. Reverse proxies can help the web server improve its performance, security, and reliability by caching content, balancing load, filtering requests, and preventing attacks. However, reverse proxies can also introduce latency and complexity to the web server's operation or cause compatibility issues with some web applications.

Transparent proxy: This is a type of proxy server that does not modify the user's requests or responses and does not hide the user's IP address. Transparent proxies are usually used by ISPs (Internet Service Providers) or network administrators to monitor, filter, or cache the user's traffic for various purposes, such as bandwidth management, content filtering, or security enforcement. However, transparent proxies can also violate users' privacy and security by exposing their online activity or injecting ads or malware into their web pages.

2. Maricor Bunal, "Geonode—Proxies for E-Commerce and Tech," Geonode Proxies, May 30, 2023, https://geonode.com.
3. Yogita Chhabra, "A Study of Recent Research Trends of Proxy Server," *International Journal of Advanced Technology in Engineering and Science* 3, no. 2 (2015): 159–64.

Anonymous proxy: This proxy server modifies the user's requests or responses and hides the user's IP address. Anonymous proxies are usually used by users who want to protect their privacy and security by preventing websites or third parties from tracking their online activity or accessing their personal information. However, anonymous proxies can also compromise the user's privacy and security by logging their activity or leaking their IP address through other means.

High anonymity proxy: This is a type of proxy server that modifies the user's requests or responses and hides the user's IP address and any other information that can identify the user or the proxy server. High anonymity proxies are usually used by users who want to achieve the highest level of privacy and security by avoiding detecting or tracing their online activity or accessing any content they want. However, high anonymity proxies can also be unreliable and slow, as they are often overloaded or blocked by websites or services that detect proxy usage.

TOR

Tor (The Onion Router) is a network of volunteer servers that allows you to browse the internet anonymously. When you use Tor, your internet traffic is encrypted and routed through multiple servers, called nodes, before reaching its destination. Each node only knows the previous and the next node in the circuit, but not the traffic's origin or destination. This means that anyone who tries to see your IP address will only see the IP address of the last node, called the exit node, not your real one. This also means you can access content hidden or censored on the internet, such as the dark web.[4]

Tor is one of the most secure and private methods to hide your IP address. It offers several benefits, such as providing a high level of encryption and anonymity, which protects your data from hackers, ISPs, and government surveillance, allowing you to access any content on the internet, including the dark web, which is not accessible by normal browsers, and being free and open source, and supported by a community of volunteers and activists.[5]

However, Tor also has some drawbacks, such as significantly slowing down your internet speed, depending on the number and location of the nodes in the circuit, being blocked or detected by some websites and services, which may prevent you from accessing them or require you to solve captchas, and exposing you to some risks and dangers, such as malicious nodes, malware, or illegal content.

One of the main drawbacks of Tor is that the encryption only applies within the Tor network. Your traffic is decrypted and sent to the final destination when it reaches the exit node. This means that the exit node can see and modify your data, and the destination

4. Roger Dingledine, Nick Mathewson, and Paul Syverson, "Tor: The Second-Generation Onion Router," Defense Technical Information Center, January 1, 2004, https://doi.org/10.21236/ADA465464.
5. Nitul Dutta et al., "TOR—The Onion Router," in *Cyber Security: Issues and Current Trends*, vol. 995, Studies in Computational Intelligence (Springer Singapore, 2022), 37–55, https://doi.org/10.1007/978-981-16-6597-4_3.

website can see the IP address of the exit node. Therefore, if you connect to a website not using HTTPS or another secure protocol, your data can be intercepted, modified, or stolen by the exit node or anyone else on the way. Moreover, the destination website or service can also block or detect the exit node, which may prevent you from accessing it or require you to solve captchas.

To avoid these risks, you should always use HTTPS or another secure protocol when connecting to websites or services outside the Tor network. You should also verify the certificates and URLs of the websites you visit and avoid entering any sensitive or personal information. Additionally, you should be careful about the content you access or share on the internet and be aware of the legality and ethics of your actions, as you may face the potential consequences.

Another way to avoid the risks of the exit node is to use Tor hidden services, which are websites or services that are only accessible within the Tor network. These hidden services have a special domain name that ends with .onion, and they do not reveal their IP address or location. When you connect to a hidden service, your traffic does not leave the Tor network; it is encrypted end-to-end. This means that no one, not the hidden service or the Tor nodes, can see or modify your data. However, hidden services also have some limitations, such as being slower and less reliable than normal websites, and hosting some illegal or harmful content. Therefore, you should be cautious and selective about the hidden services you visit, and use additional security measures to protect yourself.

Therefore, when using Tor, you should consider the following factors: the configuration and settings of the Tor browser, and whether you need to use bridges or pluggable transports to bypass censorship or firewalls, the security and privacy of the Tor browser and whether you need to use additional extensions or tools to enhance your protection, the type and location of the websites or services you access, and whether they use HTTPS or another secure protocol, and the legality and ethics of the content you access or share on the internet, and whether you are willing to face the potential consequences of your actions.

In this section, we have learned about the importance and challenges of IP address protection. We have discussed the risks of IP address exposure, such as tracking and profiling, geo-restrictions and censorship, and cyberattacks and surveillance. We have also explored the solutions for IP address protection, such as using VPNs, proxy servers, or Tor. We have also provided some guidelines and examples on using these techniques and tools effectively and safely.

To wrap up this section, let's consider a hypothetical scenario that illustrates the benefits and limitations of IP address protection. Imagine that you are a traveler who wants to access some content on the internet that is not available in your current location, such as a video streaming service, a news website, or a social media platform. You also want to protect your privacy and security from anyone who may try to see or access your online activities, such as hackers, ISPs, or government agencies.

A Cautionary Tale of IP Address Exposure

Imagine you are a journalist working on an investigative report about a corrupt politician. You have obtained some sensitive documents and evidence from a whistleblower and plan to publish your story soon. However, you are also aware that the politician has powerful allies and resources and that he may try to stop you or harm you. Therefore, you hide your IP address to protect your identity and location.

You have three options to hide your IP address: use a VPN, a proxy server, or Tor. Which one would you choose, and why?

If you choose to use a VPN, you need to make sure that you choose a reputable and reliable VPN service that has a no-logs policy and a kill switch feature. Otherwise, you may end up using a VPN service that leaks your IP address, logs your activities, or cooperates with the authorities. For example, in 2011, a VPN service called HideMyAss was accused of handing over the IP address and logs of a hacker who was involved in the Sony Pictures hack to the FBI.

If you choose to use a proxy server, you need to make sure that you use a secure and anonymous proxy server that supports HTTPS or SOCKS protocols. Otherwise, you may end up using a proxy server that exposes your IP address, modifies your data, or steals your information. For example, in 2017, a security researcher discovered that a popular proxy service called Hola was injecting ads and malware into the users' browsers and selling their bandwidth to a botnet service called Luminati.

If you choose to use Tor, you need to make sure that you use the Tor browser with the default settings and avoid downloading or opening any files or links that may compromise your anonymity. Otherwise, you may end up using Tor in a way that reveals your IP address, infects your device, or exposes you to illegal content. For example, in 2013, a hacker group called Freedom Hosting was busted by the FBI for hosting child pornography sites on the dark web, and the FBI used a malware exploit to identify the IP addresses of the visitors.

As you can see, hiding your IP address is not a simple or foolproof task. You need to be careful and vigilant about the methods and tools you use, and the risks and challenges you face. You also need to combine your IP address protection with other aspects of data privacy, such as encryption, authentication, and authorization. Only then can you build a layered data privacy plan that can safeguard your sensitive information and communication.

One of the steps that you can take to access the content and protect your privacy is to use IP address protection. You can use a VPN, a proxy server, or Tor to hide or mask your real IP address, and to connect to a server in a different country that allows you to access the content. This way, you can bypass the geo-restrictions and censorship, and enjoy the content you want on the internet. You can also prevent anyone from tracking or profiling your online activities, and from identifying or locating your device.

However, IP address protection is not enough to ensure the access and privacy of the content. You also need to use other methods and tools, such as encryption and authentication. You need to encrypt your data before sending or receiving it over the internet, and decrypt it after receiving or sending it to your device. This way, you can prevent anyone from intercepting or modifying your data, even if they manage to see your IP address. You also need to authenticate yourself and the content provider before accessing the content, and verify the integrity and origin of the data. This way, you can prevent anyone from impersonating you or the content provider, and from injecting malicious data into your communication.

By combining IP address protection with other aspects of data privacy, such as encryption and authentication, you can build a layered data privacy plan that can enable you to access and enjoy any content you want on the internet, while protecting your privacy and security from various threats and risks. You can also foster responsible and ethical communication practices, and respect the rights and preferences of the content providers and users.

Figure 10.2 IP Address Protection

10.2 MAC Address Security

A MAC address is a unique identifier that is assigned to every network device, such as a computer, a smartphone, a router, or a printer. It consists of 12 hexadecimal digits, usually separated by colons or dashes, such as 00:1A:C2:7B:00:47. A MAC address is used to communicate with other devices on the same network, such as a local area network (LAN) or a wireless network. A MAC address is also sometimes called a physical address, an Ethernet address, or a hardware address.[6]

MAC addresses are generally secure since attacks are difficult to implement and require extensive technological know-how. However, they can be used to monitor your location, disrupt your internet access, or even perform a man-in-the-middle attack[4]. In this section, we will explain the risks and solutions of MAC address security, and how to protect your devices and data from MAC address exposure.

Risks of MAC Address Exposure

One of the main risks of MAC address exposure is tracking and profiling. Since MAC addresses are unique and persistent, they can be used to identify and track your devices across different networks and locations. For example, when you connect to a public Wi-Fi network, such as at a coffee shop or an airport, the network operator can record your MAC address and associate it with your online activities, such as the websites you visit, the apps you use, or the files you download. This information can be used to create a profile of your interests, preferences, and habits, and to target you with personalized ads, offers, or messages.[7]

Another risk of MAC address exposure is network access control bypassing. Some networks use MAC address filtering as a security measure to allow or deny access to certain devices. For example, a home network may only allow devices with specific MAC addresses to connect to the router, or a corporate network may only allow devices with authorized MAC addresses to access the intranet. However, MAC address filtering is not a reliable or effective method, since MAC addresses can be easily spoofed or faked. This means that an attacker can change their MAC address to match one of the allowed devices, and gain access to the network without authorization.

A third risk of MAC address exposure is a man-in-the-middle attack. A man-in-the-middle attack is a type of attack where an attacker intercepts and alters the communication between two parties, such as your device and a website. For example, an attacker can use a technique called ARP spoofing to trick your device into sending your data to their device instead of the intended destination by pretending to have the same MAC

6. Mathieu Cunche, "I Know Your MAC Address: Targeted Tracking of Individual Using Wi-Fi," *Journal of Computer Virology and Hacking Techniques* 10, no. 4 (2014): 219–27, https://doi.org/10.1007/s11416-013-0196-1.
7. Cunche.

address as the destination. This way, the attacker can steal your data, modify your data, or inject malicious data into your communication.

No.	Time	Source	Destination	Protocol
57	2.910903	fe80::503b:ab83:1113:	fe80::e8b2:3d51:f04f:	ICMPv6
58	2.910946	fe80::e8b2:3d51:f04f:	fe80::503b:ab83:1113:	ICMPv6
59	2.968338	121.35.155.139	10.0.60.60	UDP
60	2.968513	10.0.60.60	121.35.155.139	UDP
61	3.074522	10.0.60.60	157.55.130.165	UDP
62	3.131928	fe80::e8b2:3d51:f04f:	fe80::503b:ab83:1113:	ICMPv6
63	3.137907	fe80::503b:ab83:1113:	fe80::e8b2:3d51:f04f:	ICMPv6
64	3.187286	157.55.130.165	10.0.60.60	UDP
65	3.204093	10.0.60.60	81.20.246.192	UDP

Figure 10.3 MAC Address Exposure via WireShark

Solutions for MAC Address Security

One of the main solutions for MAC address security is randomizing MAC addresses. Randomizing MAC addresses means changing your MAC address to a different one every time you connect to a network, or at regular intervals. This way, you can prevent tracking and profiling since your MAC address will not be consistent or identifiable. You can also bypass network access control since your MAC address will not be recognized or blocked by the network operator. However, randomizing MAC addresses may not prevent man-in-the-middle attacks since your MAC address may still be exposed or spoofed by an attacker on the same network.[8]

Another solution for MAC address security is disabling Wi-Fi when not needed. Disabling Wi-Fi means turning off your Wi-Fi connection on your device when you are not using it or when you are using a trusted network, such as your home network or your cellular network. This way, you can prevent MAC address exposure since your MAC address will not be broadcast or detected by any network or device. You can also save battery life since your device will not be constantly searching for or connecting to Wi-Fi networks. However, disabling Wi-Fi may not be convenient or feasible since you may need to use Wi-Fi for certain purposes, such as browsing the internet, streaming media, or downloading files.

8.

How to Randomize or Disable MAC Addresses

The methods and steps to randomize or disable MAC addresses vary depending on the type and model of your device and the operating system and software you are using. Here are some general guidelines and examples for some standard devices and platforms:

- Windows 10: To randomize your MAC address, go to Settings › Network & Internet › Wi-Fi › Manage known networks, select a network, and click Properties. Under Privacy, turn on Use random hardware addresses for this network. To disable your Wi-Fi, click the network icon on the task bar and turn off Wi-Fi.
- macOS: To randomize your MAC address, use a third-party app, such as [WiFiSpoof] or [LinkLiar]. To disable your Wi-Fi, click the Wi-Fi icon on the menu bar and turn off Wi-Fi.
- iOS: To randomize your MAC address, go to Settings › Wi-Fi, tap the information icon next to a network, and turn on Private Address. To disable your Wi-Fi, go to Settings › Wi-Fi and turn it off.
- Android: To randomize your MAC address, go to Settings › Network & Internet › Wi-Fi, tap the gear icon next to a network, and tap Advanced. Under Privacy, select Use randomized MAC. To disable your Wi-Fi, go to Settings › Network & Internet › Wi-Fi and turn off Wi-Fi.

In this section, we have learned about the importance and challenges of MAC address security. We have discussed the risks of MAC address exposure, such as tracking and profiling, network access control bypassing, and man-in-the-middle attacks. We have also explored the solutions for MAC address security, such as randomizing MAC addresses, disabling Wi-Fi when not needed, and using encryption and authentication. We have also provided some guidelines and examples on randomizing or disabling MAC addresses on different devices and platforms.

Examining MAC Address Security

To wrap up this section, let's consider a hypothetical scenario that illustrates the benefits and limitations of MAC address security. Imagine that you are a student who is working on a group project with your classmates. You need to share some files and data with your group members, and you decide to use a cloud storage service, such as Dropbox or Google Drive. However, you are also concerned about the privacy and security of your files and data, and you want to protect them from unauthorized access or modification.

One of the steps that you can take to protect your files and data is to use MAC address security. You can randomize your MAC address every time you connect to a Wi-Fi network, such as at school, at home, or at a public place. This way, you can prevent anyone from tracking or profiling your online activities, and from identifying or locating your device. You can also disable your Wi-Fi when you are not using it, or when you are using a trusted network, such as your cellular network. This way, you can prevent anyone from detecting or intercepting your MAC address, and from accessing or disrupting your internet connection.

However, MAC address security is not enough to ensure the privacy and security of your files and data. You also need to use other methods and tools, such as encryption and authentication. You need to encrypt your files and data before uploading them to the cloud storage service and decrypt them after downloading them to your device. This way, you can prevent anyone from reading or modifying your files and data, even if they manage to access them. You also need to authenticate yourself and your group members before accessing the cloud storage service and verify the integrity and origin of the files and data. This way, you can prevent anyone from impersonating you or your group members, and from injecting malicious files or data into your communication.

By combining MAC address security with other aspects of data privacy, such as encryption and authentication, you can build a layered data privacy plan that can safeguard your files and data from various threats and risks. You can also foster responsible and collaborative communication practices with your group members and complete your group project successfully.

10.3 DNS Privacy

The DNS is a service that translates human-readable domain names, such as www.example.com, into machine-readable IP addresses, such as 192.0.2.1. The DNS is essential for the functioning of the internet, as it allows users to access websites and services by using easy-to-remember names, rather than complex numbers. However, the DNS also poses a serious threat to the privacy and security of users, as it reveals their browsing habits and exposes them to various attacks.[9]

The Problem of DNS Privacy

To understand the problem of DNS privacy, we need to first understand how the DNS works. The DNS is a hierarchical and distributed system that consists of four main components: DNS resolvers, DNS root servers, DNS authoritative servers, and DNS caches.

A DNS resolver is a server that receives DNS queries from users and returns DNS responses. A DNS query is a request for the IP address of a domain name, and a DNS response is the answer to that request. A DNS resolver can be run by your ISP, your operating system, your browser, or a third-party service, such as Google Public DNS or Cloudflare DNS.[10]

9. Ramaswamy Chandramouli and Scott Rose, "Secure Domain Name System (DNS) Deployment Guide," National Institute of Standards and Technology, September 2013, https://doi.org/10.6028/NIST.SP.800-81-2.
10. Casey Deccio and Jacob Davis, "DNS Privacy in Practice and Preparation," in *Proceedings of the 15th International Conference on Emerging Networking Experiments and Technologies* (CoNEXT 19: The 15th International Confer-

A DNS root server is a server that stores the information about the top-level domains (TLDs), such as .com, .org, or .net. There are 13 root servers in the world, each with multiple copies and locations. A DNS resolver contacts a root server to find out which authoritative server is responsible for a given TLD.

A DNS authoritative server is a server that stores the information about a specific domain name, such as www.example.com. There can be multiple authoritative servers for a domain name, each with different levels of authority and responsibility. A DNS resolver contacts an authoritative server to find out the IP address of a domain name.

A DNS cache is a temporary storage of DNS responses that is used to speed up the DNS resolution process. A DNS cache can be maintained by your device, your browser, your resolver, or any intermediate server. A DNS cache can reduce the number of DNS queries and improve the performance of the DNS.

The DNS resolution process is the process of finding the IP address of a domain name by using the DNS. The DNS resolution process involves the following steps:

- When you type a domain name, such as www.example.com, in your browser, your browser sends a DNS query to your resolver, asking for the IP address of the domain name.
- If your resolver has the answer in its cache, it returns the IP address to your browser. If not, it contacts a root server, asking for the authoritative server for the TLD, such as .com.
- The root server returns the IP address of the authoritative server for the TLD to your resolver. Your resolver then contacts the authoritative server for the TLD, asking for the authoritative server for the domain name, such as example.com.
- The authoritative server for the TLD returns the IP address of the authoritative server for the domain name to your resolver. Your resolver then contacts the authoritative server for the domain name, asking for the IP address of the domain name, such as www.example.com.
- The authoritative server for the domain name returns the IP address of the domain name to your resolver. Your resolver then returns the IP address to your browser, and stores it in its cache for future use.
- Your browser then uses the IP address to connect to the website or service that you requested.

The problem of DNS privacy is that the DNS resolution process is not encrypted or authenticated by default. This means that the DNS queries and responses are sent in plaintext over the internet, and anyone who can see or intercept them can read or modify them. This exposes your browsing habits and exposes you to various attacks, such as:

ence on emerging Networking EXperiments and Technologies, ACM, 2019), 138–43, https://doi.org/10.1145/3359989.3365435.

- Tracking and profiling: Your DNS queries reveal what websites and services you visit, when you visit them, and how often you visit them. This information can be used to create a profile of your interests, preferences, and habits, and to target you with personalized ads, offers, or messages. For example, your ISP, your resolver operator, or any intermediate server can log your DNS queries and use them for marketing or analytics purposes.
- Censorship and filtering: Your DNS queries can be used to block or restrict your access to certain websites and services, based on their domain names. For example, your government, your ISP, or your network administrator can intercept your DNS queries and return false or empty responses, preventing you from reaching the websites and services that you want.
- Spoofing and hijacking: Your DNS queries can be used to redirect you to fake or malicious websites and services by changing the IP address of the domain name. For example, a hacker, a rogue resolver, or a compromised server can alter your DNS responses and send you to a phishing site, a malware site, or a site that steals your data or credentials.

The Solution for DNS Privacy

The solution for DNS privacy is to use encrypted DNS protocols, such as DNS over HTTPS (DoH) or DNS over TLS (DoT). Encrypted DNS protocols are methods that encrypt and authenticate DNS traffic, using the same technologies that are used to secure web traffic, such as HTTPS and TLS. Encrypted DNS protocols prevent eavesdropping and enhance privacy by ensuring that only the intended parties can see or modify the DNS queries and responses.

Encrypted DNS protocols work by establishing a secure connection between your device and your resolver, using HTTPS or TLS. When you send a DNS query, your device encrypts it and sends it to your resolver over the secure connection. Your resolver decrypts it and performs the DNS resolution process as usual. When your resolver receives a DNS response, it encrypts it and sends it back to your device over the secure connection. Your device decrypts it and uses it to connect to the website or service that you requested.

Encrypted DNS protocols offer several benefits, such as the following:[11]

- They protect your DNS privacy by preventing anyone from seeing or altering your DNS queries and responses, and by hiding your browsing habits and activities from prying eyes.

11. Geetika Gopi and B. Chandra Mohan, "DNS Security—Overview and Analysis," in *Advances in Automation, Signal Processing, Instrumentation, and Control*, ed. Venkata Lakshmi Narayana Komanapalli, N. Sivakumaran, and Santoshkumar Hampannavar, vol. 700, Lecture Notes in Electrical Engineering (Springer Nature Singapore, 2021), 1169–75, https://doi.org/10.1007/978-981-15-8221-9_110.

- They improve your DNS security by preventing anyone from blocking or redirecting your DNS queries and responses, and by preventing you from falling victim to spoofing or hijacking attacks.
- They enhance your DNS performance by reducing the number of DNS queries and responses, and by improving the reliability and availability of the DNS.

However, encrypted DNS protocols also have some challenges, such as:

- They require support and configuration from your device, your browser, your resolver, and your network, which may not be available or compatible with all platforms and services.
- They may conflict or interfere with other DNS features or policies, such as DNS caching, DNS filtering, or DNS monitoring, which may affect the functionality or usability of the DNS.
- They may raise some ethical or legal issues, such as the choice and trustworthiness of the resolver, the ownership and control of the DNS data, or the compliance with the local laws and regulations.

The Implementation of DNS Privacy

The implementation of DNS privacy involves configuring your devices and browsers to use encrypted DNS protocols, such as DoH or DoT. The methods and steps to configure encrypted DNS vary depending on the type and model of your device, and the operating system and software you are using. Here are some general guidelines and examples for some common devices and platforms:

- Windows 10: To configure DoH, go to Settings › Network & Internet › Wi-Fi › Properties, and scroll down to IP settings. Click Edit, and select Manual under IPv4 or IPv6. Enter the IP address of your resolver, and select the encryption type under Preferred DNS encryption or Alternate DNS encryption. To configure DoT, you need to use a third-party app.
- macOS: To configure DoH or DoT, you need to use a third-party app. Alternatively, you can use the scutil command-line tool to configure encrypted DNS manually.
- iOS: To configure DoH or DoT, go to Settings › Wi-Fi, and tap the information icon next to your network. Tap Configure DNS, and select Manual. Tap Add Server, and enter the IP address of your resolver. Tap Save. Alternatively, you can use a third-party app.
- Android: To configure DoH, go to Settings › Network & Internet › Advanced › Private DNS. Select Private DNS provider host name, and enter the host name of your resolver. Tap Save.

In this section, we have learned about the importance and challenges of DNS privacy. We have discussed how the DNS works, what information it leaks, and who can see or abuse it. We have also explored how to use encrypted DNS protocols, such as DoH or DoT, to prevent eavesdropping and enhance privacy. We have also provided some guidelines and examples on how to configure your devices and browsers to use encrypted DNS, as well as the benefits and challenges of doing so.

To wrap up this section, let's consider a hypothetical scenario that illustrates the benefits and limitations of DNS privacy. Imagine that you are a researcher who is working on a project about human rights violations in a certain country. You need to access some websites and sources that provide information and evidence about the topic, but you are also aware that the country has a strict and oppressive internet censorship regime, and that it may try to monitor or block your access to the content.

One of the steps that you can take to access the content and protect your privacy is to use DNS privacy. You can use DoH or DoT to encrypt and authenticate your DNS queries and responses, and to connect to a resolver that is outside the country or that supports the content. This way, you can bypass the censorship and filtering, and access the content you need on the internet. You can also prevent anyone from seeing or altering your DNS queries and responses, and from tracking or profiling your online activities.

However, DNS privacy is not enough to ensure the access and privacy of the content. You also need to use other methods and tools, such as IP address protection, encryption, and authentication. You need to hide or mask your IP address, using a VPN, a proxy server, or Tor, to prevent anyone from identifying or locating your device and from launching cyberattacks or surveillance against you. You also need to encrypt your data before sending or receiving it over the internet, and decrypt it after receiving or sending it to your device, to prevent anyone from intercepting or modifying your data, even if they manage to see your DNS queries and responses. You also need to authenticate yourself and the content provider before accessing the content, and verify the integrity and origin of the data, to prevent anyone from impersonating you or the content provider, and from injecting malicious data into your communication.

By combining DNS privacy with other aspects of data privacy, such as IP address protection, encryption, and authentication, you can build a layered data privacy plan that can enable you to access and use any content you need on the internet, while protecting your privacy and security from various threats and risks. You can also foster responsible and ethical communication practices, and respect the rights and preferences of the content providers and users.

10.4 Implementing E2EE Communications

Communication is an essential part of our personal and professional lives. We use various apps and platforms to send and receive messages, make and receive calls, and conduct and participate in video conferences. However, communication also involves sharing sensitive and confidential information, such as personal details, financial data, business secrets, or political opinions. Therefore, communication also requires a high level of privacy and security, to ensure that only the intended parties can access and understand the information.[12]

One of the best ways to protect your communication privacy and security is to use E2EE. E2EE is a method that encrypts your data on your device before sending it over the internet, and decrypts it on the recipient's device after receiving it. E2EE ensures that no one, not even the app or platform provider, can see or modify your data in transit or at rest. E2EE also prevents anyone from intercepting or altering your data, and from launching cyberattacks or surveillance against you.[13]

The Criteria for Choosing E2EE Communication Apps

When choosing an E2EE communication app, you should consider the following factors:

Security Reputation: Research the app's security track record. Look for apps that have undergone independent security audits or have been endorsed by privacy-focused organizations, such as the Electronic Frontier Foundation (EFF) or PrivacyTools. Avoid apps that have had security breaches or vulnerabilities, or that have been banned or criticized by authorities or experts.

Open Source: Consider using open-source apps where the code is publicly available for review. Open-source apps tend to have better security practices and faster response to bugs or issues, as they are subject to scrutiny and feedback from the community and the users. Examples of open-source apps include Signal and Wire.[14]

Encryption Protocol: Check which encryption protocol the app uses. The encryption protocol is the set of rules and algorithms that govern how the data is encrypted and decrypted. The encryption protocol should be strong, secure, and up-to-date, and should not have any known flaws or weaknesses. The Signal Protocol (used by Signal, MySudo, and others) is widely regarded as one of the most secure encryption protocols for E2EE communication.

User Base: Apps with a large user base tend to have better security practices and faster response to vulnerabilities, as they are subject to more testing and feedback from the users. They also tend to have more features and functionality, as they are subject to more demand and competition from the market. However, apps with a large user base

12. Adam Godra et al., "Practical Approach to Design and Implement a P2P and E2EE Instant Messaging System," *2023 22nd RoEduNet Conference: Networking in Education and Research (RoEduNet)*, 2023, 1–7, https://doi.org/10.1109/RoEduNet60162.2023.10274936.
13. Robert Dougherty, "Exploring E2EE: Real-World Examples of End-to-End Encryption," *Kiteworks | Your Private Content Network* (blog), August 12, 2023, https://www.kiteworks.com/secure-file-sharing/real-world-examples-of-end-to-end-encryption/.
14. Suprit Dusane, Md Iliyaz, and A. Suresh, "Implementation of E2EE Using Python," in *Emerging Technologies in Data Mining and Information Security*, ed. Paramartha Dutta et al., vol. 1348, Advances in Intelligent Systems and Computing (Springer Nature Singapore, 2023), 635–42, https://doi.org/10.1007/978-981-19-4676-9_55.

may also attract more attention and attacks from hackers, governments, or adversaries, as they pose a bigger threat or opportunity for them.

Cross-Platform Support: Choose apps that work seamlessly across different devices and operating systems, such as Windows, macOS, iOS, Android, Linux, and others. Cross-platform support ensures that you can communicate with anyone, anywhere, and anytime, without compromising your privacy or security. It also ensures that you can switch or sync your devices easily, without losing your data or settings.

Usability: Ensure the app is user-friendly and integrates well with your existing communication tools, such as email, SMS, phone, or social media. Usability ensures that you can communicate effectively and efficiently, without sacrificing your privacy or security. It also ensures that you can adopt and use the app easily, without facing any technical or practical difficulties.

Examples of E2EE Communication Apps

Here are some examples of E2EE communication apps that meet the criteria mentioned above:

Signal: Signal is a free and open-source app that offers E2EE for messages, calls, and video conferences. Signal uses the Signal Protocol, which is considered to be one of the most secure encryption protocols for E2EE communication. Signal also offers features such as disappearing messages, group chats, stickers, and voice notes. Signal has a high security reputation, as it has been endorsed by privacy advocates and experts, such as Edward Snowden, Bruce Schneier, and the EFF. Signal has a large and growing user base, as it has been adopted by many celebrities, activists, and journalists. Signal supports Windows, macOS, iOS, Android, and Linux.

Wire: Wire is a paid and open-source app that offers E2EE for messages, calls, and video conferences. Wire uses the Signal Protocol, as well as other encryption protocols, such as DTLS and SRTP. Wire also offers features such as group chats, file sharing, screen sharing, and guest rooms. Wire has a good security reputation, as it has undergone independent security audits and has been certified by the International Organization for Standardization (ISO). Wire has a moderate user base, as it has been used by some organizations and businesses, such as the European Commission and Amnesty International. Wire supports Windows, macOS, iOS, Android, Linux, and web browsers.

MySudo: MySudo is a paid app that offers E2EE for messages, calls, and emails. MySudo uses the Signal Protocol, as well as other encryption protocols, such as TLS and PGP. MySudo also offers features such as virtual phone numbers, email aliases, and custom profiles. MySudo has a good security reputation, as it has been developed by Anonyome Labs, a company that specializes in privacy and security solutions. MySudo has a small but loyal user base, as it has been used by some privacy enthusiasts and professionals, such as journalists and lawyers. MySudo supports iOS and Android.

Threema: Threema is a paid app that offers E2EE for messages, calls, and video conferences. Threema uses its own encryption protocol, called the Threema Protocol, which is based on the NaCl cryptographic library. Threema also offers features such as group chats, polls, voice messages, and QR code scanning. Threema has a good security reputation, as it has undergone independent security audits and has been praised by privacy organizations, such as Privacy International and Reporters Without Borders. Threema has a moderate user base, as it has been popular in some countries and regions, such as Switzerland and Germany. Threema supports iOS, Android, and web browsers.

Wickr: Wickr is a free and paid app that offers E2EE for messages, calls, and video conferences. Wickr uses its own encryption protocol, called the Wickr Secure Messaging Protocol, which is based on the AES, ECDH, and HMAC algorithms. Wickr also offers features such as self-destructing messages, group chats, file sharing, and voice memos. Wickr has a good security reputation, as it has undergone independent security audits and has been used by some government and military agencies, such as the US Department of Defense and the Australian Defence Force. Wickr has a small but growing user base, as it has been used by some organizations and businesses, such as Uber and OpenAI. Wickr supports Windows, macOS, iOS, Android, and Linux.

Benefits and Challenges of E2EE Communication Apps

E2EE communication apps offer several benefits, such as the following:

- **Privacy:** E2EE communication apps protect your privacy by ensuring that only you and your intended recipients can read your messages, calls, and video conferences. E2EE communication apps also prevent anyone from tracking or profiling your online activities, and from identifying or locating your device.
- **Security:** E2EE communication apps improve your security by preventing anyone from intercepting or altering your messages, calls, and video conferences. E2EE communication apps also prevent anyone from launching cyberattacks or surveillance against you, such as phishing, malware, or spying.
- **Performance:** E2EE communication apps enhance your performance by reducing the bandwidth and storage requirements of your messages, calls, and video conferences. E2EE communication apps also improve the reliability and availability of your communication by preventing network congestion or disruption.

E2EE communication apps offer many benefits for your privacy and security, but they also have some challenges, such as the following:

- Compatibility: E2EE communication apps may not work well with all devices, platforms, or networks. For example, some E2EE communication apps may not be available or supported on some operating systems, such as Windows or Linux. Some E2EE communication apps may not work well with some network settings or policies, such as firewalls or proxies. Some E2EE communication apps may not be compatible with some communication tools or services, such as email, SMS, or phone.

- Usability: E2EE communication apps may not be user-friendly or intuitive. For example, some E2EE communication apps may require additional installation or configuration, such as verifying keys or codes, or choosing a resolver or a server. Some E2EE communication apps may not integrate well with your existing communication habits or preferences, such as using emojis, stickers, or voice notes. Some E2EE communication apps may require additional steps or actions, such as switching apps or devices, or scanning QR codes.
- Trade-offs: E2EE communication apps may involve some trade-offs between privacy, security, and usability. For example, some E2EE communication apps may offer more privacy and security but at the cost of lower performance or functionality. Some E2EE communication apps may offer more performance or functionality but at the cost of lower privacy or security. Some E2EE communication apps may offer a balance between privacy, security, and usability but at the cost of higher complexity or difficulty.

These are some of the challenges that E2EE communication apps present. However, these challenges are not insurmountable, and they can be overcome or mitigated by using the appropriate criteria and tools to choose and use E2EE communication apps, according to your needs and preferences.

Beyond E2EE: Other Factors to Consider When Choosing Communication Apps

E2EE is a great feature that can protect your communication privacy and security, but it is not the only factor that you should consider when choosing a communication app. There are other factors that may affect the trustworthiness and reliability of the app, such as who owns the app, what country the app is based in, or what data the app collects or shares. For example:

Who owns the app: The owner of the app may have access to or control over the app's code, servers, or data. The owner of the app may also have some motives or interests that may influence the app's policies or practices. For example, some apps may be owned by corporations or governments that may have ties or agendas that may compromise the app's security or privacy. Some apps may be owned by individuals or groups that may have reputations or histories that may raise some concerns or doubts about the app's integrity.

What country the app is based in: The country where the app is based in may have laws or regulations that may affect the app's operations or compliance. The country where the app is based in may also have some political or social issues that may pose some risks or challenges for the app's users or providers. For example, some countries may have strict or oppressive internet censorship or surveillance regimes that may require the app to disclose or block some data or content. Some countries may have unstable or hostile relations with other countries that may expose the app to cyberattacks or sanctions.

What data the app collects or shares: The data that the app collects or shares may reveal some information about your identity, location, or activities. The data that the app collects or shares may also be used or abused by some parties for some purposes, such as marketing, analytics, or profiling. For example, some apps may collect or share some metadata, such as your phone number, your contacts, your IP address, or your device information. Some apps may collect or share some content, such as your messages, your calls, or your files.

These are some of the factors that you should consider when choosing a communication app, in addition to E2EE. You should do some research and comparison before deciding which app to use, and you should read the app's terms of service and privacy policy carefully. You should also update the app regularly, and review the app's settings and features periodically.

To help you understand and apply these factors, let's consider a hypothetical scenario that illustrates the benefits and limitations of E2EE communication apps. Imagine that you are a human rights activist who wants to communicate with your colleagues, supporters, and sources in a secure and private way. You need to send and receive messages, make and receive calls, and conduct and participate in video conferences. However, you are also aware that some of your communication may be sensitive or controversial and that some of your adversaries may try to monitor or disrupt your communication.

One of the steps that you can take to protect your communication is to use an E2EE communication app. You can choose and use an E2EE communication app that meets your needs and preferences based on the criteria that we have discussed. You can also follow the best practices for E2EE communication, such as verifying keys or codes, using disappearing messages, or using virtual phone numbers or email aliases. This way, you can ensure that only you and your intended recipients can read or hear your communication, and that no one can intercept or alter it.

However, E2EE communication apps are not perfect, and they may have some drawbacks or limitations, based on the factors that we have discussed. For example:

- The app that you use may be owned by a corporation or a government that may have ties or agendas that may compromise the app's security or privacy. For example, the app may be owned by a company that has a contract or a partnership with a government agency that may require the app to disclose or block some data or content, or to insert a backdoor or a vulnerability into the app's code or servers.
- The app that you use may be based in a country that has strict or oppressive internet censorship or surveillance regimes that may require the app to disclose or block some data or content. For example, the app may be based in a country that has a law or a regulation that may force the app to comply with some requests or

orders from the authorities, such as a warrant or a subpoena, or to follow some rules or standards, such as a filtering or a blocking list, or a key escrow or a decryption scheme.

- The app that you use may collect or share some data that may reveal some information about your identity, location, or activities. For example, the app may collect or share some metadata, such as your phone number, your contacts, your IP address, or your device information, which may be used or abused by some parties for some purposes, such as tracking, profiling, or targeting.

These are some of the challenges that E2EE communication apps present. However, these challenges are not insurmountable, and they can be overcome or mitigated by using the appropriate criteria and tools.

In this section, we have learned about the importance and challenges of implementing E2EE communications. We have discussed the criteria for choosing E2EE communication apps, such as security reputation, open source, encryption protocol, user base, cross-platform support, and usability. We have also explored some examples of E2EE communication apps, such as Signal, Wire, MySudo, Threema, and Wickr. We have also examined the benefits and challenges of E2EE communication apps, such as privacy, security, performance, compatibility, and usability.

To wrap up this section, let's consider a hypothetical scenario that illustrates the benefits and limitations of E2EE communication. Imagine that you are a business owner who wants to communicate with your employees, clients, and partners in a secure and efficient way. You need to send and receive messages, make and receive calls, and conduct and participate in video conferences. However, you are also concerned about the privacy and security of your communication, and you want to protect it from unauthorized access or disclosure.

One of the steps that you can take to protect your communication is to use E2EE communication apps. You can choose and use an E2EE communication app that meets your needs and preferences based on the criteria that we have discussed. You can also encourage your employees, clients, and partners to use the same or compatible E2EE communication app, and to follow the best practices for E2EE communication, such as verifying keys or codes, or using disappearing messages. This way, you can ensure that only you and your intended recipients can read or hear your communication, and that no one can intercept or alter it.

However, E2EE communication apps are not perfect, and they may have some drawbacks or limitations, such as the following:

- They may not work well with all devices, platforms, or networks, or with all communication tools or services. For example, some E2EE communication apps may not be available or supported on some operating systems, such as Windows or Linux. Some E2EE communication apps may not work well with some network settings or policies, such as firewalls or proxies. Some E2EE communication apps may not be compatible with some communication tools or services, such as email, SMS, or phone.

- They may not be user-friendly or intuitive, or may not integrate well with your existing communication habits or preferences. For example, some E2EE communication apps may require additional installation or configuration, such as verifying keys or codes, or choosing a resolver or a server. Some E2EE communication apps may not integrate well with your existing communication habits or preferences, such as using emojis, stickers, or voice notes. Some E2EE communication apps may require additional steps or actions, such as switching apps or devices, or scanning QR codes.
- They may involve some trade-offs between privacy, security, and usability. For example, some E2EE communication apps may offer more privacy and security but at the cost of lower performance or functionality. Some E2EE communication apps may offer more performance or functionality but at the cost of lower privacy or security. Some E2EE communication apps may offer a balance between privacy, security, and usability but at the cost of higher complexity or difficulty.

These are some of the challenges that E2EE communication apps present. However, these challenges are not insurmountable, and they can be overcome or mitigated by using the appropriate criteria and tools to choose and use E2EE communication apps, according to your needs and preferences.

List of Key Takeaways

In this chapter, we have learned about the importance and challenges of safeguarding sensitive information within our interconnected world. We have explored both personal and professional contexts, emphasizing practical strategies for protecting data. We have covered four main aspects of data privacy: (1) IP address protection, (2) MAC address security, (3) DNS privacy, and (4) implementation of E2EE communications such as commercial encrypted messaging apps, encrypted payment apps, encrypted web browsers, VPNs, and encrypted file storage. We have explained what these aspects are, why they are important, and how to use them effectively. We have also provided real-world case studies and examples to illustrate the benefits and challenges of implementing a layered data privacy plan.

By mastering these concepts, you will be equipped to navigate the complexities of data privacy while fostering responsible communication practices. You will also be able to

- understand the role and significance of IP address, MAC address, DNS, and E2EE communications in data privacy;
- identify the common threats and risks associated with these aspects of data privacy;

- apply the appropriate methods and tools to protect these aspects of data privacy in different scenarios;
- evaluate the strengths and weaknesses of different methods and tools for data privacy; and
- develop a comprehensive and customized layered data privacy plan for your own needs and preferences.

Chapter Review Questions

Directions: Refer to what you learned in this chapter to respond to the questions and prompts below.

1. What are the main risks of IP address exposure, and how can you prevent them?

   Answer: The main risks of IP address exposure are tracking and profiling, geo-restrictions and censorship, and cyberattacks and surveillance. You can prevent them by using IP address protection techniques, such as VPNs, proxy servers, or Tor, to hide or mask your real IP address, and to connect to a server in a different country that allows you to access the content you want.
2. What are the main solutions for MAC address security, and how can you implement them?

   Answer: The main solutions for MAC address security are randomizing MAC addresses, disabling Wi-Fi when not needed, and using encryption and authentication. You can implement them by changing your MAC address to a different one every time you connect to a network, or at regular intervals by turning off your Wi-Fi connection on your device when you are not using it, or when you are using a trusted network, and by encrypting your data before sending or receiving it over the internet, decrypting it after receiving or sending it to your device, authenticating yourself and your network devices before accessing the network, and verifying the integrity and origin of the data.
3. What are the main benefits and challenges of DNS privacy, and how can you overcome them?

   Answer: The main benefits of DNS privacy are preventing eavesdropping and enhancing privacy by ensuring that only the intended parties can see or modify the DNS queries and responses; hiding your browsing habits and activities from prying eyes; improving DNS security by preventing anyone from blocking or redirecting your DNS queries and responses, and preventing you from falling victim to spoofing or hijacking attacks; enhancing DNS performance by reducing the number of DNS queries and responses; and improving the reliability and availability of the DNS. The main challenges of DNS privacy are requiring support and configuration from your device, your browser, your resolver, and your network, which may not be available or compatible with all platforms and services; conflicting or interfering with other DNS features or policies, such as DNS caching, DNS filtering, or DNS monitoring, which may affect the functionality or usability of the DNS; and raising some ethical or legal issues, such as the choice and trustworthiness of the resolver, the ownership and control of the DNS data, or the compliance with the local laws and regulations. You can overcome them by using the appropriate criteria and tools, and using encrypted DNS protocols, such as DoH or DoT, according to your needs and preferences, and by consulting some resources and guides that can help you with DNS privacy.

4. What are the main criteria and examples of E2EE communication apps, and how can you use them effectively and safely?

   Answer: The main criteria for choosing E2EE communication apps are security reputation, open source, encryption protocol, user base, cross-platform support, and usability. You should look for apps that have a good security track record, that are open source or have undergone independent security audits, that use a strong and secure encryption protocol, such as the Signal Protocol, that have a large and loyal user base, that work seamlessly across different devices and operating systems, and that are user-friendly and integrate well with your existing communication tools. Some examples of E2EE communication apps that meet these criteria are Signal, Wire, MySudo, Threema, and Wickr. You can use them effectively and safely by following the best practices for E2EE communication, such as verifying keys or codes, using disappearing messages, or using virtual phone numbers or email aliases.

Applying What You Have Learned

Investigative Journalism

Imagine you are a journalist working on an investigative report about a corrupt politician. You have obtained some sensitive documents and evidence from a whistleblower and plan to publish your story soon. However, you are also aware that the politician has powerful allies and resources and that he may try to stop you or harm you. Therefore, you use a layered data privacy plan to protect your data and communication. What are the steps that you would take, and what are the methods and tools that you would use to implement your plan?

Answer: Some possible steps methods and tools that you would take and use are:

- Step 1: Hide your IP address using a VPN, a proxy server, or Tor to prevent anyone from tracking or profiling your online activities and identifying or locating your device.
- Step 2: Randomize your MAC address using a third-party app to prevent anyone from tracking or profiling your online activities and from identifying or locating your device.

- Step 3: Use encrypted DNS, using DoH or DoT, to prevent anyone from seeing or altering your DNS queries and responses and from tracking or profiling your online activities.
- Step 4: Use E2EE communication, using Signal, Wire, or MySudo, to encrypt and authenticate your messages, calls, and video conferences and to prevent anyone from intercepting or altering your data.
- Step 5: Encrypt your files and data using a third-party app, such as VeraCrypt or Cryptomator, to prevent anyone from reading or modifying your data, even if they manage to access them.
- Step 6: Use a secure and anonymous browser, such as Tor Browser or Brave, to access the internet and to prevent anyone from tracking or profiling your online activities and from blocking or redirecting your access to certain content.
- Step 7: Use a secure and anonymous email service, such as ProtonMail or Tutanota, to send and receive emails, and to prevent anyone from intercepting or altering your emails.

Personal Travel

Imagine that you are a traveler who wants to access some content on the internet that is not available in your current location, such as a video streaming service, a news website, or a social media platform. You also want to protect your privacy and security from anyone who may try to see or access your online activities, such as hackers, ISPs, or government agencies. Therefore, you decide to use a layered data privacy plan to access and enjoy the content. What are the steps that you would take, and what are the methods and tools that you would use to implement your plan?

Answer: Some possible steps methods and tools that you would take, and use are:

- Step 1: Hide your IP address using a VPN, a proxy server, or Tor to bypass geo-restrictions and censorship and access the content you want on the internet.
- Step 2: Randomize your MAC address using a third-party app to prevent anyone from tracking or profiling your online activities and from identifying or locating your device.
- Step 3: Use encrypted DNS, using DoH or DoT, to prevent anyone from seeing or altering your DNS queries and responses, and from tracking or profiling your online activities.
- Step 4: Use E2EE communication, using Threema, Wickr, or Wire, to encrypt and authenticate your messages, calls, and video conferences, and to prevent anyone from intercepting or altering your data.
- Step 5: Encrypt your files and data, using a third-party app, such as VeraCrypt or Cryptomator, to prevent anyone from reading or modifying your data, even if they manage to access them.

- Step 6: Use a secure and anonymous browser, such as Tor Browser or Brave, to access the internet, and to prevent anyone from tracking or profiling your online activities, and from blocking or redirecting your access to certain content.
- Step 7: Use a secure and anonymous email service, such as ProtonMail or Tutanota, to send and receive emails, and to prevent anyone from intercepting or altering your emails.

Image Credits

Fig. 10.1: Generated using DALL-E.

Fig. 10.2a: Copyright © 2023 Depositphotos/vovan13.

Fig. 10.2b: Copyright © 2024 Depositphotos/Orxbyte.

Fig. 10.2c: Copyright © 2014 Depositphotos/vectomart.

Fig. 10.3: Imgur, "MAC Address Exposure" http://i.stack.imgur.com/9Qppk.png. Copyright © by Imgur.

Printed by Libri Plureos GmbH in Hamburg,
Germany

9 798823 356725